METROPOLITICS

METROPOLITICS

A Regional Agenda for Community and Stability

Myron Orfield

Brookings Institution Press
Washington, D.C.

The Lincoln Institute of Land Policy
Cambridge, Mass.

Library of Congress Cataloging-in-Publication data

Orfield, Myron.
    Metropolitics : a regional agenda for community and stability /
Myron Orfield.
        p.   cm.
    Includes bibliographical references and index.
    ISBN 0-8157-6640-8 (cl : alk. paper).
    1. Metropolitan areas—United States. 2. Regional planning—
United States. 3. Inner cities—United States. 4. Community
development—United States. 5. Urban policy—United States.
I. Title.
HT334.U5074   1997
307.′76′0973—dc21   96-45202
                                                       CIP

9 8 7 6 5 4 3 2 1

The paper used in this publication meets the minimum requirements of the American National Standard for
Information Sciences—Permanence of Paper for Printed Library Materials, ANSI Z39-48-1984.

Typeset in Times Roman

Composition by Cynthia Stock
Silver Spring, Maryland

Printed by R. R. Donnelley and Sons Co.
Harrisonburg, Virginia

The Brookings Institution

The Brookings Institution is an independent, nonprofit organization devoted to nonpartisan research, education, and publication in economics, government, foreign policy, and the social sciences generally. Its principal purposes are to aid in the development of sound public policies and to promote public understanding of issues of national importance. The Institution was founded on December 8, 1927, to merge the activities of the Institute for Government Research, founded in 1916, the Institute of Economics, founded in 1922, and the Robert Brookings Graduate School of Economics, founded in 1924.

The Institution maintains a position of neutrality on issues of public policy to safeguard the intellectual freedom of the staff. Interpretations or conclusions in Brookings publications should be understood to be solely those of the authors.

The Lincoln Institute of Land Policy

The Lincoln Institute of Land Policy is a nonprofit and tax-exempt educational institution established in 1974. Its mission as a school is to study and teach land policy, including land economics and land taxation. The Institute is supported by the Lincoln Foundation, established in 1947 by John C. Lincoln, a Cleveland industrialist. Mr. Lincoln drew inspiration from the ideas of Henry George, the nineteenth-century American political economist and social philosopher.

Integrating the theory and practice of land policy and understanding the forces that influence it are the major goals of the Lincoln Institute. The Institute explores the fundamental forces affecting land use and development: governments' strategies for managing change, community and individual rights and responsibilities, taxation and regulation, the functioning of markets, patterns of human settlement and economic production, and transportation systems.

For Jeanne

Contents

CONTENTS

Foreword

Myron Orfield is one of the most revolutionary politicians in urban America. A 35-year-old Minnesota state representative, attorney, part-time law professor, and full-time champion of regionalism, Orfield has forged the first enduring political alliance in America between declining central cities and older, threatened, blue-collar suburbs.

A few academicians and journalists may have pointed out how urban poverty has been spreading from inner city to inner suburb, but Orfield has developed the most compelling and comprehensive documentation of this trend and translated it into effective political action. The political coalition he has organized between legislators from Minneapolis–Saint Paul, their declining blue-collar suburbs, and what Orfield terms "developing, low–tax capacity suburbs" has become a dominant force in the Minnesota legislature. In short, Orfield has split the suburbs politically.

Orfield has also pioneered the use of a political tool: maps that, jurisdiction by jurisdiction, trace the decline of central cities and many older, inner-ring suburbs and the rise of affluent outer-ring suburbs. With the help of employees of the Minnesota state legislature and the state's planning agencies, Orfield has produced 300 maps of the Twin Cities area alone.

In addition, Orfield has been spreading the gospel of central city–older suburb alliances (and the benefits of his mapping strategy) across the country. Since his political breakthrough in the Minnesota legislature, he has been invited to speak dozens of times in more than twenty metro areas. With local foundation support, he has mapped metrowide economic and social trends in Baltimore, Philadelphia, Pittsburgh, Cleveland, Chicago, Portland, Oregon, Seattle, and San Francisco.

The case Orfield's maps make for regional reform is graphic and compelling. But what is as important is that, with the credibility of a successful politician who has converted analysis into public policy, Orfield is an even more effective expert witness in presenting his own material in business forums, citizen assemblies, and legislative hearings.

Finally, though focused on the Twin Cities, *Metropolitics* lays out a comprehensive case for regional policy reforms. Census tract by census tract across the seven counties and 187 municipalities that form the bulk of the Twin Cities region, Orfield charts the widest array of demographic, educational, economic, and fiscal trends. The list ranges from poverty among children under age five to allocation of state highway funds. It is truly a checklist of critical concerns that add up to a comprehensive portrait of vast disparities among communities in many metropolitan areas. All public policy activists and concerned citizens can use *Metropolitics* as a starting point for their own communities. Strike out "Minneapolis–Saint Paul," write in another region's name, and begin filling in the data blanks. The book serves as a detailed road map for analyzing and understanding most urban regions in America.

Metropolitics, of course, is both a book and a continuing political process—a story without a last chapter. But there are vital lessons for the rest of urban America that Orfield and his allies have learned.

The first is the choice of political arena: the state legislature. Many Americans do not fully understand that how local governments are organized and what they are empowered to do is determined by state legislatures. Local governance in urban America is not the constitutional province of the federal government. The U.S. Constitution is silent on the issue of local government; under the Tenth Amendment local governance is a power "reserved to the States respectively, or to the people."

In highly fragmented metro areas, absent the creation of an elected regional government like Oregon's Portland Metro, there is no local public body to speak for the interests of the entire region. It is only at the state level that a local citizen's interests are placed in a framework that addresses his or her interests as a citizen of the entire state or of a metropolitan region. State legislatures *must* serve as regional policy bodies because they are the only ones that can. Legislatures must set new ground rules for how myriad local governments must share common responsibilities for common problems.

Through *Metropolitics* we also learn that making progress on hard, divisive issues is based rarely on friendly, consensual agreement, but more often on building political coalitions. Those coalitions are most durable when based on each member's political self-interest—that is, the individual's perception of the interests of the constituencies he or she represents. The glue that held the Minnesota legislative coalition together was underlying social, economic, and political self-interest.

The mathematics of local self-interest would also favor potential winning coalitions almost everywhere. University of Minnesota geographer John S. Adams has shown that almost every large metro area is characterized by the "favored quarter"—a slice of the region where most high-end commercial and residential development occurs. In Chicago the "favored quarter" is the northwestern suburbs around Schaumburg and Hoffman Estates. ..n Memphis it extends through east Memphis to Germantown and Collierville. In Atlanta it grows out through the Buckhead area of north Atlanta into Cobb County—and so on.

But the existence of the "favored quarter" also means the existence of the unfavored three-quarters. The concept of "metropolitics" is built on uniting the political weight of the unfavored three-quarters.

In four short years (1993–96), Minnesota's "metropolitics" coalition racked up a remarkable legislative record. It enacted two regional fair-share housing bills, approved a new regional revenue-sharing formula pooling tax revenues from high-end housing, changed the state tax code to end abuse of tax increment financing by wealthy suburbs and protect farmers against pressure to subdivide their land, and revised how regional sewer services are funded. The coalition vastly expanded the powers of the Twin Cities Metropolitan Council (a regional planning and coordinating agency first established by the Minnesota legislature in 1967) by placing regional sewer and transportation agencies with annual budgets totaling $600 million under its direct administration. The "metropolitics" coalition came within one vote on the Minnesota House floor of converting the gubernatorially appointed Metropolitan Council into a popularly elected regional government like Portland Metro. Beyond that one Senate vote, the coalition most often was stymied by one other missing vote—Minnesota Governor Arne Carlson's. Only vetoes by the governor prevented more sweeping redefinition of regional benefit-sharing and regional burden-sharing from taking effect.

In recent years the Minnesota legislature has been engaged in the battle over all the crucial regional issues. Orfield and his colleagues have shown how to put together a winning coalition. More than specific regional issues (such as land use planning, fiscal disparities, or affordable housing), successfully building this political coalition constitutes the most important regional reform model in the United States. In *Metropolitics* Myron Orfield lays out a blueprint of how such coalitions can be built nationwide.

DAVID RUSK
Former mayor of Albuquerque

Acknowledgments

There are many friends and colleagues who helped me bring this book to publication. I would like to particularly thank Michael O'Keefe of the McKnight Foundation, Terry Saario of the Northwest Area Foundation, Marion Etzwiler of the Minneapolis Foundation, and Paul Verret of the Saint Paul Foundation for jointly funding much of the research and writing. Without Michael O'Keefe as a firm and early supporter, this project would not have happened. I would also like to thank David Lanegran of Macalester College for encouraging me to write this book, for reading drafts, and for talking about cities. He has been a wonderful friend and mentor. Angie Bernhard, who was my legislative assistant from 1993 to 1996, did a brilliant job helping me through the process of passing bills and planning legislation. She was my associate in all of this—from crunching endless numbers for tax base–sharing debates, to making maps at a moment's notice, to pulling members out of the hallway to vote on bills. She is now in graduate school (in urban studies!), and I miss her. To her predecessor Kristin Hanson, my legislative assistant in 1992–93, and her successor, Crystal Henle, my present LA, I also owe a tremendous debt. The nonpartisan staff of Minnesota House Research and of Minnesota Planning supplied magnificent support throughout the legislative debate. I am particularly grateful to Deb Dyson, Kathy Novak, Steve Hinze, Tim Strom, Tom Todd, and Richard Fong.

My brother Gary, in addition to being a wonderful, thoughtful sibling, has had a tremendous influence on how I think about metropolitan patterns (and many other things) and has given valuable advice on every step in the process.

Both Anthony Downs and David Rusk, whose books on regionalism had an enormous influence on this one, provided vital insights that much improved this manuscript. Henry Richmond also provided important advice, help, and friendship throughout. It was primarily through Henry's organization, the National Growth Management Leadership Project, that the research on other U.S. cities was supported. Henry's strength of character and vision about the future of the country is breathtaking and has more than once renewed my confidence. His advice on regionalism (and land use in particular) was instrumental both in the writing of this book and in the actual process of legislation.

Alice E. Ingerson of the Lincoln Institute of Land Policy provided comments that greatly improved the organization and substance of the manuscript and was endlessly patient with my questions about the process of completing my first book. Kathleen A. Lynch, my author's editor, helped me organize my thoughts, smooth my prose, and unmix my metaphors. In the process, she helped turn a long draft into a concise working manuscript. I am also grateful to a patient and talented team at the Brookings Institution Press, which is copublishing this book—particularly to Steph Selice, manuscript editor; Nancy Davidson, acquisitions editor; and Norman Turpin, production manager. They were assisted by several freelancers: Cindy Stock, desktop publisher; Stacey Seaman, verifier; Robert E. Elwood, indexer; and Phil Schwartzberg, map designer.

I would also like to thank John Harrigan, Paul Jargowsky, John Adams, Judith Martin, Edward Goetz, Frank Hornstein, Alan Malkis, Tim Thompson, William Morrish and Catherine Brown, Robert Liberty, Douglas Massey, Christopher Leinberger, Peter Calthorpe, Robert Tennessen, John Brandl, Gerald Heaney, Susan Tincher, Gretchen Nicholls, George Galster, Will Craig, Tom Luce, john powell, Todd Swanstrom, John Logan, Michael Ames, and Robert Einsweiler for reading and making valuable comments on all or parts of the original manuscript. Thanks also go to Larry Agran for his suggestion of *Metropolitics* as the title of this book.

Most of all, I would like to thank my wife, Jeanne Farrar, to whom this book is dedicated, for her endless emotional support throughout the process of working on legislation and writing this book. Her critical and meticulous mind sharpened my ideas and my arguments daily. She is my best friend and the center of my life. I had hoped to finish this book before the birth of our son Sam, but he showed up a little early. His smiles and wonderful presence have encouraged me to finish it so that I can play with him. Finally, I would like to thank my parents, Lindy and Myron Orfield, Sr., for their love and support and their confidence in me—and for their example.

MYRON ORFIELD

1

"It Couldn't Happen Here . . ."

I t couldn't happen here." Not in Minneapolis-Saint Paul, the political home of Hubert Humphrey; Minnesota, America's sane
heartland. . . . The Twin Cities was immune to urban decline, inner-
suburban decay, urban sprawl—and the polarization that has dev-
astated and divided older, larger regions. After all, we were not
Chicago, Detroit, or Milwaukee. We were reform minded, and our philanthropic and governmental centers were coordinated and responsive.
Then the 1980s hit, marking our Twin Cities with identical patterns of regional polarization.

If it could happen here, no American region is immune. Once polarization occurs, the concentration of poverty, disinvestment, middle-class
flight, and urban sprawl grow more and more severe. The increase of real
property wealth in certain outer suburbs, aided by truly massive regional
infrastructure expenditures, and its decline in the central city and inner
suburbs represent an interregional transfer of tax base from some of the
most poor and troubled communities in American society to some of the
most thriving and affluent. The problems associated with these patterns
are more complex and detrimental than any other set of challenges facing
American society. There is essentially no federal urban policy left to deal
with this polarization or its costs.

Impelled by this awareness, a powerful coalition has been building
in the Twin Cities. During the 1993–95 sessions of the Minnesota State
Legislature, the central cities, declining inner suburbs, and low–tax base,
developing suburbs have stretched across the divide in support of a regional reform agenda that includes sharing of property tax bases, fair
housing, reinvestment, land use planning, transportation and transit reform, and revitalized regional governance. Throughout the community,
hundreds of churches, environmental, good-government, and civil rights
groups have linked their energies and agendas to this program. Large
parts of the agenda have been enacted, and the movement's energy is
growing.

1

The tools being forged to address the problems of decline and polarization in the Twin Cities might well serve as a model for reform in all of the nation's metropolitan areas.

The Push-Pull of Regional Polarization

Throughout the United States, people move "up and out," taking their economic and social resources with them and leaving behind an increasingly dense core of poverty in the city and rapidly growing social needs in older suburbs. The same patterns of polarization are present in every region in some form. Pushed by concentrated need, pulled by concentrated resources, polarization gathers force.

In blighted central city neighborhoods and decaying inner suburbs, poverty and social needs concentrate, racial segregation increases, and poor people grow more isolated from the functional economy and the middle class. The concentration of poverty amplifies its effects on individuals, destabilizes schools, intensifies crime, and costs local government precious resources at the very moment needs are increasing.

At parts of the metropolitan periphery, resources congregate, protected by land use restrictions that control entry to the community. Those who are the best off economically need social services the least, but they do need workers for local jobs and roads or transportation systems to deliver the workers and support concentrated business activity. They also need expensive wastewater treatment systems to support new residential and commercial development. Politically influential and bolstered by development interests, these most affluent suburban communities get the infrastructure they want, and the less well-off metropolitan communities pay disproportionately.

On another part of the metropolitan fringe lie the developing middle-class suburbs, filled with middle- and working-class families. These areas are developing rapidly, with lots of new less expensive housing but little commercial development. When the time comes to pay for all the new schools and infrastructure necessary to build a new community, these communities often find themselves financially overextended.

Push of Concentrated Need

Virtually all of the nation's metropolitan regions have areas of dense poverty at their cores.[1] The concentration of poverty, *ghettoization*,[2] increased dramatically in U.S. cities in the Northeast during the 1970s and in the Midwest during the 1980s.[3] Not only are these distressed areas expanding in size, but the degree of poverty concentration and racial segregation is also intensifying within them.[4] In the 1980s, the Twin Cities became the nation's fourth fastest ghettoizing region.[5] Its extreme poverty tract (or ghetto) areas tripled in number and size from 11 census tracts in 1980 to 32 in 1990 and from 24,420 to 79,081 people. Surrounding these very poor neighborhoods, an area in deep transition increased from 43 to 57 census tracts and from 102,682 to 153,700 people.[6]

The residential concentration of poverty creates social repercussions far greater than the sum of its parts. Physical separation from jobs and middle-class role models and dependence on a dysfunctional welfare system reinforce social isolation and weaken work skills. Poor individuals living in concentrated poverty are far more likely to become pregnant as teenagers, drop out of high school, and remain jobless than young people living in socioeconomically mixed neighborhoods.[7] Freed from poor neighborhoods and schools and given economic opportunities in low-poverty communities, their educational and employment prospects improve dramatically.[8]

Schools are the first victim and the most powerful perpetuator of metropolitan polarization. Local schools become socioeconomically distressed before neighborhoods become poor; rising poverty among a community's school children predicts the future of its adults. Schools cannot perform when all the children come from poor homes. When middle-class families and pundits say that cities have bad schools, what they often mean is that cities have schools full of poor children. Middle-class families, the bedrock of stable communities, will not tolerate high concentrations of poverty in their schools.

In this light, both Twin Cities' central cities are struggling under a disproportionate share of concentrated poverty—and segregation. Between 1982 and 1994, the Minneapolis school system went from 33 percent to 52 percent of its children on free or reduced-cost lunch and from 34 percent to 59 percent minority student enrollment. Saint Paul experienced similar changes.[9] Both central cities lost one-third of their preschool white children.

As poverty concentrates in poor central city neighborhoods and older suburbs, crime grows dramatically. Minneapolis census tracts with more than 25 percent of their residents below the federal poverty line accounted for 71 percent of the city's violent crime in 1987–89, even though only 32 percent of the city's people lived there.[10] In the poorest neighborhoods, violent crime rates were ten times higher than the metro average and thirty times the suburban average. Many of the neighborhoods that underwent socioeconomic change during the 1980s saw violent crime grow between 50 percent and 70 percent in a five-year period. When neighborhood concentrations of poverty passed a critical mass, violent crime crime rates increased exponentially.

In 1995, the city of Minneapolis had a higher murder rate than New York City.[11]

Throughout the nation, as social needs and problems multiply in core cities, the vital human and financial resources to address them disappear.[12] In Minneapolis residential property around the expanding poverty core lost from 15 to 25 percent of its value over a five-year period, while housing values in exclusive suburbs soared.[13] As middle-class customers leave and poverty becomes more concentrated, businesses lose through crime, physical decline of the neighborhood, and loss of property value. Polluted brownfields (former business sites with pollution-based barriers to redevelopment), inability to expand, and lack of rapid access to radial highways further dim their prospects.

The Twin Cities region created more than 240,000 net new jobs during the 1980s and was one of the only northern U.S. metropolitan economies to create significant net new manufacturing employment. Yet Minneapolis and Saint Paul together lost more than 20 percent of their manufacturing jobs in a single decade.[14] Unemployment grew rapidly in both central cities.

Contrary to popular belief, socioeconomic instability does not stop neatly at central-city borders. As it crosses into inner suburbs, especially into suburbs that were once blue-collar and middle-class neighborhoods, it accelerates and intensifies. In the Twin Cities metropolitan area, growing concentrations of poverty and economic instability firmly established themselves in working class inner-ring suburbs, particularly those north of Minneapolis and south of Saint Paul. Like older metropolitan areas elsewhere, Twin Cities working-class suburban communities have less hopeful prospects than do the cities they surround. Though first hit by social and economic change, central cities have a fiscal, governmental, and social infrastructure to slow these powerful trends. Lacking the central city's central business district and elite neighborhood tax base, social welfare and police infrastructure, and network of organized political activity, inner suburbs often decline far more rapidly.

Following the pattern of older, larger regions, by 1994 nine of eleven metro inner-suburban school districts had more than 20 percent of their children on free lunch and were gaining poor children faster than Minneapolis.[15] Eight were gaining minority students faster. Eighteen of 29 inner-ring cities experienced significant flight of white preschool children over the decade. During the 1980s, not only did the inner suburbs have a serious crime rate 20 percent higher than in the middle-class suburbs, they were also the only place in the region where crime was increasing, except for the poorest central-city neighborhoods. Moreover, to the extent that these inner-ring communities developed with more than a purely residential tax base, many had far more dramatic job losses than the central cities. Their older industrial and manufacturing sites (like the disadvantaged central-city locations) were also burdened by brownfield pollution, lack of space for expansion, and poor access to radial roads. Finally, as the severity of their problems deepened, their tax bases—small to begin with—grew less certainly than those of the central cities.

Pull of Concentrated Resources

At the edge of metropolitan regions, developing communities engage in as restrictive and as low-density a pattern of land use practices as their economic circumstances will bear. Like virtually all neighborhoods and communities since time immemorial, developing neighborhoods assiduously try to exclude "undesirables" such as apartment dwellers and build a broad rich tax base to keep services high and taxes low. Not all communities are uniformly successful, however, in their efforts toward exclusivity.

The "favored quarter" (a term coined by real estate consultants) dominates regional economic growth and garners a disproportionate share of the region's new roads and other developmental infrastructure. Its housing markets are highly restrictive, its social needs small and often declining. However, it has too few local workers for local jobs and traffic congestion that cannot be solved by new highways. In the white-collar sector moving out from the affluent neighborhoods of the city, growing communities corner the market in low-density executive housing and/or business tax base with low service requirements. Fiscal zoning is the process by which communities zone or plan to develop expensive housing and/or commercial-industrial property with low service demands so as to increase their tax base per household and keep their costly social needs (and taxes) down.

Christopher Leinberger and his colleagues at Robert Charles Lessor and Co., one of the nation's most successful real estate consulting firms, have made a great deal of money locating the "favored quarter" for businesses in certain metropolitan areas. These quarters—developing suburban areas—have mastered the art of skimming the cream from metropolitan growth while accepting as few metropolitan responsibilities as possible. As these communities grow affluent and their tax base expands, their exclusive housing market often causes their relatively small local social needs to decline.

Robert Charles Lessor and Co. looks for areas with concentrations of housing with average values above $200,000, high-end regional malls, and the best freeway capacity. In the Twin Cities, the favored quarter is a group of developing suburbs to the south and west, on and beyond the I–494 beltway. While the cities and many of the inner suburbs lost jobs over the decade, the southern and western developing suburbs, with 27 percent of the region's population, gained 61 percent of its new jobs. At the heart of this quarter, Eden Prairie, Minnetonka, and Plymouth, with 7 percent of the region's population, created 26 percent of its new jobs.[16]

Affluent developing communities use their economic power and local authority to restrict the access of prospective moderate- and low-income residents. Almost all of the southern and western developing cities have extensive, multilayered barriers to affordable housing. Communities burgeoning with new entry-level jobs have no land zoned for new apartment buildings, require large expensive lots for single-family homes, and impose other regulatory barriers that prevent workers from reaching for opportunity—and the marketplace from responding to their quest for affordable housing. A planner for one of these communities announced the intention of not building single-family housing units costing less than $140,000, because such housing would not "pay its own way" in terms of social services.[17]

Through exclusive housing markets, these communities welcome throngs of middle- and upper-income migrants and businesses from core communities but restrict the access of those less fortunate. With such powerful advantages, these communities can quickly drain off wealth and productive energies from the rest of the region. So though the concentration of poor children soared in middle- and working-class core communities, many southern and western cities had a smaller percentage of poor children at the end of the decade than at the beginning.[18] Their school systems, in particular, enjoy insulated, stable prosperity and high achievement financed by growing protected tax bases. As the central cities and inner suburbs become more socioeconomically challenged and diverse, these districts become wealthier and less diverse. The favored quarter's low crime rates steadily decline.

During the 1980s, the central cities and inner suburbs saw property value increases 31 percent below the metropolitan average increase. Conversely, the southern and western developing suburbs experienced the region's largest property tax base growth. To illustrate this economic strength, Eden Prairie and Minnetonka, two southwest communities, together had the same commercial-industrial tax base as Saint Paul ($1.5 billion), but only one-third as many residents and (unlike Saint Paul) virtually no poor people.

As suburbs without affordable housing dominate regional job growth, a mismatch develops between where the jobs are and where the people are who need them. Local southern and western chambers of commerce state that thousands of jobs go unfilled for lack of workers. More and more employees are bused hours each way to minimum-wage jobs in the southern and western suburbs. Some workers call these buses "Soweto Expresses." These workers complain that they are good enough to work in affluent communities but not good enough to live there or to send their children to those schools.

To support the development of the new southern and western cities, state, metropolitan, and local governments have spent billions of dollars building freeways and sewer systems over the last two decades. These expenditures have exacerbated social and economic polarization in the Twin Cities.

Of the twenty-five largest regions in the country, the Twin Cities has the second lowest population density and some of the least congested freeways.[19] Nevertheless, during the 1980s, $1.09 billion was spent on new highways, 75 percent serving the southern and western developing suburbs.[20] During the 1990s, virtually all of the metro transportation budget has been earmarked to expand capacity in the I–35W and I–494 corridors, again to the south and west.[21] Yet expanding lane capacity cannot solve the mismatch between opportunity and housing that contributes to congestion, real or imagined. Cars owned by people who cannot afford to live close to their work clog the beltways. As long as most new jobs are created in communities without affordable housing, only coordinated transportation and land use policy reform that promotes such housing will lessen the stress.

In a similar mismatch, a system of sewer financing was put in place in the mid-1980s through which the core of the region subsidized the construction and operation of sewer capacity at the fringe, in the most exclusive suburban areas. By 1990, 131,488 acres (23 percent of the land) remained undeveloped in the area served by sewers.[22] Most of this excess capacity was in the struggling middle-income suburbs. Instead of directing growth to these areas, between 1987 and 1991 the region provided sewer service to an additional twenty-eight square miles of land (18,000 acres) at the request of cities and developers.[23] Despite the system's abundant unused capacity, the region spent approximately $50 million on new sewer capital costs, a disproportionate share of it in the southern and western quadrant.[24] By 1992, the central cities were paying more than $6 million a year to help move their middle-class households and businesses to the edge of the region.[25] A regionally financed sewer system could have served as the linchpin of effective planning.

On the opposite side of a region's favored quarter lie the blue-collar, middle-income developing communities. Despite their struggles to build expensive housing and commercial industrial properties, they end up with only modest homes, apartment buildings, and trailer parks, and few businesses. They would like to win the fiscal zoning battle but cannot. These communities develop without the resources for adequate schools and other public services.

The patterns of metropolitan polarization play a cruel joke on these middle-income families seeking a better life at the edge of the region. As they flee the socioeconomic dislocations of the central cities and inner suburbs, they arrive in rapidly growing school districts with small tax bases. Because their tax base is inadequate and their neighborhoods have throngs of young children needing to go to school, their local governments will build almost anything that stands simply to pay the bills. Perhaps in part because of overcrowding and minimal spending per pupil, these districts have some of the highest drop-out and lowest college attendance rates in the Twin Cities region.

Increasing Momentum of Polarization

These multilayered forces inexorably drive subregions apart. The poorer the central cities and inner suburbs are, the faster they grow even poorer. The more successful the favored quarter is, the faster it grows more successful.

In Twin Cities communities, restrictive fiscal zoning and competition for tax base have created growing disparities in the property wealth that supports local services. The central cities and inner-ring and working-class suburbs all had $1,800 of annual tax capacity per household to support public services. The southern and western developing suburbs, with $2,749 of average capacity, had one-third more tax base per household and less social need.[26] Virtually everywhere social needs are present and substantial, governmental tax resources are comparatively small and growing slowly, stagnating, or declining. Virtually everywhere governmental resources are large and rapidly growing, social needs are small and growing slowly, holding stable, or declining.

An area with high social needs and low resources is generally not a nice place to live, with poor services and high taxes. Conversely, an area with high resources and low social needs *is* a nice place to live, with good services and low taxes. This process of polarization fuels itself as high-income individuals with broad residential choices and businesses seek out pleasant places, good services, and low taxes and avoid unpleasant places, poor services, and high taxes. As the favored quarter captures more and more high-income residents, its base increases, taxes go down, and/or services improve. It becomes an even more attractive area. But as individuals and businesses leave areas with high social need and high taxes, the base shrinks and tax rates go up. The incentive to get out grows.

Polarization's Unquantifiable Costs

Polarization on a regional scale exacts its costs in terms of human and governmental waste, overtaxed and overregulated business climate, environmental destruction through irrational use of land, and balkanization of political life. How can we set a true price on these costs?

What is the human cost of locking people in areas of concentrated poverty—in hopeless places without role models or connection to the broader economy, places with titanic levels of crime and disorder, places with no way out? What does it cost when people have no choice but to live in places where their lives can only become worse, where they are programmed to fail, and where that very failure will only increase already deep social and racial divisions?

In the United States, each generation builds a new ring of cities at the edge of our metropolitan areas, as a central city or an inner ring of suburbs becomes isolated and declines. How do we estimate this cost? How do we value the decline of once-vibrant cities and neighborhoods, the devaluation of buildings, streets, roads, parks, and schools that each generation builds and abandons? In the clearest sense, the increase of property wealth in outer suburbs and the stagnation or decline of central city and inner-suburban values represents, in part, an interregional transfer of tax base. As such, the loss of value in older, poorer communities is one of the costs of economic polarization and urban sprawl. But there is much more than this.

The closing of vast numbers of schools in the core of the region, while scores are built at its periphery, symbolizes the magnitude of the flight to the edge and the massive waste involved. Between 1970 and 1990, total Twin Cities metropolitan school enrollment fell by 81,000, owing to the generational population decline after the baby boom. During this period, the central cities and the inner-ring and diverse second-ring suburbs together closed 132 schools, while 50 new schools were opened at the edge of the metropolitan area.[27]

Business underwrites a good part of this decline and sprawl. It takes the hit when the central city or inner suburbs grow worse and suffers from the lack of available workers at job sites and from association with a divided, declining region. It pays the price of restricted and arbitrary housing markets in the developing suburbs.

Locally, the vast supply of developmental infrastructure put into restrictively zoned communities creates land use patterns that are low density, economically inefficient, and environmentally dangerous. Between 1970 and 1984, the population of the metro area grew by 9.7 percent, while the share of land devoted to urban uses increased by 25.1 percent. Between 1982 and 1987, 86,832 acres of farmland (136 square miles) succumbed to metropolitan development.[28] The Prairie Du Chien, a main aquifer serving the southern and western quadrant, shows signs of severe groundwater pollution and depletion.[29] Correspondingly, thousands of acres of polluted industrial land lie fallow at the core, unable to compete economically with virgin land at the exterior.

As physical and economic chasms widen, so too does political polarization. For example, each year the Minnesota Children's Defense Fund rates legislators on their willingness to support the issues of children, particularly poor children. During the 1991 session, representatives of central city and middle-income suburban districts in the Minnesota House on average scored over 80 percent on the Defense Fund scorecard. Representatives of the southern and western developing suburbs scored an average of 20 percent.[30] Over time, as regions grow more distinct socially, politically, and racially from each other, they stop speaking a common language. Without deliberate intervention, cooperation becomes impossible.

Benefits of Cooperation

Nationally, the National Civic League, academics, and Ripon or Rockefeller Republicans have for decades preached the gospel of metropolitanism. The message of cost-effective regional planning, supported by local business leadership, had a strong influence in the Twin Cities twenty-five years ago. In the 1990s, columnist Neal Peirce has popularized good-government metropolitanism. He did this by broadening its base among editorial boards and local chambers of commerce—by emphasizing the economic interdependence of metropolitan areas and the need for regional economic coordination to compete effectively in the new world economy, rather than social polarization between cities and suburbs or equity concerns.[31] On another front, David Rusk, former mayor of Albuquerque, New Mexico, has simply and effectively connected the issues of metropolitanism and social equity.[32] He has shown that regions that have created metropolitan governments by annexation or consolidation are less segregated by race and class, economically healthier, and simply more equitable for a region's people.

Anthony Downs of the Brookings Institution has assembled his own research together with the recent groundbreaking work of urban poverty scholars, economists, transportation experts, and land use planners. With this, he makes compelling new arguments for metropolitan government, broad metropolitan-based reforms in fair housing, transportation, land use, property tax base sharing, and metropolitan governance.[33] Hank Savitch, Ronald Vogel, Richard Voith, William Barnes, and Larry C. Ledebur have argued that there are deep interconnections between metropolitan economies, even between central city and favored quarters. Peter Calthorpe, an urban planner from San Francisco, has created a compelling esthetic vision of how inclusive, regionally responsible communities concerned about transit-oriented development could look.[34] These ideas—particularly Rusk's—have received extraordinary coverage in the national media and have stimulated a nascent national discussion. In Washington, U.S. Housing and Urban Development Secretary Henry Cisneros is pushing the federal government to strengthen metropolitan coordination of affordable housing, land use, environmental protection, and transportation issues. President Clinton has issued an executive order to begin this process.[35]

The Regional Agenda for Community and Stability

Only through a strong, multifaceted, regional response can regional polarization be countered. To stabilize the central cities and older suburbs, six substantive reforms and one structural reform must be accomplished on a metropolitan scale. They are interrelated and reinforce each other substantively and politically.

The first three reforms are the most significant in terms of the socioeconomic stability of the core: fair housing, property tax-base sharing, and reinvestment. Together, these reforms deconcentrate poverty, provide

11

resource equity, and support the physical rebuilding necessary to bring back the middle class and restore the private economy. The second three reinforce and allow the first three reforms to operate efficiently and sustainably: land planning and growth management, welfare reform and public works, and transportation and transit reform. Together, these reforms provide for growth that is balanced socioeconomically, accessible by transit, economical with governmental resources, and environmentally conscious. These reforms can be most effectively administered and sustained by an elected metropolitan coordinating structure. Finally, a panoply of tax and public finance reforms should occur to overturn the perverse incentives created by generations of a highly fragmented, overregulated local marketplace. The proliferation of cities in the Twin Cities metro area—there are now 187 municipalities with land use powers—regulating the land use practices of one market leads to such overregulation. This results in barriers in the new suburbs to the affordable housing or mixed-use developments that market demand in job-rich communities would create in a less regulated setting.

Central control versus local autonomy within federated systems has been a core political dilemma throughout American history. Each major adjustment in the existing balance of power has been divisive—the Articles of Confederation and the Constitution, the Civil War and the Fourteenth Amendment, the New Deal and the Great Society, and most recently the Contract with America. In Minnesota, the centrally important regional reform of tax base sharing has been bitterly resisted by contributing suburbs. This resistance has been taken all the way to the U.S. Supreme Court and to every legislative session since 1971. In the end, though the notion of building a total win-win regional consensus is appealing in theory, in practice sustained regional reform clearly demands the formation of enduring coalitions that can weather intense opposition and controversy.

In this light, the regional agenda in Minnesota is more than the musings of good-government academics and luncheon speakers. It is the political platform of an increasingly powerful local coalition. Community leaders are deeply aware of the severe consequences of the decline and polarization that have occurred in older, larger metropolitan areas. The Twin Cities has a legacy of metropolitan cooperation and reform that, though squandered during the 1980s, still has force. Perhaps most important, due in part to the research reported in this book, it has become clear that Twin Cities suburban communities are not a monolith with common experiences and political needs. The emergence of these patterns has created a metro-majority political coalition between the central cities, which make up one-third of the region's population, and the inner suburbs and middle-class developing suburbs, which make up another third.

The creation of such a coalition between the central cities and inner and low–tax base suburbia is no mean feat. These middle-income (often working-class) suburbs, which have been a loose cannon politically since 1968, hold the balance of power on these regional issues and arguably on most political issues in the United States. Our most distinguished political commentators have written about the central significance of this group in holding and maintaining a ruling political coalition.[36]

On the merits, these middle-income, blue-collar suburbs are the largest prospective winners in regional reform. To them, tax base sharing means lower property taxes and better services, particularly better funded schools. Regional housing policy means, over time, fewer units of affordable housing crowding their doorstep. Once understood, this combination is unbeatable. However, in the face of this coalition stand long-term, powerful resentments and distrust, based on class and race and fueled by every political campaign since Hubert Humphrey lost the White House in 1968—and Archie Bunker became a Republican.

In Minnesota, after two years of constant cajoling and courting and of constant repetition of the growing inequities among the suburbs, the middle-income, working-class, blue-collar suburbs joined the central cities and created a political coalition of great political power in the legislature. In 1994, this coalition passed the Metropolitan Reorganization Act, which placed all regional sewer, transit, and land use planning under the operational authority of the Metropolitan Council of the Twin Cities.[37] In doing so, it transformed the Met Council from a $40-million-a-year planning agency to a $600-million-a-year regional government operating regional sewers and transit, with supervisory authority over the major decisions of another $300-million-a-year agency that runs the regional airport. That same year, in the Metropolitan Land Use Reform Act, metro area farmers were insulated from public assessments that would have forced them to subdivide farm land for development. In both 1993 and 1994, the legislature passed sweeping fair housing bills (both vetoed), but in 1995 a weakened version was finally signed. In 1995, the legislature passed a bill that significantly increased the regional tax-sharing system known as "fiscal disparities." That bill was vetoed.

The legislative process has indeed been controversial, but the urge toward reform is growing. Social equity groups representing poor residents in older communities and environmental groups wishing to protect land and water from development pressures are beginning to come together around this regional agenda. These groups sense a common connection in their individual struggles against the waves of chaos that overwhelm their individual efforts. In 1994, the Alliance for Metropolitan Stability was formed, an organization including regional churches, environmental groups, communities of color, community development agencies, and other good-government groups. As the alliance gains visibility and develops a common language and agenda, the potential for broad-based regional action increases.

The mapping of demographic and economic data, in ways that had to wait for the recent development of inexpensive technology, helped support these legislative coalitions between central cities, inner suburb, and low–tax base developing suburbs. Simple colored maps allowed policymakers to quickly create images of both demographic patterns and the implications of fiscal and land use policies. Had this technology not been available, much of what is presented in this book (both in terms of understanding the pattern of regional polarization and the resulting legislative action) would have been more difficult to achieve.

This book is a call to action not only in the Twin Cities, but also to local, state, and national policymakers who face rapid polarization in metropolitan communities across the country. The relevance of the Twin Cities experience can be placed on a continuum. Polarization and decline in the Twin Cities, though less severe than in New York, Chicago, or Detroit, are worse than in most younger, smaller regions and even some regions of similar size, age, and complexity. The central-city schools are dominated by poor minority children; every night, as in every metropolitan region, the local television news is dominated by the same stories about poor minority crime and violence in the inner city. The same dynamics that have divided and conquered older, larger regions are firmly rooted here as well, and the local coalitions that are beginning to take action in response can be built elsewhere. Although the Twin Cities in the early 1990s had the rudiments of a regional planning layer, these regional debates (particularly those on equity) could have taken place without it. Also, the same dynamics that have divided and conquered older, larger regions are firmly rooted here as well, and the local coalitions that are beginning to take action in response can be built elsewhere.

This book presents new research on the interaction of schools, crime, fiscal disparity, and governmental structures in a midsize metropolitan region. It is intended to provoke questions for further study in the context of the political world's reaction to academic theories about reform.

2

The Core: Concentrated Poverty and the Challenge of Regionalism

Concentrated poverty is a cancer that is growing around the very heart of the Twin Cities. It is deepening in intensity and spreading in scope. The most recent census shows that this cancer has broken the central-city membrane, and its early stages are established in the inner suburbs.[1] Virtually every older metropolitan region in the United States has experienced what Minneapolis and Saint Paul are just discovering—left unchecked, the cancer spreads relentlessly outward from the city core.[2]

Sectoral Development of American Metropolitan Areas

American metropolitan areas develop along class lines in socioeconomic wedges, reaching out from central-city neighborhoods deep into suburbia, say students of American metropolitan housing markets from Homer Hoyt through John S. Adams.[3] As cities initially form, the working class settles within walking distance of industry. The middle class forms neighborhoods "upwind" of heavy transport and manufacturing areas on sites close to white-collar, downtown jobs. The upper class settles (and tends to remain) in neighborhoods removed from the other two groups, on land with attractive topographical features and in houses equipped with every amenity currently available.

The most rapid turnover in home ownership occurs in middle-class housing markets as promotions and pay increases allow owners to move into "newer and better" housing. Middle-class sectors therefore appear as asymmetrical bulges of housing construction at the region's periphery.

Among working-class people, simple home ownership is a major goal, wages peak early, and demand for move-up housing is low.

A household move to a new unit at the periphery creates a vacancy at the old address, to be filled by another household, which leaves a vacancy at its old address, and so on. Building new housing at the periphery sets in motion vacancy chains reaching far back into the city's central core. Thus the more rapid peripheral growth of middle-class sectors leaves excess housing and low demand at the center of its vacancy chain. As demand declines, so too does price, opening up opportunities for the region's poor people. Gradually, working-class neighborhoods extend into working-class first- and second-tier suburbs, middle-class neighborhoods into middle-class suburbs, and upper-class neighborhoods into upper-class suburbs. These patterns once followed street car lines and radial access roads beyond the city into the first-tier suburbs. However, as circumferential highways became the shaping force of metropolitan development, the influence of sectoral patterns began to wane in suburbs beyond the beltways (map 2-1).[4]

In this way, core middle-class neighborhoods are the first to become impoverished and ultimately become extreme poverty tracts (also known as ghettos). As these neighborhoods grow poor, social and economic decline accelerate, pushing the middle class out while the vacancy chain simultaneously pulls these residents outward.[5] Working-class and upper-class neighborhoods, with less growth and turnover, remain stable longer than middle-class neighborhoods do. But once decline starts, these neighborhoods quickly collapse. Ironically, as the various economic classes leave central-city areas, all the social and economic changes that occur in the core of their sectoral housing markets eventually follow them through the vacancy chains out into the suburbs.

Poverty in the Twin Cities

In the Twin Cities, as in most large cities around the country, extreme-poverty tract and transitional-poverty neighborhoods exploded in size and population during the 1970s and 1980s. The first neighborhoods to fall were distressed census tracts where more than 40 percent of the people live below the federal poverty line—these are extreme-poverty or *ghetto neighborhoods*.[6] Next were the surrounding *transitional-poverty neighborhoods*, where between 20 percent and 40 percent of the people live in poverty.[7] By 1980 the Twin Cities ghetto or extreme-poverty tract areas included eleven census tracts surrounding both downtown areas. During the 1980s, 21 contiguous tracts became part of the ghetto, as their population swelled from 24,420 to 79,081 (maps 2-2 and 2-3). Transitional-poverty areas also increased, from 43 census tracts with 102,682 people to 57 census tracts with 153,700 residents. To put this in perspective, taken together, the ghetto populations of Minneapolis (61,054) and Saint Paul (17,834) were one-twelfth as large as the massive New York City ghetto (952,484), one-fifth the size of Detroit's (375,548), and almost half the size of Milwaukee's (140,831).[8] On the other hand, they were not quite twice as large as Newark's ghetto (49,189); three times the size of Boston's (28,738), Kansas City's (24,049), and Indianapolis's (23,297) ghettos; and five times as large as the ghettos of San Francisco (12,127) and Portland, Oregon (15,764).[9]

Extreme-poverty tract and transitional-poverty areas together account for 11 percent of the Twin Cities' population, but 36 percent of its poor people live there.[10] These neighborhoods have an extremely high combination of welfare households, single parents, unemployed males, school dropouts, low–birth weight children, teenage mothers, personal and narcotics-related crimes, women without prenatal care, female-headed households, and homicides.[11]

Concentrated poverty is intrinsically connected with racial segregation and an array of social problems.[12] During the 1980s, the concentration of blacks in Twin Cities extreme-poverty tracts increased faster than in any other U.S. metropolitan area with more than 1 million people except Milwaukee, Detroit, and Buffalo.[13]

The Ghetto and Segregation

A few more statistics sharpen this picture. The Twin Cities region is 92 percent white, 4 percent African-American, 1 percent American Indian, and 3 percent Asian. The extreme-poverty tracts are 48 percent white, 24 percent African-American, 19 percent Asian, and 7 percent American Indian. The transitional-poverty area is 69 percent white, 19 percent African-American, 7 percent Asian, and 3 percent American Indian.

Poor African-Americans are more than twice as likely as poor whites to live in the extreme-poverty tracts and about 20 percent more likely to live in transitional-poverty areas. Specifically, 40 percent of poor African-Americans (18 percent of poor whites) live in the ghetto; 43 percent (37 percent of poor whites) live in the poverty areas.

In 1990 the Twin Cities had 7,248 African-American households above the metropolitan median income. Of these African-American middle-class households—people who have more choices about where they will live—almost half (40 percent) lived in the suburbs. Only 18 percent of these households chose to live in majority–African-American census tracts.[14]

Minneapolis is home to about two-thirds of the 4,000 central-city African-American households with incomes above the median. These middle-class African-Americans are concentrated in neighborhoods that are not yet segregated: in the southside, Central (47 percent African-American), Bryant (62 percent African-American), and Regina (52 percent African-American); in the northside, Willard Hay (65 percent African-American) and Hawthorne (31 percent African-American). Middle-class African-Americans in the Twin Cities rarely choose to live in majority–African-American census tracts, but they often live in more socially distressed neighborhoods than whites of similar income. Seven percent of African-American households above the median income live in the two central-city ghettos; another 23 percent, in transitional–poverty area census tracts.

The Concentration Effects of Poverty

Concentrated poverty multiplies the severity of problems faced by communities and poor individuals.[15] As neighborhoods become dominated by joblessness, racial segregation, and single-parentage, they become isolated from middle-class society and the private economy.[16] Individuals, particularly children, are deprived of local successful role models and connections to opportunity outside the neighborhood. A distinct society emerges with expectations and patterns of behavior that contrast strongly with middle-class norms, and the "exodus of middle- and working-class families from ghetto neighborhoods removes an important 'social buffer.'"[17]

Individuals who live in concentrated poverty are far more likely to become pregnant as teenagers,[18] to drop out of high school,[19] and to remain jobless[20] than their counterparts in socioeconomically mixed neighborhoods. In the social isolation of concentrated poverty, distinctive speech patterns develop,[21] making interaction with mainstream society difficult and complicating education and job searches.[22] An "oppositional culture" emerges that appears to reject many closely held middle-class mores.[23]

Poor young men and women from broken families, without connections to outside opportunity or hope for a better life, engage in self-reinforcing, promiscuous sex in a search for affection or status. Single parentage in poor neighborhoods is part of conforming to peer group expectations. At first, the infant represents a focus of love, identity, and purpose in an otherwise bleak setting; later, the child becomes another burden in a life overwhelmed by hopelessness. In neighborhoods where adult independence is hard to achieve and home life may be dysfunctional, the welfare benefit paid for a child represents a way out of the family apartment.[24]

In neighborhoods lacking successful middle-class role models, gang leaders, drug dealers, and other antisocial figures are often the only local residents with money and status.[25] Tightly knit gangs replace nonexistent family structures. These factors interact with anger, frustration, isolation, boredom, and hopelessness, and create a synergism of disproportionate levels of crime, violence, and other antisocial behavior.[26]

The growing oppositional culture holds down those who try to find a way out. Individuals who attempt to succeed through steady work at modest employment are often singled out and derided by communities where failure dominates.[27] Ridiculed by peers, children can soon lose their desire to achieve academic success at school.[28]

Crime: The Last Resort?

Concentrated poverty and its attendant social problems in distressed city neighborhoods sustain America's notoriety for violent crime.[29] Like all other urban maladies sweeping into inner suburbs, crime accelerates and intensifies. Saturation-style crime reporting in the media amplifies the alarm of city dwellers and strengthens the forces of race- and class-based polarization as the middle class moves out.

In the Twin Cities metropolitan region, the crime rate declined 8 percent during the 1980s. This overall regional decline hid conflicting trends among different types of metropolitan communities. In middle-income and gentrifying city neighborhoods and most other places, crime dropped. In transitioning poor central-city neighborhoods and in declining inner suburbs, it continued to make inroads. The serious crime rate in the central cities was almost half again as high as the metropolitan rate and more than double the suburban rate.[30] Of all the suburbs, the inner ring fared worst. Violent crime (a subset of serious crime) was even more concentrated in cities and their poorest neighborhoods.

In the Twin Cities metropolitan region, nearly one-third of the people live in the central cities, but they are responsible for nearly half of all crime. Crime in Minneapolis (11,754 crimes per 100,000 people) was 42

Table 2-1. Average Number of Violent Crimes, Minneapolis Area, 1983–89, 1993

Minneapolis neighborhood crime rate (per 100,000 residents)	Percentage of city population	Average number of violent crimes, 1993	Percentage of city violent crimes	Percentage increase, 1983–89
< 3,000 crimes	21	229	62	69
< 3,000 crimes and > Minneapolis rate	12	138	17	52
< Minneapolis rate and > metro rate	25	30	13	42
< metro rate and > suburban rate	29	12	6	62
< suburban rate	14	6	1	20

Source: Minneapolis Police Department.

percent higher than in Saint Paul (8,264). The 8 percent regional increase in the central-city crime rate reflected a 16 percent increase in Minneapolis, mitigated by a 4 percent decline in Saint Paul. Violent crime is disproportionately concentrated in distressed city areas.

One-third of Minneapolis residents live in neighborhoods with serious and violent crime rates below the metropolitan average, and one-sixth live in neighborhoods where crime is below the suburban average. With 16 percent of the Twin Cities metropolitan population in 1990, Minneapolis accounted for 34 percent of the region's serious crimes and 53 percent of its violent crimes. Thirty-two percent of the residents of Minneapolis live in distressed neighborhoods, where more than 25 percent of the residents have incomes below the federal poverty line. From 1987 to 1989, these core neighborhoods account for 53 percent of the city's serious crimes and 71 percent of its violent crimes. This city core, with 5 percent of the region's population, accounts for 18 percent of its serious crimes and 38 percent of its violent crimes. In the poverty core, the serious crime rate (20,197 per 100,000 people) is one and a half times the Minneapolis rate (12,281) and more than three times the metro rate (5,981). The core's violent crime rate (3,391) is more than twice the Minneapolis rate (1,540) and seven times the metropolitan rate (478).

Violent Crime

Violent crime is far more concentrated than serious crime in the city's most socioeconomically distressed neighborhoods (map 2-4). Based on a three-year average crime rate for 1987–89, the central-city violent crime rate (1,290 per 100,000 residents) is two and a half times the regional rate

(478) and almost eight and a half times the suburban rate (149). Minneapolis's violent crime rate (1,540) was almost twice Saint Paul's (918).[31]

In contrast to the tremendous violence in the poorest neighborhoods of the city, violent crime is the lowest in many middle-class neighborhoods only a few miles removed from the poorest areas but without concentrated poverty. The coincidence of concentrated poverty and violent crime suggests some solutions. On one extreme, twelve Minneapolis neighborhoods at or near the most socioeconomically distressed part of the city had an average of 229 violent crimes from 1987 to 1989. In this category, the Downtown West, Near North, and Phillips neighborhoods have violent crime rates more than ten times the metropolitan average and more than 30 times the suburban average. As these neighborhoods grew poorer, they saw a 69 percent increase in violent crime between 1983 and 1989. In contrast, eleven middle-class neighborhoods, mainly in the southwestern part of the city outside the poverty core, had an average of only six violent crimes a year. In three of those neighborhoods, Waite Park, Page, and Fulton, crime was two-thirds the suburban violent crime rate.

The Inner Suburbs

Serious crime in the Twin Cities inner suburbs was 17 percent higher than in the nearest group of suburbs, and two-thirds of the inner suburbs had crime rates above the suburban average (map 2-5). The northern inner-ring suburbs of Minneapolis were the most troubled by crime. Brooklyn Center's serious crime rate of 8,231 per 100,000 residents was nearly as high as Saint Paul's, and it was increasing (29 percent over the decade) almost twice as fast as the Minneapolis rate. Close behind were Columbia Heights, Fridley, Brooklyn Park, Blaine, Roseville, Maplewood, and West Saint Paul, all of which had serious crime rates of between 6,000 and 8,000 crimes per 100,000 residents.[32] Spring Lake Park, with a serious crime rate of 5,242, saw a staggering 282 percent increase over the decade. In Chicago and Philadelphia, where these trends have played themselves out further into the future, there are many inner-declining suburbs with crime rates significantly higher than the central cities they surround.

In the remaining three groups of suburbs, serious crime rates declined approximately 15 percent. The mid-developing suburbs, with a serious crime rate of 4,408 per 100,000, had 12 percent of the metropolitan population and 8 percent of its crime. The southern and western developing suburbs had 27 percent of the Twin Cities population and 17 percent of its crime. The safest part of the region, the east metro suburbs, had 5 percent of the population and 3 percent of its serious crime—2,714 per 100,000 residents.

The Media and Crime

For most metropolitan residents, local television is the largest source of news—"crime, weather, and sports," as one commentator aptly described it.[33] Crime stories are inexpensive to cover, easy to explain, and generate high ratings. During several of the most recent ratings sweeps, the top two stories on half the local newscasts in the Twin Cities were about crime (figure 2-1). Coverage, often sensationalistic and repetitive, frequently returns to the scene of a brutal crime two or three nights in a row.[34]

Over and over again, metrowide polling in the Twin Cities indicates that the public's single biggest concern is crime. Dramatic new penalties have caused prison populations in Minnesota to increase 287 percent from 1978 to 1993.[35] Crime and prison costs are one of the few areas in state government where there are tremendous amounts of new spending (maps 2-4 and 2-5).

During the 1996 legislative session, almost nine straight hours were spent on the Minnesota House floor considering more than 50 amendments to the crime bill—a bill that took a large percentage of the new money the state spent during the session. Representatives from suburbs with small and declining crime rates offered complicated bills about gang activity. Representatives from rural areas, within the reach of metropolitan television, sponsored bills about drive-by shootings. Such threats are by no means present in their own communities.

On an average night, almost 1 million Twin Cities adults tune in to televised news programs. As the combined readership of metropolitan newspapers continues to decline, television increasingly represents the most important source of public information. Local TV news programs bear a 71 percent chance of featuring at least one crime story in the first three stories broadcast.[36] Crime and destruction have come to dominate both national and local programming. According to the Center for Media and Public Affairs, the 1993 national evening broadcasts of ABC, NBC, and CBS contained 1,632 crime stories, up 208 percent from the previous year. Meanwhile, the violent and nonviolent crime rates on American streets have declined since the early 1980s.[37]

For most Americans, local news provides no alternative to this violent sensationalism. A study published by the Rocky Mountain Media

Figure 2-1. Crime Coverage in Local Television News

Number of stories

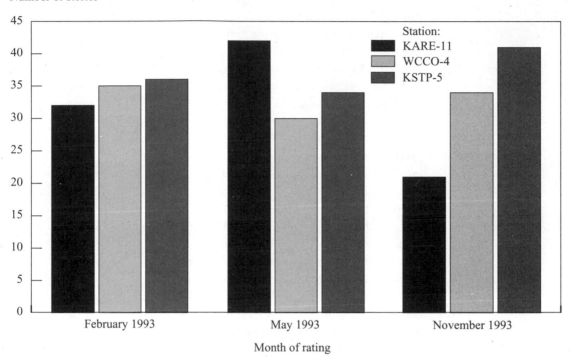

Month of rating

Source: KARE-11 TV, Minneapolis.

Watch analyzed 50 television news programs in 29 cities, all recorded on the evening of January 11, 1995. An average of 28.5 percent of total news time was devoted to crime alone, and 53.8 percent covered stories of crime, war, or disaster—collectively known as the "mayhem index."[38]

The Rocky Mountain Media Watch report included two of the Twin Cities metropolitan area's commercial television stations in its sample: WCCO-4 and KARE-11. Thirty-five percent of KARE's broadcast was consumed by crime, war, and disaster, and WCCO devoted a hefty 62.7 percent to mayhem. Local stations are pushed toward crime coverage because it represents attention-grabbing material while requiring little or no labor costs spent on background research and because crime's sensationalism garners high Nielsen ratings in a competitive market. A 1992 study found that many news managers believe that crime coverage constitutes valuable news. They also think presenting violence is necessary in news in order to remain professional and objective.[39]

Twin Cities TV news gives priority to mayhem in evening newscasts, granting it more time than any other category of substantive news. Heavy coverage of crime comprises the largest portion of mayhem. In this light, it is not uncommon for a station to revisit the same crime story on successive nights. When a young man was murdered walking home from the YWCA in uptown Minneapolis, stations covered the original story. A follow-up story interviewed many of his friends and family. A third story interviewed people in the area where the crime occurred, asking them how safe they felt in their own homes and in the neighborhood. The final story reported that police had no new leads in the case.[40]

Scholars agree that the less direct experience people have with a given issue, the more they rely on the news media for information and interpretation. According to Minnesota Planning, metropolitan residents do not generally have high levels of exposure to crime.[41] They are therefore likely to turn to the media for information about the issue. Minnesota Planning found in 1994 that residents of Hennepin and Ramsey counties held expectations of victimization that were in some cases more than six times their true likelihood of victimization. The disproportionate levels of crime covered by television news programs, then, are significant not only in their large audience and skewed coverage, but in their ability to form perceptions and set the public agenda. This can create a real barrier to regional coordination and discussion.

Middle-class TV viewers are working harder for declining real wages, are losing pension and health benefits, and cannot afford to send their children to college. Job security itself is also rapidly declining. Viewers come home exhausted after driving farther from work and spending more time in the car than any previous generation. When these people are subjected, night after night, to repetitive stories showing poor people (often people of color) committing violent crimes—and see few other types of news—perceptions harden, social and racial tensions increase, and the division between the city and older suburbs on the one side and newly developing outer suburbs on the other accelerates. The inner-suburban fear of the city hardens, and the realignment of middle-income and lower-middle-income voters shifts to a more conservative agenda.

In the last decade, responding to both the perception and the reality of increased criminal activity, the state of Minnesota, like the federal government and most other states, has lengthened sentences and embarked on large prison-building projects.[42] These very large expenditures and their small effects strongly suggest that it is time to seek solutions to crime by reducing the concentration of its breeding ground, the poverty core. Providing individuals with access to opportunity and freedom from the negative influences of local oppositional culture is likely to cut crime and in the process help to stabilize the socioeconomic conditions at the core.

The *Gautreaux* Case: Access to Opportunity

One outstanding social experiment, Chicago's Gautreaux project, provides evidence that poor individuals can dramatically change their lives if freed from extreme-poverty and distressed neighborhoods and provided with opportunities to improve their lives. Under a 1976 court order in the case of *Hills* v. *Gautreaux*, thousands of single-parent African-American families living in Chicago public housing were provided housing opportunities in predominantly white, middle-class neighborhoods.[43] Under the consent decree in a massive fair housing lawsuit originally brought in 1966, more than 4,000 low-income households were given housing opportunities in Chicago and its suburbs. By random assignment, more than half of these households moved to affluent suburbs that were middle class and virtually all white; the other participants moved to neighborhoods that were all poor and either exclusively African-American or low-income and integrated. The pool of Gautreaux families therefore provides an almost perfect sample to study the effects of suburban housing opportunities on poor city residents.[44]

James Rosenbaum and colleagues from Northwestern University have intensively studied the Gautreaux families.[45] Their research established that the low-income women who moved to the suburbs "clearly experienced improved employment and earnings, even though the program provided no job training or placement services."[46] Soon after the moves, the new suburbanites were about 15 percent more likely to be employed. Employment was easier to find in the suburbs because there were more jobs, they said. Greater safety for themselves and their children was the second most important factor mentioned. One woman, whose only previous employment had been in the Navy, said "I can advance now. When I was discharged from the service, life stopped. You can't walk up and down the streets in the city." Another suburban mover quit the job she had before she moved because, she said, "I'd have to use the subway late at night. I was just scared." Another noted, "I've moved up. You don't get robbed here, so I can better myself."[47]

Finally, the suburban movers said that simply living in the suburbs gave them a stronger motivation to improve themselves and get jobs. "[The housing project] deteriorates you. You don't want to do anything . . . [Living in the suburbs] made me feel that I'm worth something. I can do anything I want to if I get up and try it," said a young women who had re-cently been promoted at work. Another woman, a clerical worker in both city and suburbs, believed that moving had motivated her to pursue new opportunities: "It was a different type of environment. Most of the people around me were more advanced than I was. . . . I wanted a promotion. So more education was the answer."[48]

Rosenbaum found that the children of the suburban movers dropped out of high school less frequently than the city movers (5 percent versus 20 percent) and maintained their grades despite the higher standards of suburban schools. These children were much more likely to be on a college track (40.3 percent versus 23.5 percent), and 54 percent of them went to college, compared with 21 percent who stayed in the city. In terms of employment, 75 percent of the suburban youth had jobs, compared with 41 percent in the city. Moreover, the suburban youth had a significant advantage in pay and were more likely to have a prestig-ious job with benefits. Finally, 90 percent of the suburban youth were either working or in school compared with 74 percent of the city youth.[49]

The participants' comments were illuminating. The suburban mov-ers noted that their new environments stimulated motivation in school. "[My daughter] wouldn't have the drive, the challenge, the desire to ad-vance that's needed to get ahead in life . . . if we hadn't moved," said one mother. "She wouldn't be in college now." Some of this motivation came from higher expectations in the suburbs. "A lot more is expected from you out here. A lot of emphasis on school. You have to succeed. If you don't go to school, you're not going to make anything of yourself," said one young suburban mover.[50]

Many women also noted that teachers, less overwhelmed by local problems, could typically provide more help: "His suburban teacher tries to help each individual as they need it. They didn't do that in the city." Many students remarked on the influence of positive role models. "I saw that most of the kids in my classes wanted to go to college, and their older brothers and sisters were in college, so I thought I could do that too," said one. In contrast, their peers in the city were negative role models. "My friends back in Chicago are skipping [school] a lot. I would probably be hanging around with them," stated one girl.[51]

The acceptance of these poor African-American families in affluent, predominantly white suburbs was neither painless nor immediate. At the outset, about 52 percent of the suburban movers reported incidents of racial harassment, compared with 23 percent in the city.[52] However, these inci-dents rapidly tapered off. Both suburban and city movers reported similar degrees of support and assistance from neighbors (24.8 percent suburban versus 25.0 percent city) and essentially no difference in terms of their contact with neighbors. The suburban movers were slightly more likely to have friends in their new neighborhoods than were the city movers, and the suburban movers had more than twice as many white friends and slightly fewer African-American friends. Over time, the degree of integration continued for suburban movers, and resegregation did not occur.[53]

The relevance of the *Gautreaux* case and the follow-up study done with the participants seems clear: opportunities for fair housing *can* make a difference to individuals from extreme-poverty or distressed areas.

Business Follows the Middle Class

The core of poverty grows denser as people who can choose leave the blighted neighborhood. Progressive social disorganization intensifies crime, business disinvestment, and loss of property value around the core. As the middle class leaves, fewer customers patronize local retailers, and the value of local housing as well as commercial property plummets. Even grocery stores disappear from the poorest metropolitan neighborhoods.[54] As an example of these trends, during the 1960s, Chicago lost 500,000 white residents, 211,000 jobs, and 140,000 private housing units, while its suburbs gained 800,000 white residents, 500,000 jobs, and 350,000 housing units.[55] As the West Side of Chicago was enveloped in an expanding core of poverty during the 1960s, 75 percent of its businesses disappeared.[56] By 1980, the West Side's ghetto North Lawndale neighborhood included "48 state lottery agents, 50 currency exchanges, and 99 licensed bars and liquor stores, but only one bank and one supermarket for a population of some 50,000."[57] Any private entrepreneurs who stay justify their exorbitant prices by their "high risk of doing business." In the extreme-poverty tracts or ghetto areas, social needs (and hence property taxes) begin to accelerate on a shrinking value base. As local property taxes become highest in the least desirable parts of the metropolitan area, the flight of the middle class and the private economy accelerate.

Jobs Follow Business

Larger industrial and service businesses are disadvantaged by high taxes, deteriorating public infrastructure, crime, loss of property value, lack of room for expansion or parking, lack of rapid access to radial highways, and the cost of urban environmental issues.[58] Employers say that workers who remain in stressed ghetto neighborhoods are less and less suited to fill available jobs—if there are any, because jobs also flee with the businesses (see chapter 5).

Job training or creation programs must struggle against the oppositional culture. To the extent such programs succeed, individuals—even those who find jobs in the neighborhood—often move to less poor residential areas.[59] Physical rehabilitation programs can improve the quality of shelter and the appearance of the neighborhood, but they cannot unravel the tangle of pathology that is bound to these neighborhoods by concentrated poverty.

A Failed Leg Up

Not even the largest and most successful Community Development Corporation (CDC) initiatives in the country have changed the basic downward spiral of poor, segregated neighborhoods. In his study of the twenty-five CDCs that the nation's philanthropic community judged most successful, David Rusk found that, despite large CDC investment, family and individual poverty rates and median household income have moved farther from metropolitan norms, and these communities have grown more segregated.[60] Although individuals may have benefited and CDC efforts may have made these communities better than they might otherwise have been, the initiatives are woefully inadequate against the enormous forces of metropolitan polarization.

In terms of business development, areas of concentrated poverty have great difficulty competing with developing suburbs with middle-class customers, low taxes, cheap land at rising prices, room for expansion and parking, new highways, and relative freedom from crime and environmental problems. Thus, even when enormous financial resources have been devoted to enterprise zones or inner-city tax abatements, viable business opportunities that employ core residents have been, at best, difficult to generate.[61] In the end, the lack of a social mortar to hold neighborhoods together and build communities makes economic development in extreme-poverty tracts or ghetto areas all but impossible.

Political Diversity of Metropolitan Areas

Metropolitan reforms are no longer possible because the suburbs have taken over American politics, assert political commentators, scholars, and even serious reformers.[62] Representing more than 50 percent of the American population and more than 70 percent of the Twin Cities metropolitan area, "the suburbs" do have great political power. Contrary to the pessimists' assumptions, however, the suburbs are not monolithic and do not necessarily share common social experiences and political needs. Their experiences and needs are almost as diverse as those of the nation itself (table 2-2).

Internal Diversity of the Central Cities

The Twin Cities central core is a place of overwhelming transience, social isolation, and decline. When residents vote, they overwhelmingly vote Democratic. In older cities, for lack of a watchful electorate, there is the constant danger of corrupt political representation. Perhaps because local problems are presumed to be insoluble, these neighborhoods usually have the lowest voter turnout in the state.

North and Northeast Minneapolis and the East Side of Saint Paul were once tightly knit, ethnic, working-class neighborhoods. Today, they are in the throes of rapid social and economic change. Politically, these neighborhoods are passing from an old guard that is white, socially conservative, and dominated by organized labor to younger, more socially liberal whites and people of color.

South Minneapolis and the Highland Park area in Saint Paul's southwestern quadrant are still solidly middle class and unthreatened by immediate change. Because of the self-selection of middle-class people who decide to stay, this part of the Twin Cities is decidedly more liberal and Democratic than it was a generation ago. Its legislators include some of the Minnesota legislature's strongest liberal voices on issues such as ethics, gun control, and the environment.

Neighborhoods in the central cities with many residents who are professionals include Kenwood and much of southwest Minneapolis and the Macalester/Groveland and Merriam Park areas of Saint Paul. Here are some of the region's most desirable housing stock, the trendiest restaurants and shops, and shrines of pop culture. Because incomes are higher than in the poorest neighborhoods, these areas are often characterized as exclusive. However, their housing stock is so diverse (a mix of expensive and moderately priced houses and rental units) that median income remains well below levels in the affluent suburbs. These former Republican bastions have become Democratic, but their elected officials are more concerned about property taxes than are politicians in other parts of the city.

Table 2-2. Selected Twin Cities Regional Statistics

	Central cities	Inner-ring suburbs	Mid-developing suburbs	East developing suburbs	Southwest developing suburbs
Persons, 1990	640,618	564,359	245,490	118,418	578,903
Households, 1990	271,139	224,625	78,924	41,107	213,550
Percentage of region's population, 1990	29.8	26.3	11.4	5.5	27.0
Median household income, 1989 (thousands of dollars)	25.8	36.1	42.1	47.3	47.2
Percentage change in median household income, 1979–89	0.4	–4.7	2.3	8.4	1.8
Percentage children under 5 in poverty, 1989	31.9	10.6	6.3	4.8	4.4
Percentage change in children under 5 in poverty, 1979–89	62.3	16.3	0.7	3.1	5.9
Percentage female-headed households with children, 1990	30.8	19.1	10.9	11.9	11.3
Percentage change female-headed households, 1980–90	21.4	32.7	29.2	17.6	18.2
Percentage change in white children ≤ age 5 in 1980 to ages 10–14 in 1990	–36.5	–12.0	21.0	36.1	33.2
Percentage change in jobs, 1980–92	0.7	18.2	72.4	64.1	71.1
Market value per household, 1994 (thousands of dollars)	74.2	91.7	114.6	142.7	159.3
Percentage change in market value per household, 1980–94	–8.3	2.5	78.1	75.2	69.7

Source: Bureau of the Census, 1980, 1990; Minnesota Department of Jobs and Training, Research and Statistics Office, *Twin Cities Area Average Covered Employment, First Quarter 1992* (Minneapolis, June 25, 1993); Minnesota Department of Revenue, unpublished data.

Local Metropolitan Subregions

Over generations of urban growth, four distinct types of suburban communities have emerged in the Twin Cities metropolitan area: socioeconomically declining inner suburbs; low–tax capacity developing suburbs at mid-region; commercial high–tax capacity developing suburbs in the southern and western region; and residential high–tax capacity developing suburbs in the eastern region.[63]

The socioeconomically declining inner-ring suburbs (the *inner suburbs*) are a collection of fully developed working- and middle-class suburbs where 26 percent of the metropolitan population lives. Many of these communities are beginning to feel the effects of the socioeconomic changes spreading outward from the city and are ill equipped to handle new problems.

The inner-suburbs are the only part of the Twin Cities metropolitan region—including the central cities—where income has declined. In median income, the inner suburbs ($36,000) are closer to the central cities ($26,000) than to the high–tax capacity suburbs ($47,000). At $1,800 of tax capacity per household, even after the application of local fiscal equity measures, the inner suburbs have about one-third less than the high–tax capacity suburbs.[64] Their total property wealth expanded 2.5 percent over the decade, about 25 percent below the regional average.[65] This lethargic increase came in the face of rapidly increasing social needs. Their crime rate, for example, is almost twice as high as in the wealthy residential suburbs.[66]

Single mothers head 20 percent of all inner-suburban families, about twice the average rate in developing suburbs. With 11 percent of their children already living below the federal poverty line, the inner suburbs are gaining poor children faster than the central cities (figure 2-1). Columbia Heights, a community just north of Minneapolis, provides a particularly striking example of the spread of childhood poverty in the inner suburbs. Its concentration of poor children in 1990 (21 percent) was the same as in Minneapolis in 1980, but Columbia Heights is growing poor almost twice as fast.

While some upper-income inner suburbs such as Edina and Mendota Heights are among the region's most stable communities, middle-class and particularly working-class inner suburbs are less stable than central cities for economic, organizational, and cultural reasons:

—*Central cities have a comparatively stable resource base.* Central cities are the first to feel social and economic change and decline, but their central business districts and stable, gentrifying neighborhoods provide them with some tax base for responding. Inner-ring, post–World War II suburbs are often bedroom communities without commercial-industrial base or stable housing values. As poverty and instability arrive, the relatively few available resources rapidly evaporate.[67]

—*Cities have social and governmental systems in place to deal with poverty and social change.* Most welfare and other social networks are located in central cities, which also have large, well-equipped police forces. These agencies provide vital assistance in containing and lessening the severity of social distress. When social problems slip suddenly across city borders, they often hit the unprepared inner-ring suburbs like a freight train.

—*Central cities are heterogeneous and retain pockets of stability and gentrification.* American cities originally reflected the social and economic mix of their respective metropolitan areas, with a range of elite, middle-class, and working-class neighborhoods. Upper-class neighborhoods retain their appeal for older elite and young urban professionals.

Middle- and working-class suburbs are homogenous and do not have elite or gentrifying neighborhoods.

—*Central cities housing was built to last.* Housing in central cities, particularly in elite and upper-middle-class neighborhoods, was built to last and to please the eye. Fashioned of stone and brick, the exteriors were durable. Interior amenities such as hardwood floors and built-in cabinetry are still in demand and expensive to duplicate. Most post–World War II expansion suburbs are a collection of rapidly assembled, inexpensively constructed homes. They are not unique and do not compete directly with more modern housing in outer-edge cities that lack social stress.[68]

—*Central cities have institutions and social amenities.* These attractions range from universities and the stable communities connected with them, to the fine arts and popular entertainment, and to a wide variety of restaurants and a well-landscaped urban park system. These all interact well with unique housing stock to foster diverse stable communities. Inner-ring, inexpensive housing is usually arranged in grids that rarely include entertainment, parks, or other amenities.

Politically, the inner suburbs house a mix of Democrats and Republicans. Initially, affluent inner suburbs such as Roseville and Golden Valley were solidly Republican. Roseville has moved to a Democratic margin under a relatively gentle inner-suburban transition, and Golden Valley, though still Republican, is gaining Democrats. Edina, with some of the region's most expensive and exclusive housing, remains among the state's most Republican districts.

The northern inner suburbs, settled as working- and middle-class suburbs, were strongholds of organized labor and Democratic from the outset. Recently, under the onslaught of social and economic changes, these suburbs have become politically volatile, like the Macomb County, Michigan, suburbs outside Detroit that Stan Greenberg discusses in his book *Middle Class Dreams.*[69] The margins of old-line labor Democrats grow slimmer every year. In Brooklyn Park, Brooklyn Center, and Columbia Heights, the antiwelfare, anticrime, anti–affirmative action presence is powerful and growing as large numbers of poor people (particularly people of color) move in. Many of the closest legislative races in the 1994 election were in the northern inner suburbs.

The midregion, low–tax capacity developing suburbs *(mid-developing suburbs)* tend to be extensions of middle- and working-class neighborhoods beyond the beltways. These rapidly developing communities, with a property tax base resting mainly on inexpensive single-family homes and apartment buildings, do not have sufficient resources to support basic public services.

The Twin Cities mid-developing suburbs represent about 11 percent of the region and about 25 percent of the developing suburbs. This group has 6 percent children living in poverty and 11 percent familes headed by single mothers, slightly higher than the other developing suburbs. At $42,000, median income is higher in mid-developing suburbs than in the inner suburbs, but 10 percent lower than in the high–tax capacity suburbs ($47,000).[70] These communities are characterized by inexpensive housing, with a median home price of $80,000, about 40 percent below median home value in the high–tax capacity suburbs ($130,000).[71] The mid-developing suburbs therefore have about the same tax capacity as the central cities and inner suburbs.[72] However, because they are growing fast and building streets, sewers, schools, parks, and other infrastructure, they have little money left for basic public services such as education and police forces. Ironically, by the time these suburbs begin to reduce their debt service for public infrastructure costs, they are already well down the path of socioeconomic decline. This group of suburbs has the second lowest per pupil school spending in the region and very high drop-out rates.[73] Their crime rate of 4,408 is about midway between that of the inner suburbs and the high–tax capacity suburbs.[74]

The mid-developing suburbs are classic swing districts, leaning toward the Democrats on economic issues and toward the Republicans on social issues. In the Twin Cities, the northern part of these districts has a comparatively strong antiabortion presence. Their male residents, frequently avid sportsmen, often oppose gun control. Property tax increases are highly unpopular in these areas, where the budgets of young working-class families are stretched to the limit. Although education is important to parents, school referendums seldom pass.

The *commercial high–tax capacity developing suburbs* in the Twin Cities form the "favored quarter" (or as it is locally known, the Fertile Crescent) of the area's south and west. Although this subregion is sometimes referred to as the "southwestern" region, it is really a crescent of southern and western suburbs that sweep in an arc from Maple Grove (actually northwest of Minneapolis) down along the I–494 beltway, all the way to the city of Eagan and the communities beyond. (See subregions map at map 2-6.) To the east lie the *residential, high–tax capacity developing suburbs,* with a broad, rich property tax base and comparatively few socioeconomic needs. The crime rate is low in the south and west (3,831 per 100,000 residents), but higher than in the east developing suburbs (2,714), which are the lowest in the region.[75] Childhood poverty is below 5 percent, single parentage below 12 percent. More than half the cities in these growing communities had smaller concentrations of poor children at the end of the decade than at the beginning, quite possibly a result of local zoning and metropolitan transportation policies friendly to the middle class but restrictive toward poor residents (maps 2-7 and 2-8).[76] Over time, households that cannot make it over suburban housing barriers tend to collect in the central cities and the older suburbs. The high–tax capacity suburbs have a $47,000 median household income— almost twice as high as in the central cities, 23 percent higher than in the inner ring, and 10 percent higher than in the mid-developing suburbs. With $2,500 of tax capacity per household, they have about one-third more tax wealth than the other subregions.

The southern and western developing suburbs have dominated metropolitan commercial growth for the past two decades.[77] During the 1980s, this subregion, which has 27 percent of the region's people, created 61 percent of its new jobs. Eighty percent of the funds spent on new metro highways during the decade ($830 million out of $1 billion) and most of the new sewer construction budget was built to benefit the southern and 23 percent more CI growth western development boom. The southern and western developing suburbs had the most property value per household of all the regions, at $159,260. Although the east and southern and western developing suburbs have similar property tax wealth per household, the value of the east suburbs is based far more in its residential property.

The southern and western component of this group is strongly (but not entirely) Republican. Home to many regional business leaders, it is a Republican campaign coffer. It is also the one area in the state where the majority of voters and about one-third of the Republican elected officials are pro-choice. In the rest of the state, virtually all the other Republican officeholders are antiabortion. The eastern part of the region tends toward political conservatism, but the election results are closer.

Income Polarization and Politics

Underlying this spatial polarization was the polarization of household income. Throughout the United States, the rising tide of the 1980s lifted the large, fast boats, but only added ballast to mid-sized boats and almost swamped the small ones. During the 1980s, those in the bottom three quintiles of household income lost ground, those in the fourth stayed even, and those in the fifth saw their household income increase by nearly one-third (table 2-3).

As the incomes of many Americans shrank, health care costs climbed out of reach, and private pensions became less well funded and

Table 2-3. U.S. Family Income
Constant 1992 dollars[a]

Income group quintile	1977	1985	1992	Percentage change, 1977–92
Lowest	8,495	7,353	7,434	–12.50
Second	18,885	16,798	16,955	–10.20
Middle	27,788	25,988	25,670	–7.60
Fourth	36,563	36,367	37,094	1.50
Highest	63,546	76,252	82,455	29.8
Overall	30,948	32,364	33,722	9.1

Source: United States House of Representatives, Ways and Means Committee, *1991 Greenbook*, table 19, p. 1306.
a. Average real income after taxes.

less common. Young adults entering the work force found jobs with benefits or decent wages increasingly difficult to locate and land. Education and training have also become harder to finance. Labor Secretary Robert Reich blames this loss of economic status and opportunity on changing technology, increased global competition, and the steep political decline of the American labor movement.[78]

A disappointed, frustrated middle class reacted angrily to the civil rights movement and the Great Society. Beginning in the 1966 midterm elections after the signing of the Civil Rights Act and reaching maturity in the 1968 election, Republican strategists divided the second- and third-quintile voters against those in the poorest quintile. In a powerful series of campaign ads, they asserted that Democratic programs both favored poor citizens (particularly those of color)—and did so at the expense of the hard-working, increasingly foundering middle class. These programs that raised and protected poor people were unraveling the middle-class social order, they argued. This campaign began with Kevin Phillips's appeal to the "forgotten American" in the 1968 presidential race, reached a crescendo with the wickedly brilliant cynicism of the Willie Horton ads in the 1988 Republican presidential effort, and reemerged more recently in California Governor Pete Wilson's media war on affirmative action.

In the older, more divided regions of the country, these divide-and-conquer tactics succeed in working-class city neighborhoods and older suburbs undergoing social changes. They are beginning to work here. Central cities usually vote Democratic; white-collar suburbs, Republican. Stan Greenberg writes of the inner suburbs, the land of the second and third quintiles, who voted for Kennedy in 1960 and Johnson in 1964. By

1968, many had switched to Nixon and the Republicans. These communities of middle-class whites, raised up by the union movement and the New Deal, now had homes and neighborhoods to protect—homes and communities directly in the path of metropolitan decline.

In the late 1960s, in older, larger regions of the country, poor people—those in the lowest economic quintile—rolled into these areas, fleeing the declining core city. People in the second and third quintile groups felt a deep threat to the value of their houses—their main assets—and to their neighborhoods, which were the center of their world. As they resisted these incursions in Macomb County, Michigan, in western inner Cook County, Illinois, and in inner southeastern Delaware County, Pennsylvania, they aligned with more conservative economic and political forces than their economic circumstances would normally indicate. These increasingly conservative, working-class inner suburbanites outside of large cities feared for their homes and neighborhoods. Their racism was wrong, but their fear that disorderly metropolitan change would severely hurt—perhaps destroy—their communities was well founded. In another part of suburbia, in their insulated, exclusive neighborhoods, the upper economic quintiles watched the lower and mid-quintiles fighting among themselves. The more they fought, the more insulated and affluent the top economic group became.

Spatial and income polarization marry in unpredictable and angry politics. In 1992, the middle class supported Bill Clinton and, to some degree, Ross Perot. In Minnesota, the lowest three income quintiles supported Clinton, but in declining numbers as income rose; George Bush's strength lay in the top two quintiles (figure 2-2). Perot took 20 percent of the vote of each group. The central cities, inner suburbs, and low–tax capacity suburbs went Democratic in both statewide and legislative elections; the affluent, high–tax capacity suburbs supported Bush and the Republicans.

By 1994, throughout the country, many middle-income voters turned to Newt Gingrich and the Republican Party, not so much because of the inherent force of the Contract with America—which few voters had even heard of—but perhaps because their economic prospects were not improving. In the only close Minnesota statewide race, between Ann Wynia and Rod Grams for the U.S. Senate, Wynia lost the race among middle-class voters, particularly those earning between $20,000 and $50,000. In the 1994 election to the Minnesota State Legislature and two special legislative elections since, the Democrats lost eight metro House seats, all in the inner and low–property value suburbs.[79]

Figure 2-2. Minnesota Voting in the 1992 Presidential Election, by 1991 Family Income

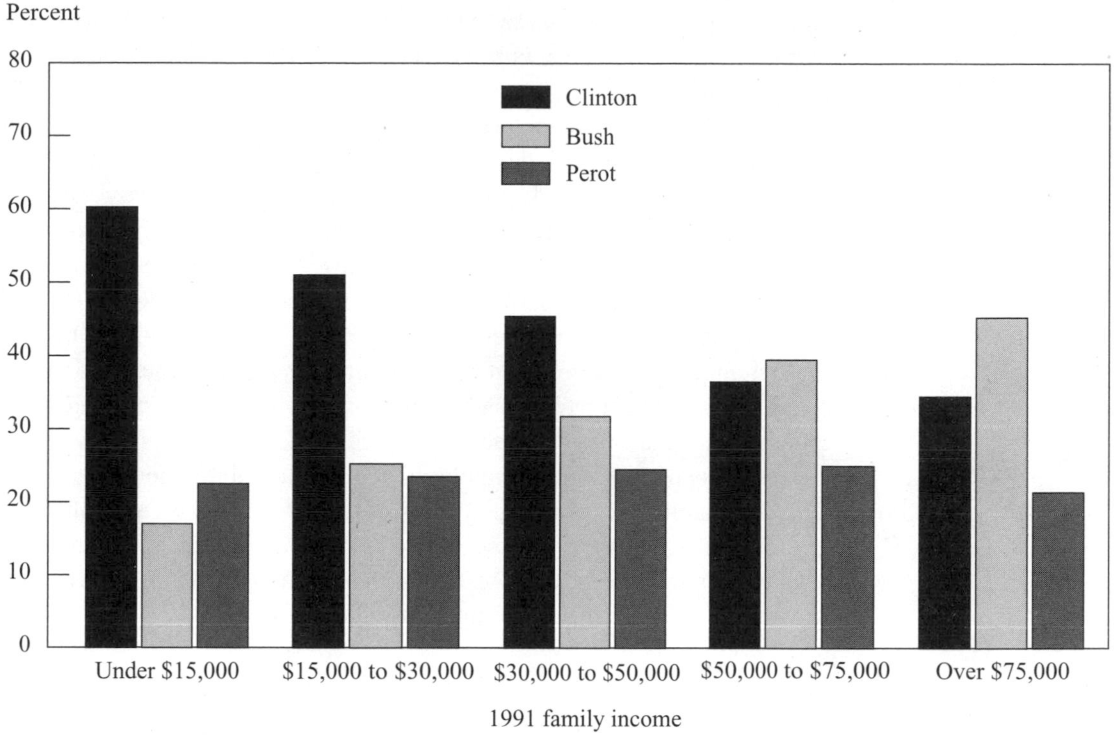

Percent

1991 family income

Source: Adam Pertman, "Reagan Democrats Go for Clinton," *Saint Paul Pioneer Press,* November 4, 1992, p. 8A.

The challenge of regionalism, then, is no mean feat:

—To unite the central cities with the middle- and lower middle-class voters in the declining and low–property tax value suburbs;

—To show them that tax base sharing lowers their taxes and improves local services, particularly schools; and

—To convince them that fair housing will limit their commitment to poor citizens to manageable regional standards and thereby stabilize residential change in their communities.

For middle-class inner suburban neighborhoods, which have their fair share of the region's poor residents already, regionalism promises to *limit* their commitment to affordable housing and end overwhelming waves of poor people arriving from the city. Once inner-suburban legislators understand this message, they can become powerfully supportive.

For years, however, their constituents have dreaded the arrival of changes from the region's core, and they have campaigned against the city in their elections. At the outset, these inner suburbs are not powerfully disposed to believe that an alliance with their previous enemy is either wise or politically expedient.

In the end, spatial polarization and income polarization augment each other. In some ways, the desperate struggle for exclusivity in the affluent suburbs (increasingly the realm of the economically powerful) is part and parcel of an effort by the upper class to reduce its responsibilities to society in terms of a progressive tax policy. As the privileged have less and less contact with those less fortunate, their attitudes harden. Their intensely exclusive zoning practices may be a last-ditch effort to act through municipal government before opting for private "gated" communities, as the affluent have already done in many older, more polarized regions of the United States—and in the third world.[80]

As social and economic polarization spreads throughout the Twin Cities, instability is growing. The intensity of debate on schools and crime are good indicators of the scope and depth of middle-class anxiety. It is the rapid increase of poor children in local schools, however, that sounds the first warning of imminent middle-class flight.

3

The Schools:
Early-Warning Signal

Income and social polarization in the Twin Cities are nowhere more apparent than in its forty-eight school districts, especially those in the inner suburbs. In the middle-income, outer-ring suburbs, which are struggling to develop on an inadequate tax base, spending per pupil is the lowest in the region, and social and academic challenges are multiplying. Only the affluent suburban systems enjoy insulated, stable prosperity—financed by local business.

Schools are not just instruction and textbooks but a complex web of social networks that reinforce student success or failure.[1] Just as concentrated poverty holds down neighborhoods, in schools it inhibits individual success and academic achievement. Fast-track, well-funded suburban schools move students toward success on a stream that places high value on hard work, goalsetting, and academic achievement.[2] Monolithically poor central-city and inner-suburban schools sweep children toward failure on undercurrents that reinforce antisocial behavior, drifting, teenage pregnancy, and dropping out.[3] Socioeconomically mixed schools improve poor children's academic achievement, high school graduation rates, and (most significantly) their access to further technical training, higher education, good jobs, and many other middle-class benefits.[4] The change in demographics from white to African-American in a basically blue-collar suburban district can be one of the most unsettling events in American politics.[5]

Deepening poverty and other socioeconomic changes show up in schools before they do in neighborhoods and in elementary schools before junior high and high schools. Elementary school enrollment patterns therefore sound an early warning of impending flight by the middle class, the first group to leave a neighborhood when schools fail. Perceived school quality is a key factor in attracting or retaining middle-class residents (and the businesses that cater to them), and thus in maintaining property values, which in turn fund schools—in a potentially vicious circle.

School Subregions

Because socioeconomic change is further advanced in the region's school systems than in its neighborhoods, and because school districts divide affluent suburbs between the middle class and more affluent residents, the categories used here to describe schools differ slightly from those used to describe cities (map 3-1).[6] The *central-city* and *inner-suburban* categories are roughly the same.

In the developing suburbs, however, two rings of school districts are growing poorer instead of one. The diverse *second ring* of school districts is less poor and racially diverse than the inner ring but much more so than the other groups of districts. The *fast-growing* districts are characterized by rapid growth in the past decade, rapid projected growth in the next, or both, and include the mid-developing suburbs and the less affluent parts of the southern, western, and east developing suburbs. Eleven percent of the population of the region lives in growing, middle-income cities without enough tax capacity for adequate public services, but 21 percent of metropolitan students attend schools in fast-growing districts with low tax capacity and per pupil spending rates.

In the affluent *southern and western developing* districts lives 33 percent of the region's residents, but only 11 percent of the students attend schools there. Per pupil spending is high and student diversity and poverty extraordinarily low. If restrictive housing markets perpetuate great social and economic disparities, school districts appear to slice affluent communities into even more exclusive school districts.

School Spending

The education bill for kindergarten through twelfth grade (K-12) is the largest state appropriations bill—$5.8 billion each biennium and 32 percent of the state budget. Legislators from fast-growing districts compete strenuously for positions on the education committee and struggle for funding for their school districts. In 1957 Minnesota moved to an educational formula through which the state ensures every district a basic foundation amount per pupil.[7] A number of categorical aids further target funds to high-need districts. Inflation has gradually eroded this aid, and disparity has increased among the metropolitan districts (map 3-2). On the high end, Saint Louis Park spends $7,021 per pupil, while north suburban Forest Lake spends more than one-third less ($4,611).[8] Because fast-growing districts spend so much of their resources just to construct new school buildings, their school operating (noncapital) expenditures can vary even more than per pupil spending.[9] These disparities, though large, are much smaller than the 3:1 disparities of Chicago and other metropolitan areas with less significant school equity systems.

The huge portion of state resources absorbed by the K-12 bill and the variation in spending among metro districts might suggest a more direct connection between spending and school performance. Paradoxically, the lowest-spending districts seem to be among the best at attracting, retaining, and graduating middle-class students. Many of the highest-spending districts have the highest flight and drop-out rates. This paradox is due partly to the cost of special support for poor students in declining districts (for example, special education or enrichment programs, day care, health care, and nutrition programs).

It is also worth noting that the variation in school funding in Minnesota is not as great as it is in many regions, where segregated inner-city and inner-suburban schools literally do not have enough resources to maintain their physical plant or purchase books and equipment. (This is not meant to imply that the disparities in school performance would not be worse without these funds.)

Neither does school spending appear to reflect a community's dedication to schools. High property wealth (business property in particular) accounts for the local variation in school spending. "We love CI [commercial-industrial property], because you can hit it twice as hard and it can't vote," confided one school board member.

Polarization in Metropolitan School Districts

Throughout the country, schools in large industrial central cities are segregated and poor. This pattern is so pervasive that by 1990, even in Portland, Oregon (with a population less than 3 percent African-American metrowide), elementary school enrollment in the poorest neighborhoods was more than 70 percent African-American.

Busing

In the Twin Cities, extensive school busing in Minneapolis preempted drastic racial segregation and had the general effect of dispersing poverty.[10] Without busing, enrollment in "neighborhood" schools around the northern and southern cores of poverty would have been totally poor and minority today, instead of more than 60 percent. Schools in predominantly white middle-class neighborhoods would be virtually all white and middle-class instead of having more than 30 percent non-Asian minority students. Saint Paul, with a smaller minority population and less residential segregation, used voluntary magnet schools to preempt racial concentrations. Its less extensive efforts are reflected in wider socioeconomic disparities in its schools.[11]

Busing in the Twin Cities began on order of the local federal district court in 1972 to desegregate the Minneapolis public schools.[12] At that time, Minneapolis had 15 percent minority students. In 1983, responding to the imminent threat of a desegregation lawsuit in Saint Paul, the Minnesota State Board of Education assumed legal responsibility for desegregating Minnesota's schools by promulgating the state desegregation rule.[13]

Under this "15 percent rule," a school district is deemed "segregated" and experiences a "reduction in state aids" if the minority population in one of its school buildings exceeds the minority population of the district as a whole by more than 15 percent. The rule creates responsibilities only for individual school districts; it does not contemplate any interdistrict or metropolitan obligation for desegregation. Minneapolis (with the highest percentage of non-Asian minority students and the greatest residential segregation) is the only district in the Twin Cities with an extensive desegregation plan. Saint Paul, which has never been under a court order, has neighborhood schools with voluntary magnets to encourage integration. The suburbs all have neighborhood schools.

When the state desegregation rule was adopted, the central cities had more than one-quarter minority students, and the inner ring was just beginning to have a minority presence. Since then, rapidly increasing central-city and inner-suburban minority school populations, together with metropolitan housing and migration patterns, have made effective desegregation impossible within the boundaries of the central cities and will do so shortly in the inner suburbs. By 1993, the Robbinsdale and Osseo school districts were already in violation of the state desegregation rule.

As the concentration of minority students exceeded 50 percent in Minneapolis, the system faced the difficult job of trying to maintain integration while preventing white flight to suburbs with few poor or minority children. It elected to bus poor African-Americans into the ethnic working-class northeast section of the city before fully engaging the more middle-class southwest. It also created a desegregation plan interconnected with a school choice plan that required an extraordinarily complex system of school busing. Similar though less extreme maneuvering occurred in Saint Paul.

Central Cities

Central-city schools in the Twin Cities enroll 22 percent of the region's children of elementary school age but 55 percent of the poor children in that age group (map 3-3). Between 1982 and 1994, children receiving free and reduced-cost lunch in the Minneapolis Public Schools rose from 33 percent of enrollment to 52 percent; Saint Paul "caught up," moving from 28 percent poor children to 55 percent. During this period, the concentration of minority children also increased—from 34 percent to 59 percent in Minneapolis and from 29 percent to 49 percent in Saint Paul (map 3-4).

These similar minority percentages hid ethnic differences. Minneapolis had 47 percent non-Asian minority students versus 27 percent in Saint Paul.[14] Generally, Asian students have a more stable family structure, higher test scores, better graduation rates, and tend to present schools with fewer challenges than African-American, Hispanic, and American Indian students. Asians throughout the country are more integrated with whites than are African-Americans or Hispanics.[15] However, a large percentage of the Asian students in the Saint Paul schools were recent Hmong immigrants. The Hmong, coming from a less sophisticated agrarian background than most Asian immigrants, have many of the same socioeconomic and related difficulties as African-Americans, Hispanics, and American Indians. In the end, both central-city school systems face similar challenges.

By 1994, the elementary schools closest to the expanding core of poverty were the poorest schools in each of the Twin Cities. In Saint Paul, fifteen elementary schools had more than 70 percent of their children on free lunch programs. The poorest school was East Consolidated, with 95 percent poor children. In Minneapolis, a larger and poorer school system, only eight schools had more than 70 percent poor children as students. Waite Park, with 85 percent of its children on free or reduced-cost lunches, was the city's poorest elementary school.

Concentrations of children on free lunch increased in schools in both cities between 1982 and 1994, but the most dramatic changes occurred in middle-income and working-class neighborhood schools in the northeast section of Minneapolis (from 37 percent to 60 percent) and the East Side of Saint Paul (from 33 percent to 55 percent). In one school in the northeast, Waite Park Elementary, this indicator shot up from 21 percent in 1982 to 85 percent in 1994. In Minneapolis, these changes were the result of both residential decline and the decision of the Minneapolis schools to bus poor African-American children into the northeast before fully engaging the more affluent sections of the city.

Corresponding almost directly to the increases in poor students, the central-city graduation rates are shockingly low. Of children entering the ninth grade, 33 percent in Minneapolis and 28 percent in Saint Paul do not graduate.[16]

Though poverty in core areas deepened and elementary schools in middle-income neighborhoods underwent stunning transitions into majority poverty status, the middle-class lakes area of southwest Minneapolis and the Macalester/Groveland area of Saint Paul experienced their own unsettling movement, with the student body becoming roughly one-third poor and non-Asian minority. Despite great internal disparities in city schools, the average resident of a middle-class city neighborhood still sent her child to a school that was five to ten times poorer than a suburban school within her financial reach. This fact took an extraordinary toll in terms of middle-class flight.

During the 1980s, Minneapolis lost 41 percent of its white preschool enrollment.[17] Saint Paul lost 32 percent. The largest percentage loss of white children occurred in a halo of census tracts around the expanding poverty cores of both cities (maps 3-5 and 3-6). In many transitional neighborhoods in Minneapolis, between 75 percent and 100 percent of white preschool children disappeared between census reporting periods. In Saint Paul, the most highly transitional areas lost between one-half and three-quarters of their preschool white children. The farther away a neighborhood was from the poverty core, the less dramatic the level of flight. Some middle-class and gentrifying neighborhoods in Minneapolis and Saint Paul registered a small increase in white children.

The 1980 Minneapolis Homeowners Survey reported that 14 percent of households with children planned to move out of the city within five years. By 1986, 23 percent of them were planning to move.[18] More than one-third of the parents in virtually every middle-class north and northeast neighborhood had plans to leave the city. In the middle-class south Minneapolis neighborhoods, between 25 percent and 35 percent of households with children were preparing to leave. Poor parents living near the cores of poverty who did not have the financial means to leave were less likely to be planning a move.[19] By 1993, 45 percent of the households with children planned to leave the city within five years.[20] Between 37 and 50 percent of householders with preschool children intended to move from the working and middle-class south Minneapolis neighborhoods (map 3-7).

As the level of white flight and African-American immigration intensified, so too did the segregation of African-American children. In 1980, the ratio of African-American to white preschool children exceeded 2:1 in two census tracts in Minneapolis's Near North neighborhood and two in the Summit-University and Thomas Dale area of Saint Paul. By 1990, Minneapolis had 19 core tracts with a ratio greater than 2:1, and St. Paul had four. The African-American to white ratio exceeded 3:1 in seven tracts in Minneapolis, including a 32:1 ratio in the Near North neighborhood. Saint Paul had four tracts (the same four) with a ratio greater than 3:1, the highest (19:1) in the Summit-University neighborhood. In both cities, the census tracts with the highest concentrations of poverty were the most racially segregated in terms of preschool children.

Few people realize that the central-city schools spend $7,060 per pupil, 15 percent more than any other group of districts in the Twin Cities. Spending on central-city schools is also high in Chicago, Atlanta, and many other cities throughout the United States. No matter where it occurs, higher spending does little to attract or retain middle-class students. The existing level of poverty and student diversity are overriding deflectors.[21]

In the Twin Cities, because both central cities have low tax bases, state aid supplies a large part of this extra per student spending. If some of this largesse comes from heartfelt compassion, the rest derives from a form of blackmail practiced by both central-city districts. Every few years, they threaten the legislature with a metropolitan desegregation lawsuit. In response, the education committees, with strong support from suburban members, approve increased funding for the city schools. Talk of the lawsuit then cools for a time. This ugly bargain is repeated in region after region throughout the United States.[22] "We'll keep them here, if you send us money" is one of the most self-destructive parts of regional polarization.

The crisis of city and inner-suburban schools often proceeds without any relevant facts. In older metropolitan areas, post hoc analysis has revealed that test scores ratchet downward in synchronization with increasing poverty.[23] By 1994 the central cities, with more than half of their students living in poverty, were experiencing a huge loss of middle-class students. During the 1980s, this growing instability coincided with enormous parental and public concern about the quality of the central-city schools. Perhaps because they were afraid of the potential reaction, school administrators did not forthrightly discuss changes in their school populations or their implications, and neither system employed testing systems that provided accurate information on student performance. Experts told the school board and parents that test scores were stable or declining slightly. In reality, the testing data were so incomplete and so heavily manipulated that no one really knew how these changes were affecting students.[24]

This dearth of relevant facts combined with growing and often explosive parental discontent. The ensuing reform discussions, centered on curriculum, bureaucracy, and teacher accountability, was in many ways isolated from the reality of what was occurring in the schools in the 1980s.[25] A series of reforms, some very expensive, were instituted to correct the "problems" of the central-city schools. None of these reforms directly addressed the schools' overwhelming transformation to majority poverty status as a result of polarization in the regional housing market. Whether the reforms had any effect at all on slowing the loss of middle-class families was hard to know, so quickly were they abandoned and often without any evaluation. In any event, they clearly did not turn the tide.

Improvements came neither from an exhausting and costly public campaign for a Minneapolis school referendum in the early 1990s directed at reducing class sizes nor from large property tax increases. In Saint Paul, a similar referendum repeatedly failed to win voter approval. Recognizing the need for stable schools and facing a declining tax base, mayoral candidates and other desperate city officials in both cities began to call for a return to segregated neighborhood schools as the final solution to the school problem. This solution was no more likely to succeed than any of the other failed ideas. Moreover, it presented the additional threat of deepening social and racial divisions in an increasingly segregated metropolitan area.

During the 1993 mayoral election in both central cities, there was palpable public concern that city schools were not holding middle-class families and that without these families the cities would fail. Although the mayor of neither Minneapolis nor Saint Paul has authority over education, the candidates campaigned, more than ever before, on plans to save the schools. The liberals promised more money and programs, the conservatives better management. Neither faction could name any city where these types of proposals had helped to stabilize school populations, although dozens of older, larger cities faced these same transformations.

In early 1995, Mayor Sharon Sayles Belton, Minneapolis's first African-American mayor, began (like many other big-city mayors across the country) a series of pointed attacks on the local school system. At the center of Belton's attack was a demand to return to neighborhood or "community" schools—whether these schools would be segregated or not. For this, she was praised by the city's middle-class neighborhoods, particularly in the northeast. She enjoyed the enthusiastic support of the conservative establishment and its think tank, the Center for the American Experiment, which was resisting a plan by the State Board of Education for metropolitan school desegregation.

Many saw the mayor as a voice of reason and a realist who would return "community" to city neighborhoods. The Minneapolis chapter of the National Association for the Advancement of Colored People, the Urban League, and the emerging Center for Race and Poverty at the University of Minnesota vigorously opposed the mayor's effort. However, because she was the most prominent local African-American leader, their efforts were greatly weakened.

As the debate continued, the mayor moved to endorse a plan to desegregate the city housing market. In mid-1995, the school board, the city council, and the mayor reached a compromise that allowed the city's middle-class neighborhoods to have a more neighborhood-centered program, without abandoning desegregation entirely. The municipal triumvirate also pressed for more affordable housing in the middle-class neighborhoods of the city and regionwide. In the end, this move gave the city's middle-class neighborhoods breathing room in terms of their schools. However, because housing progress would be slow and uncertain, the compromise would greatly intensify the concentration of poverty and segregation in the poorest neighborhoods of the city. In response, in the summer of 1995 the Minneapolis Chapter of the NAACP filed a lawsuit against the State of Minnesota and the Metropolitan Council, under the Minnesota State Constitution for an interdistrict or metropolitan remedy for housing and busing problems.[26]

Inner Suburbs

During the 1980s, the largest social and racial transitions and flight of middle-class families in the nation did not occur in central cities, but in the inner suburbs of Washington, D.C., Atlanta, and Chicago (see chapter 8).[27] In line with these national trends, as social and racial instability crossed into inner-suburban school districts, it accelerated and intensified in the Twin Cities. Virtually all of the Twin Cities' inner-suburban districts, representing 15 percent of metropolitan enrollment (and several second-ring districts), were gaining poor and minority children at an unsettling pace in the face of uncertain or declining tax bases. Nine of the eleven inner districts had more than 20 percent of their students on free lunch and were gaining poor children faster than Minneapolis (map 3-8). Eight were gaining minority students faster (map 3-9).

During the 1980s, the most stunning suburban increases in poverty and racial diversity occurred in a cluster of northern inner-ring suburban systems bordering the middle-income neighborhoods of north and northeast Minneapolis. Virtually every elementary school in the districts of Brooklyn Center, Robbinsdale, Columbia Heights, Fridley, and Spring Lake Park underwent concussive transformations. Like the changes internal to the city, poverty and instability dissipated as distance between the schools and the central-city borders grew.

The population of poor children in the elementary schools of Brooklyn Center, a small school district close to the Minneapolis city limits, went from 17 percent to 39 percent of the student body. By 1994, Brooklyn Center had 25 percent non-Asian elementary minority enrollment. The poorest and most racially diverse suburban district, Brooklyn Center was growing socially and racially diverse at a much faster rate than Minneapolis. In the adjacent Robbinsdale district, with an elementary school enrollment of more than 5,700, the concentrations of poor children tripled (from 7 percent to 25 percent) and minority children doubled (from 7 percent to 14 percent). Richfield, an inner suburb on the south side, received families fleeing south Minneapolis following socioeconomic transition in the housing market. During the 1980s, its schools moved from 8 percent minority elementary school children to 20 percent and from 10 percent poor children to 24 percent.

The high school nongraduation rate in the inner suburbs closely tracked the percentage of poor children in the central cities. In comparatively high poverty schools like Robbinsdale (–15 percent, or a 15 percent decrease from the number of ninth graders who enroll to the number of twelfth graders who graduate four years later), Spring Lake Park (–11 percent), Columbia Heights (–14 percent), South Saint Paul (–14 percent), and Richfield (–14 percent) school districts, roughly one in seven students does not complete high school.

White flight was not just a central-city problem (map 3-10). Eighteen of the 29 inner suburbs also lost white preschool children during the decade. There were large losses in inner-suburban Fridley (–24 percent), Brooklyn Center (–21 percent), Saint Louis Park (–29 percent), Hopkins (–29 percent), Richfield (–23 percent), and South Saint Paul (–14 percent), cities whose boundaries roughly matched school districts by the same names.

A comparison of white flight in Edina and Saint Louis Park is instructive. Both were affluent communities that developed concurrently.

Map 1-1. Twin Cities Metropolitan Area

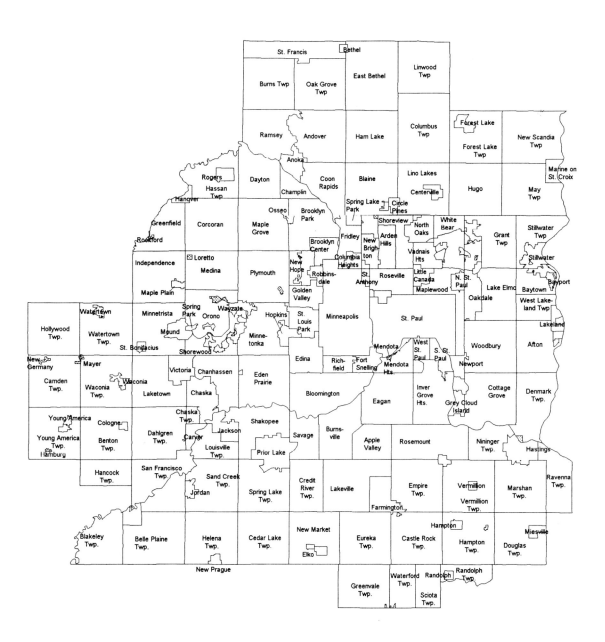

Source: Geographic Information Systems Subcommittee, Minnesota State Legislature.

Map 2-1. Adams Sectoral Housing Model

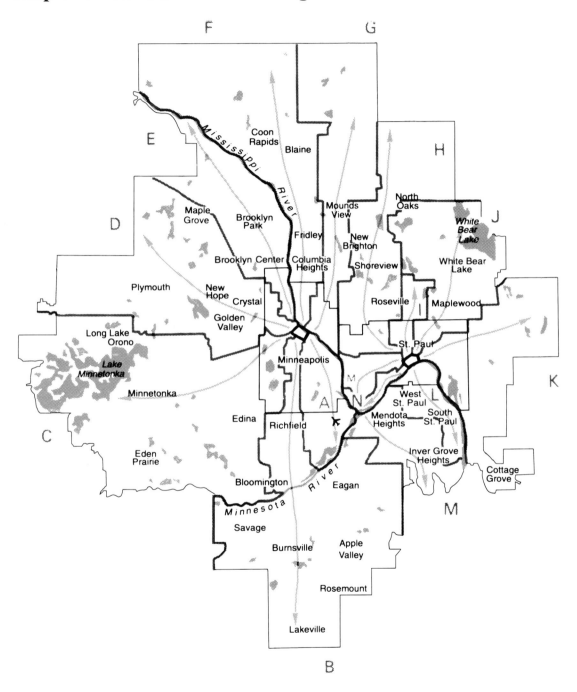

Source: Reprinted from John S. Adams and Barbara J. VanDrasek, *Minneapolis–St. Paul: People, Place, and Public Life* (University of Minnesota Press, 1993), p. 105. By permission, University of Minnesota Press.

Map 2-2. Concentrated Poverty in Minneapolis and Saint Paul,[a] 1979

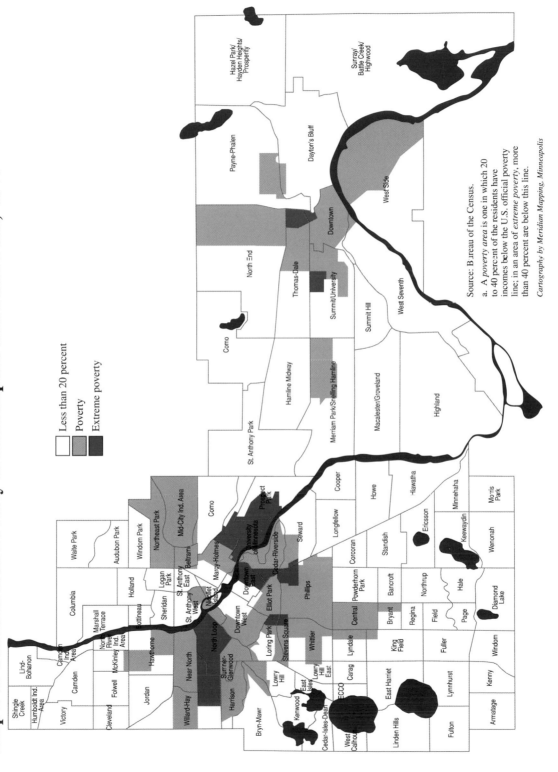

Less than 20 percent

Poverty

Extreme poverty

Source: Bureau of the Census.

a. A *poverty area* is one in which 20 to 40 percent of the residents have incomes below the U.S. official poverty line; in an area of *extreme poverty*, more than 40 percent are below this line.

Cartography by Meridian Mapping, Minneapolis

Map 2-3. Concentrated Poverty in Minneapolis and Saint Paul,[a] 1989

Less than 20 percent

Poverty

Extreme poverty

Source: Bureau of the Census.

a. A *poverty area* is one in which 20 to 40 percent of the residents have incomes below the U.S. official poverty line; in an area of *extreme poverty*, more than 40 percent are below this line.

Cartography by Meridian Mapping, Minneapolis

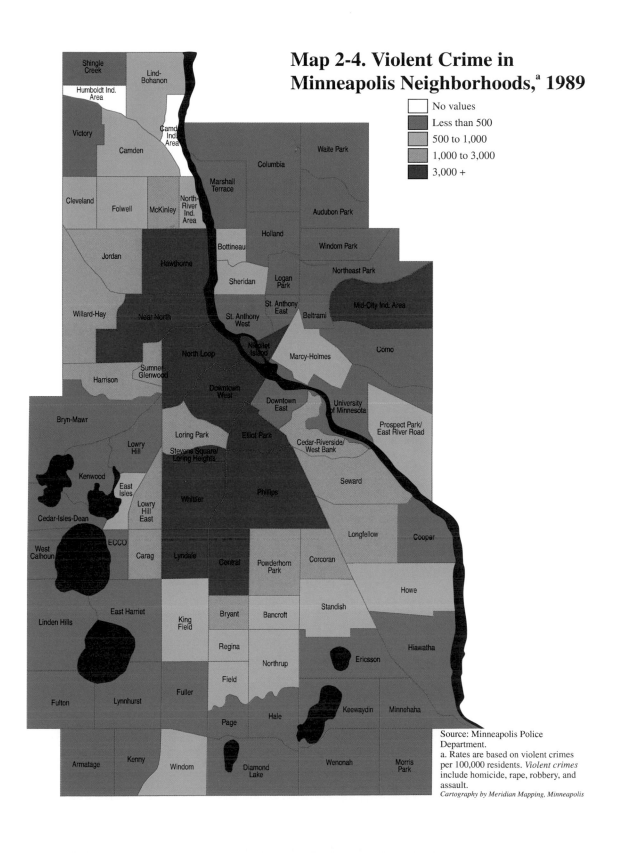

Map 2-4. Violent Crime in Minneapolis Neighborhoods,[a] 1989

No values
Less than 500
500 to 1,000
1,000 to 3,000
3,000 +

Shingle Creek
Lind-Bohanon
Humboldt Ind. Area
Camden Ind. Area
Victory
Camden
Waite Park
Columbia
Marshall Terrace
Cleveland
Folwell
McKinley
North-River Ind. Area
Audubon Park
Holland
Windom Park
Jordan
Bottineau
Hawthorne
Sheridan
Logan Park
Northeast Park
St. Anthony East
Willard-Hay
Near North
St. Anthony West
Beltrami
Mid-City Ind. Area
Nicollet Island
Como
North Loop
Marcy-Holmes
Sumner-Glenwood
Harrison
Downtown West
Downtown East
University of Minnesota
Bryn-Mawr
Loring Park
Elliot Park
Prospect Park/East River Road
Lowry Hill
Stevens Square/Loring Heights
Cedar-Riverside/West Bank
Kenwood
East Isles
Lowry Hill East
Whittier
Phillips
Seward
Cedar-Isles-Dean
Longfellow
Cooper
West Calhoun
ECCO
Carag
Lyndale
Central
Powderhorn Park
Corcoran
Howe
East Harriet
Bryant
Bancroft
Standish
Linden Hills
King Field
Regina
Hiawatha
Northrup
Ericsson
Field
Fulton
Lynnhurst
Fuller
Keewaydin
Minnehaha
Page
Hale
Armatage
Kenny
Windom
Diamond Lake
Wenonah
Morris Park

Source: Minneapolis Police Department.
a. Rates are based on violent crimes per 100,000 residents. *Violent crimes* include homicide, rape, robbery, and assault.
Cartography by Meridian Mapping, Minneapolis

Map 2-5. Serious Crime in the Twin Cities[a]

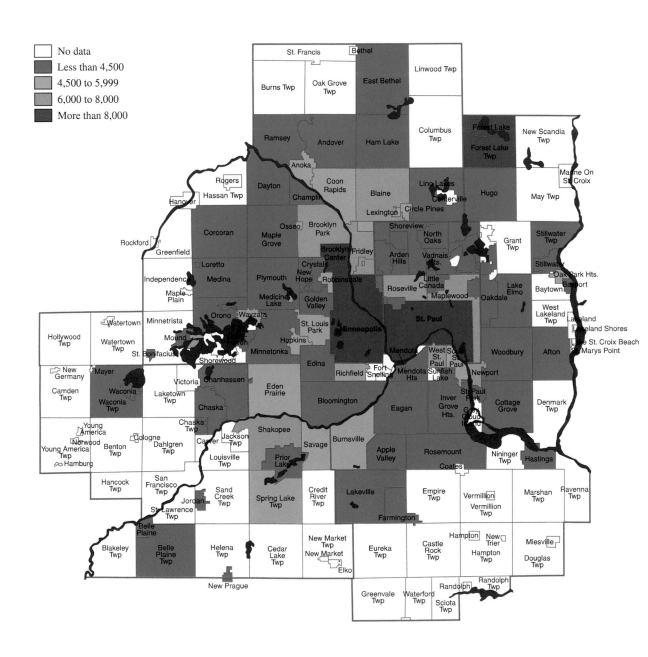

Legend:
- No data
- Less than 4,500
- 4,500 to 5,999
- 6,000 to 8,000
- More than 8,000

Source: Minnesota House of Representatives, House Research Office;
Minneapolis Police Department, Bureau of Criminal Apprehension.

a. Rates based on serious crimes per 100,000 residents for 1989, 1990, and 1991 (averaged).
Serious crimes (Part I) include homicide, rape, robbery, assault, burglary, theft, and arson.

Cartography by Meridian Mapping, Minneapolis

Map 2-6. Twin Cities Metropolitan Subregions, 1996

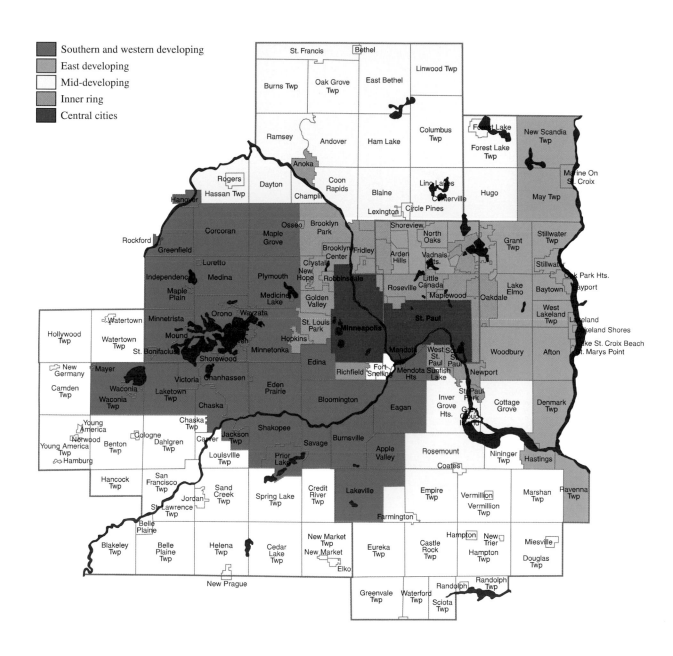

Southern and western developing
East developing
Mid-developing
Inner ring
Central cities

Source: Cities assigned to regions by the author.

Cartography by Meridian Mapping, Minneapolis

Map 2-7. Poor Preschool Children in the Twin Cities, 1989

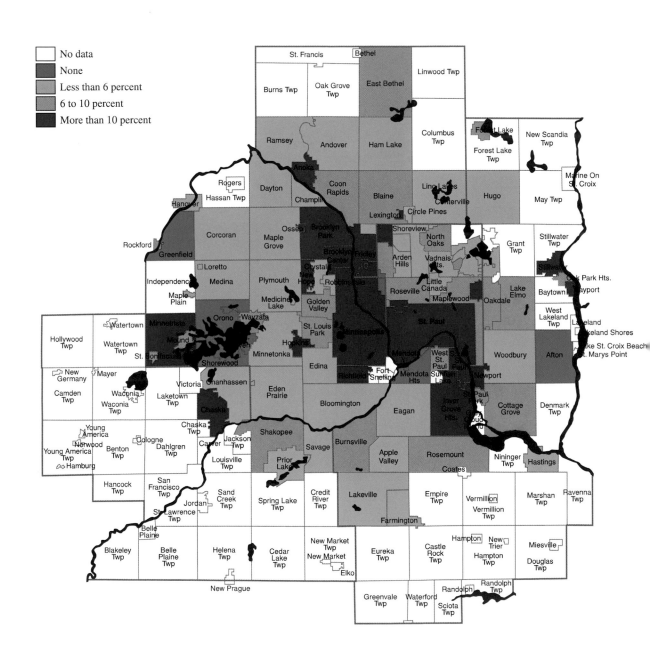

No data

None

Less than 6 percent

6 to 10 percent

More than 10 percent

Source: Bureau of the Census.

Cartography by Meridian Mapping, Minneapolis

Map 2-8. Poverty Trends among Preschool Children in the Twin Cities, 1979–89

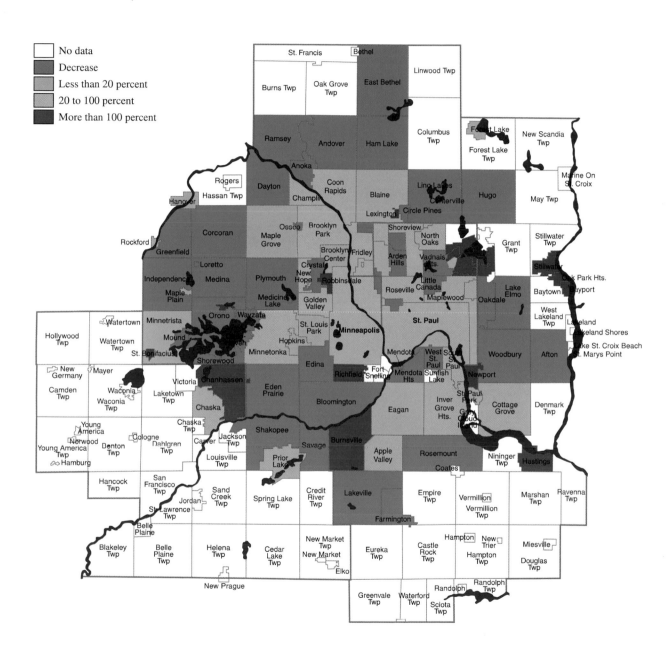

Legend:
- No data
- Decrease
- Less than 20 percent
- 20 to 100 percent
- More than 100 percent

Source: Bureau of the Census.

Cartography by Meridian Mapping, Minneapolis

Map 3-1. Twin Cities School District Subregions

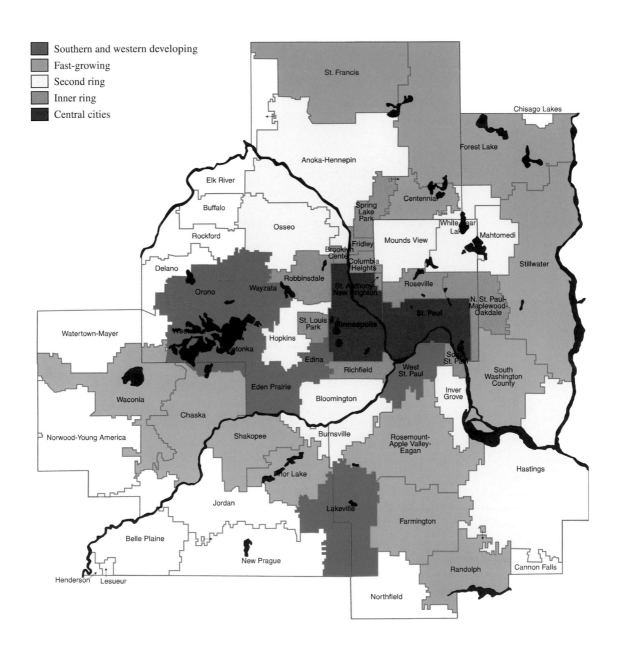

Legend:
- Southern and western developing
- Fast-growing
- Second ring
- Inner ring
- Central cities

St. Francis

Chisago Lakes

Forest Lake

Anoka-Hennepin

Elk River

Buffalo

Rockford

Osseo

Centennial

Spring Lake Park

White Bear Lake

Mahtomedi

Stillwater

Fridley

Mounds View

Brooklyn Center

Columbia Heights

Delano

Robbinsdale

St. Anthony-New Brighton

Roseville

Orono

Wayzata

N. St. Paul-Maplewood-Oakdale

St. Louis Park

Minneapolis

St. Paul

Watertown-Mayer

West

Hopkins

Minnetonka

Edina

Richfield

West St. Paul

So. St. Paul

Eden Prairie

Bloomington

Inver Grove

South Washington County

Waconia

Chaska

Shakopee

Burnsville

Rosemount-Apple Valley-Eagan

Hastings

Prior Lake

Norwood-Young America

Jordan

Lakeville

Farmington

Belle Plaine

New Prague

Randolph

Cannon Falls

Henderson   Lesueur

Northfield

Source: School districts assigned to regions by the author.

Cartography by Meridian Mapping, Minneapolis

Map 3-2. Twin Cities Metro Spending per Pupil,[a] by School District, 1991

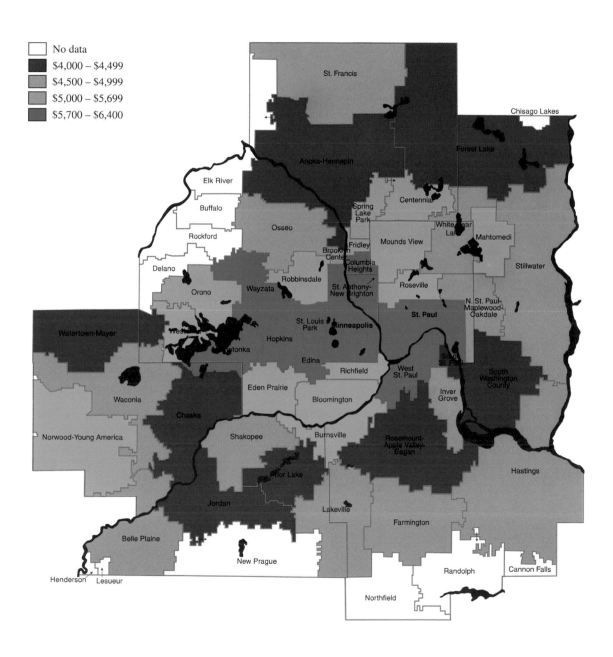

Legend:
- No data
- $4,000 – $4,499
- $4,500 – $4,999
- $5,000 – $5,699
- $5,700 – $6,400

Source: Minnesota Department of Children, Families and Learning.

a. Total expenditures include operating, capital, and debt-service expenditures.

Cartography by Meridian Mapping, Minneapolis

Map 3-3. Children Receiving Free and Reduced-Cost Lunches in Minneapolis and Saint Paul Elementary Schools,[a] 1993

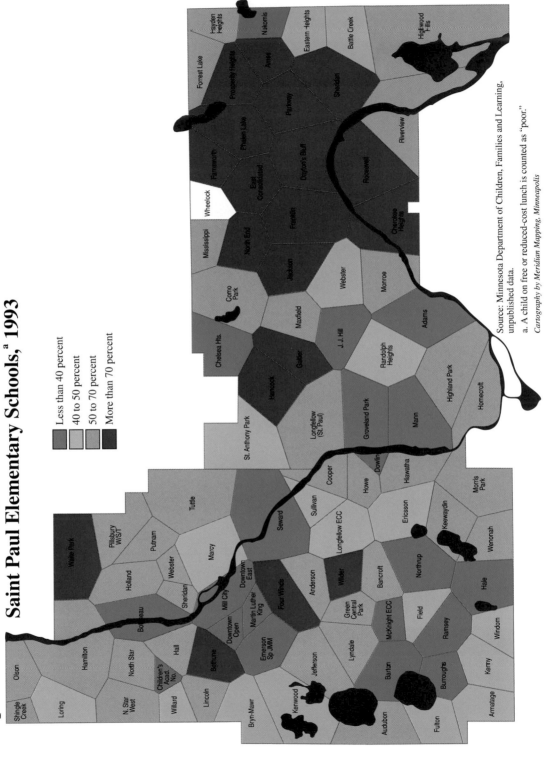

Less than 40 percent
40 to 50 percent
50 to 70 percent
More than 70 percent

Source: Minnesota Department of Children, Families and Learning, unpublished data.

a. A child on free or reduced-cost lunch is counted as "poor."

Cartography by Meridian Mapping, Minneapolis

Map 3-4. Minority Enrollment in Minneapolis and Saint Paul Elementary Schools, 1993

Less than 45 percent
45 to 55 percent
55 to 60 percent
More than 60 percent

Source: Minnesota Department of Children, Families and Learning, unpublished data.

Cartography by Meridian Mapping, Minneapolis

Map 3-5. Migration of White Preschool Children in Minneapolis and Saint Paul Neighborhoods,[a] 1990

No white children

−5 to 250

−25 to −6

−50 to −26

−100 to −51

Source: Bureau of the Census.

a. Migration is determined by subtracting the number of white 10- to 14-year-olds residing in a census tract in the 1990 census from the number of white children up to age four residing in the same location in the 1980 census.

Cartography by Meridian Mapping, Minneapolis

Map 3-6. Ratio of Black to White Preschool Children in Minneapolis and Saint Paul Neighborhoods, 1990

No white children
0 to 0.25
0.26 to 0.75
0.76 to 2
2.01 to 50

Source: Bureau of the Census.
Cartography by Meridian Mapping, Minneapolis

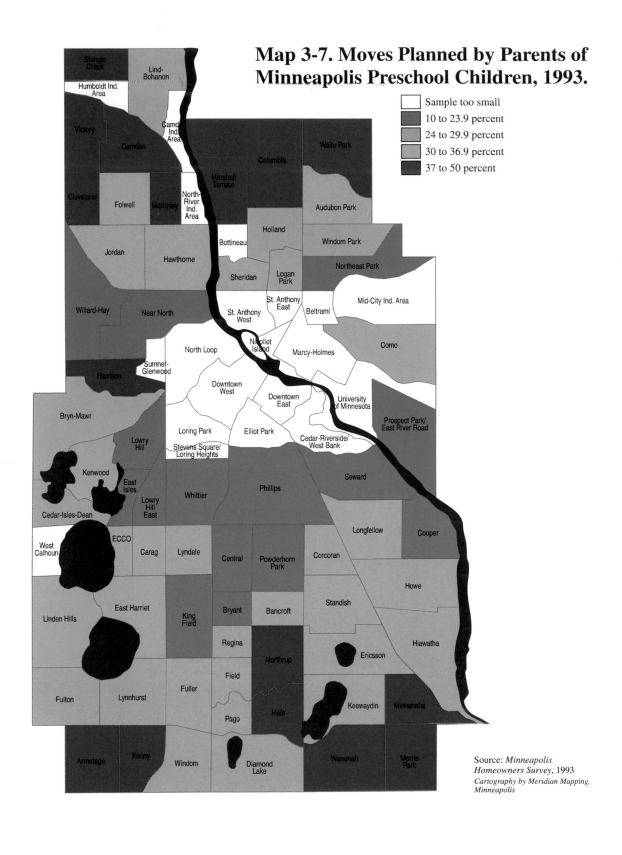

Map 3-7. Moves Planned by Parents of Minneapolis Preschool Children, 1993.

Sample too small
10 to 23.9 percent
24 to 29.9 percent
30 to 36.9 percent
37 to 50 percent

Source: *Minneapolis Homeowners Survey*, 1993
Cartography by Meridian Mapping, Minneapolis

Saint Louis Park had a more diverse housing market; Edina was highly exclusive. Between 1982 and 1994, as Saint Louis Park's school system went from 9 percent poor children to 23 percent and from 5 percent minority children to 11 percent, Edina's remained at 1 percent poor and moved from 2 to 5 percent minority. During this time, Saint Louis Park lost one-third of its white preschool children, while Edina gained 43 percent more school-age white children than were born in the community. In the end, this shows that communities that remain affluent and exclusive are highly attractive to young families with children, while older suburbs with growing poverty are not.

Spending $5,829 per pupil, with tremendous aid from the state's equity system, the troubled inner-ring districts were second in regional spending. Saint Louis Park, a district with significant socioeconomic change and large-scale white flight, was the highest spending suburban district. Columbia Heights, which during the 1980s increased from 15 percent poor elementary school children to 32 percent, was spending 120 percent of the metropolitan average. As in the central cities, this comparatively high level of spending seemed to do nothing to stabilize the composition of the student body.

Parents and local school administrators in the inner ring understand, to varying degrees, the transitions occurring in their schools, but few grasp the metropolitan pattern of these changes or their implications in terms of community stability. The general public and the media are almost completely unaware of what is happening in these schools. As some districts struggled to make programmatic changes to deal with the growing population of poor children, others simply endured this crisis in silence. These inner-suburban systems feared that acknowledging problems associated with increased poverty would only aggravate parental concern and hasten middle-class flight from their schools. By the mid-1990s, seeing their schools strongly affected by social and racial transformation (despite above-average funding), some inner-suburban school officials began looking to regional housing and land use reform to stabilize the middle-class presence in their districts.

Diverse Second Ring

One northern suburban city manager used to quip that working families who fled the inner suburbs into developing low–tax base suburbs were "jumping out of the frying pan and then back into it." As the metropolitan housing market continues to segment along class lines, outer-ring, middle-income communities are dominated by lower-value housing and small commercial tax bases. As single parentage and shrinking real wages become middle-class realities, these newer communities face unexpected social needs, while at the same time building new schools and associated infrastructure.

The diverse second-ring districts enrolled 110,000 students in 1994, 30 percent of the students in the Twin Cities metropolitan region. These districts, with 13 percent of their children on free lunch, stood midway between the wealthiest and the most rapidly declining groups in the suburbs. Cutting across different socioeconomic varieties of suburbs, the diverse second-ring districts were hybrids. Many schools, clearly in trouble, were losing enrollment, but other schools in the same district were growing.

Of all school districts in this subset, Osseo underwent the greatest socioeconomic and racial change. Seven elementary schools in its inner southeastern quadrant had more than 22 percent of the children on free lunch and six of these had an enrollment of more than 15 percent non-Asian minority students in 1994. Osseo responded to these shifts with changes in attendance boundaries and decisions about school buildings that cumulatively isolated poor, minority children in the inner southeastern quadrant in older buildings operating at less than capacity in Brooklyn Park. Simultaneously, the district was building elaborate schools in the outer northwestern quadrant in the city of Maple Grove. By 1993 Osseo and several other second-ring diverse districts were essentially legally segregated, in violation of the Minnesota State Board of Education's desegregation rule. Elm Creek Elementary in Maple Grove had only 8 percent poor and 2 percent minority students in 1994.

At the same time, Zanewood Elementary in the Osseo school district went from 37 percent of its students on free lunch in 1992 to 43 percent in 1993, and its minority enrollment climbed from 34 to 38 percent. Today teachers and administrators at Zanewood have a battle-hardened look about them. Hired a decade ago into an all-white, middle-income suburban school, today they teach in increasingly poor, multiracial classrooms. Unlike their central-city counterparts, they were not trained to respond to issues related to poverty and racial diversity.

To the south of the two central cities, second-ring Bloomington and third-ring Burnsville felt the leading edge of the socioeconomic and racial housing transition moving through south Minneapolis and Richfield.[28] In both school districts, once among the region's most elite, the concentration of poor and minority children roughly doubled. In Bloomington's rapidly changing eastside housing market, several elementary schools had enrollments of nearly one-third poor and minority children. Some of Burnsville's schools were not far behind.

Some of the diverse districts experienced only growing poverty without racial change. Here the concentration of lower-income whites, with a large percentage of children from single-family homes, created schools with high levels of disorder and delinquency—schools where few students were college bound and dropping out was commonplace. The stresses and strains of these diverse, often blue-collar, districts with low property wealth were exemplified by legislation sponsored by State Representative Charlie Weaver of Anoka to control guns in schools. Weaver was an astute politician whose legislation mirrored the fears faced by parents in these suburban districts.[29]

The diverse second-ring districts spent $5,408 per pupil, which was close to the metropolitan average. Only the Hopkins district, with a large commercial base, spent much more than the average—$6,256 per pupil (12 percent more than the regional average). Per pupil spending was lower than the metropolitan average in such districts as Anoka-Hennepin (89 percent of the average), Mahtomedi (93 percent), Osseo (96 percent), and Hastings (85 percent). The northern outer-ring suburban and the east metro districts, with very low property tax bases, faced increasing socio-economic challenges and may well have been harmed by polarization of the metropolitan tax base. Perhaps in the schools with high drop-out rates among students from middle- and working-class families, where poverty had not concentrated, a few more guidance counselors or slightly smaller classes could have kept these students who were from struggling families in school.

Many of the low-value northern suburban districts, with lower-middle-income constituencies, were concerned about their school systems' lack of resources to meet burgeoning difficulties. But property tax increases were politically unpopular with district residents. As their legislators began to understand that tax base sharing would improve the resource base for schools and lower taxes, many became strong proponents.

Fast-Growing Districts

The fast-growing districts enrolled 21 percent of metropolitan school children, and almost half of them attended schools in two large districts, Rosemount and South Washington County. Ten percent and 14 percent of these districts' elementary school children, respectively, were on free lunch. Again, poverty rates corresponded directly to high noncompletion rates.[30]

Even with their enormous cost of physical expansion (in Rosemount, fourteen new schools in twenty years), these districts spent the least in the region per pupil—$5,050. In this light, low-poverty, low-spending districts in fast-growing southern and eastern areas such as Rosemount and South Washington County did a better job attracting, retaining, and graduating middle-class students than did higher-spending districts in the central city and in inner-suburban areas. At the same time, some of the northern fast-growing districts with higher poverty rates and lower property wealth had higher nongraduation rates than the inner suburbs and face increasing social challenges, with fewer resources.

Legislators in these districts that are dominated by young families were centrally interested in securing money for school operating and capital expenses. When they realized that tax base sharing would allow them more resources for their school without the accompanying tax increases—that is, that tax base sharing would help solve one of their basic problems—they often became supporters.

Southern and Western Developing Districts

The southern and western developing districts, with 12 percent of metropolitan enrollment, consist of a mix of wealthy, fast-growing areas and wealthy, stable districts. These school districts have the best of both worlds—a predominantly upper-middle-class student body and high per-pupil spending. In 1992, spending $5,651 per pupil, they were the third-highest–spending region after the central cities and second ring. As a group, they are the least racially and socioeconomically diverse districts in the metropolitan area. Less than 7 percent of their elementary students are on free lunch; less than 3 percent are from non-Asian minority groups.

In 1994, inner-ring Edina was the metropolitan area's wealthiest school district, with only 1 percent of its students on free lunch and less than 5 percent minority enrollment. As the southern and western fast-growing housing market had become increasingly restrictive over the preceding decade, several of its districts became less poor and racially diverse. The southern and western developing nongraduation rate was only 1 percent. However, owing to the substantial number of high school students transferring into these districts, this figure may underestimate the actual drop-out rate.

With their high-income constituencies and large property-tax bases, the southern and western communities were contributors to the state aid system and believed that their school systems and constituents would be better off if such a system were less generous. Their prevailing political theme was to cut off statewide aid and regional equity mechanisms and push school funding back to the local property-tax base. Based on local resources, these districts could have both higher spending and lower local taxes.

Enrollment and Facilities

The enrollment and school facilities data offer a striking insight into the scope of middle-class flight and the financial costs of abandoning school districts and neighborhoods to build new schools and communities. Between 1970 and 1990, metropolitan school enrollment fell by 81,000, owing to the generational population decline after the baby boom. The central cities lost one-third of enrollment and the inner ring nearly half, but the developing suburban school population grew by almost 60 percent. As a result of these shifts, the central cities and inner-ring and second-ring suburbs together closed 132 schools, while 50 new schools were opened at the edge of the metropolitan area (map 3-11).

This process is unending. Between 1992 and 1999, the central cities expect 17 percent growth in school-age population percent growth.[31] The diverse second-ring districts project 11 percent growth overall, but schools in inner-suburban territory, losing large parts of their enrollment, project little growth. Districts more balanced between fast-growing and declining areas were losing students and buildings at one end of the district and gaining them at the other. Outer-ring districts will simply continue to grow.

The fast-growing districts project a 26 percent expansion between 1992 and 1999.[32] Massive Rosemount, on the heels of 65 percent growth during the 1980s, expects further growth of 25 percent between 1992 and 1999. The fast-growing districts would add 20 schools (net) over the period, 14 of them just in Rosemount. By 1997, this group plans to build eight more schools at a cost of more than $104.4 million. During this period, the fast-growing, second-ring, and south and west developing areas will build 16 new schools at a cost of more than $384 million.[32]

South and west developing districts project the same rate of growth (27 percent) as the fast-growing districts from 1992 to 1999.[33] The growth projections of the south and west developing inner districts show the fundamental difference between wealthy and middle-income inner suburban systems. Older suburbs—Edina, Mendota Heights (in the West Saint Paul district), and Minnetonka—developed at the same rate as Columbia Heights, Brooklyn Center, and the northern inner ring. All these districts lost enrollment in the post–baby boom slump and cyclical graying experience. However, as metropolitan enrollment began to increase and the graying cycle ended, suburbs such as Columbia Heights and Brooklyn Center were replacing middle-class students with poor ones. These suburbs expect little growth to 1999. Exclusive residential areas like Edina, Mendota Heights, and Minnetonka bounced back with strong increases in middle-class enrollment and growth projections. Similarly, newly developing south and west districts like Lakeville and Eden Prairie project stunning growth (44 percent and 69 percent, respectively) by 1999.

The cycle continues. Poverty and its problems become concentrated in certain school districts, middle-class residents flee, old schools close, new schools are built farther out, and poverty moves outward. Schools are the first indicator and the most powerful perpetuator of regional polarization, but this polarization ultimately begins and ends in regional housing markets.

4

Affordable Housing and the Tax Base

Regional polarization and affordable housing are inextricably connected. The Twin Cities metropolitan region has a little more than half the affordable housing needed by the lowest income groups, and most of it is located in the cities and inner suburbs (table 4-1 and figure 4-1). Poor people who can find affordable housing live in it; many others must live in housing they cannot afford. In both cases, the presence of a disportionate share of low-income earners and the housing they live in increases the demands for local services and limits the tax base of their communities, the main source of financing these services. On the other hand, in the areas with large tax bases, where there is less social need and where most of the new jobs are, there is little affordable housing. Is this unequal distribution of affordable housing "fair" to people, communities, and the region?

Regional "Fair Share"

A regional "fair share" is determined by allocating to every jurisdiction an even share (by population) of the region's total need for affordable housing. Local, state, and federal housing subsidies usually apply to three categories: units that are affordable to households earning 30 percent, 50 percent, and 80 percent of the metropolitan median income ($11,000, $18,000, or $29,000 a year in the Twin Cities metro area in 1990). Much of society considers $36,000, the metro median income, a middle-class income, yet affordable housing projects in this range frequently meet with stiff opposition.

In the Twin Cities in 1992, 11.57 percent of metropolitan households live at or below 30 percent of the metropolitan median income,

Table 4-1. Affordable Housing, by Income and Region, Twin Cities Metropolitan Area

Location	30 percent of metro median		50 percent of metro median		80 percent of metro median	
	Households	Available housing	Households	Available housing	Households	Available housing
Twin Cities metro region	11.6	6.6	21.6	46.3	38.6	81.5
Central cities	20.6	14.0	35.3	67.2	55.5	91.3
Inner ring	9.8	4.0	20.3	49.2	38.9	88.4
Mid-developing	5.7	2.8	11.4	43.7	25.2	77.3
East developing	6.2	3.0	12.2	30.5	25.9	66.8
Southwest developing	5.3	2.7	11.1	23.1	24.1	67.6

Source: Minnesota House of Representatives—House Research.

21.57 percent live at or below 50 percent, and 38.58 percent at or below 80 percent.[1] If each metropolitan community had its fair share of affordable housing, 12 percent of its housing would be affordable at 30 percent, 22 percent at 50 percent, and 39 percent at 80 percent of median household income.

The Twin Cities region has twice as much housing as is needed for households at 50 percent and 80 percent of the median, and virtually every subregion meets its fair share of such housing. However, there is only half as much housing as needed for households below 30 percent of the median, for those earning incomes of $11,000 or less.[2] Moreover, in many localities where jobs abound, suitable housing is most scarce for the entry-level employees who will fill them.

The central cities have almost twice (178 percent) their fair share of households of people below 30 percent of the median income (20.57 percent), but only 121 percent of their fair share of housing units affordable at this level (14.06 percent). As a result, there is affordable housing for only 66 percent of the central cities' poorest households. If this shortfall seems scandalous, the central cities come closest of all subregions to meeting the need for this type of housing.[3] The cities' vast oversupply of affordable housing is daunting. (In this usage, oversupply means an excess over what this part of the region would have if it had the regional average proportions of affordable housing and poor households.) At 30 percent of the median income, the central cities have 5,815 too many affordable units and 24,396 too many poor households. With such a huge unmet need for affordable housing regionwide, the overabundance of such housing draws households at the lowest level of the income scale into the central cities.

Figure 4-1. Need for Affordable Housing in the Twin Cities Metropolitan Region

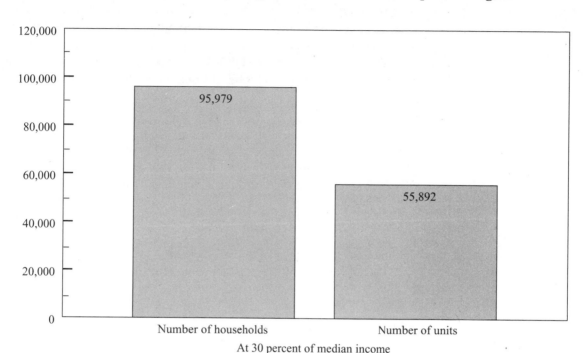

At 30 percent of median income

Source: House Research Department, Minnesota House of Representatives.

The inner suburbs as a group have roughly their share of low-income households and more than their share of affordable units, except for the lowest income groups. Specifically, the inner suburbs have 84 percent of their fair share of households below 30 percent of median income (9.77 percent), yet only 34 percent of their fair share of affordable units at this level (3.98 percent). Twelve of the thirty inner suburbs have more than their fair share of affordable housing at the lowest levels of income.

Many proponents of "in-place" strategies for dealing with poor people—either residents of developing suburbs who want to keep out affordable housing, or city dwellers who want to preserve the status quo of racial segregation and concentrated poverty for political or programmatic reasons—insist that poor residents do not want to live in the suburbs. However, with affordable units available to only 40.69 percent of the inner-suburban residents who need them, the shortage of affordable housing for the poorest households is greater in the inner suburbs than in the central cities. The fact that so many more of the poorest households are liv-

57

ing beyond their means in the inner suburbs must reflect their preference. This is particularly striking, because the inner suburbs are not places of great economic opportunity. They are a poor household's only alternative to central-city housing.[4]

The mid-, south, west, and east developing suburbs have most of the Twin Cities new entry-level jobs, but only about half their fair share of poor households (5.25 to 6.24 percent) and one-quarter of their fair share of affordable housing for these households (less than 3 percent). With half of the poorest households having affordable units available, there is more demand for local housing (that is, more people willing to live beyond their means) than in the central cities, but less than in the first ring of suburbs. This difference between developing communities and the first ring of suburbs may perhaps be explained by a lack of information about these communities reaching the region's needy residents or to the greater prevalence of housing discrimination (by income or race) in developing communities than in the city or older suburbs.

Each developing subregion had wide internal variations. Older satellite cities that developed independently of the metropolitan area (until urban sprawl reached their borders) have more than their fair share of affordable units at the lowest income level, while newly developing affluent suburbs have some of the lowest amounts of such housing. Some old satellite cities in the southwest, for example, have at least their fair share of low-income households, while some wealthy exclusive suburbs have some of the poorest regional records.[5]

Some cities that did not have their metropolitan fair share of low- and moderate-income housing nonetheless did a better job at providing housing for local poor residents than others. For instance, in the south and west, Eagan, Burnsville, and Apple Valley had only between 30 percent and 45 percent of their fair share of low-income households, but they had enough units to accommodate virtually every such household that lived in these cities. This record reflects the strong efforts of the Dakota County Housing and Redevelopment Authority, a governmental entity that struggles diligently (albeit with limited funds) to provide for such housing.[6]

Barriers to Affordable Housing

The shortage of affordable housing in the developing suburbs is due largely to barriers erected by individual communities in the form of zoning provisions, development agreements, and development practices. Explicit *zoning codes* use lot sizes, minimum room sizes, fees, and development time tables to increase costs and otherwise deter the construction of affordable housing. *Development agreements* contain additional requirements, costs, and delays above and beyond those set in public codes. Informal *local development practices* often accomplish what formal codes and agreements cannot by imposing further requirements or construction delays.

Two studies, commissioned by groups with competing interests in the metropolitan housing debate, contain an inventory of some of the most common obstacles to affordable housing in the developing suburbs. One, the Minnesota State Planning study (State Planning), done for the Governor's Task Force on Metropolitan Housing Policy, examined fifty-seven metropolitan cities representing a cross-section of fully developed, developing, core cities, and rural metropolitan communities.[7] The other, prepared by the Center for Urban and Regional Affairs (CURA) for the Legal Aid Society of Minneapolis in conjunction with the *Hollman* v. *Cisneros* metropolitan housing lawsuit, examined exclusionary zoning patterns in the ten suburban areas with the highest job growth.[8] Eight of the ten communities were in the southern and western developing suburbs: Plymouth, Eden Prairie, Minnetonka, Maple Grove, Lakeville, Shakopee, Burnsville, and Edina. In addition, CURA studied Woodbury in the east-developing region and Coon Rapids in the mid-developing region. Both studies reported that large lot sizes, minimum floor areas, development fees, and a variety of other exclusionary practices imposed significant barriers to affordable housing.

For single-family structures, the Metropolitan Council recommends lots of 7,500 square feet (85 feet on each side, or 100 feet by 75 feet). State Planning discovered that 85 percent of the developing suburbs require larger lots.[9] Lot-size requirements also exceeded the Met Council's recommendation in all ten high-growth suburbs studied by CURA. Minnetonka required the largest lots (22,000 square feet), three times the size recommended by the Met Council guidelines.[10] Cutting lot size from 10,800 square feet to 7,200 square feet would save an average of $3,600 dollars per unit in land costs and $3,750 in utility fees.[11] Smaller lots would also reduce costs of street maintenance, snow plowing, garbage pickup, and other municipal services.[12]

For a *multifamily structure,* an apartment building with four or more units, the Met Council recommends a density level of twenty units per acre. Higher densities save land costs, and large buildings permit economies of scale, for example, in terms of heating. Both factors help to make rents affordable. State Planning found that 70 percent of the developing communities had maximum multifamily densities lower than recommended by the Met Council.[13] Nine of ten CURA communities had lower multifamily density limits. Woodbury, the most restrictive suburb, had a ten-unit-per-acre maximum density. Half of the CURA high-growth cities have increased their multifamily minimum lot area requirements since 1977.[14]

For health and safety purposes, the state building code requires a minimum of 625 square feet for a two-bedroom home and 700 square feet for a three-bedroom home. The standards for multifamily development are 500 square feet for a two-bedroom unit and 560 square feet for a three-bedroom apartment. Excluding land, building a typical multifamily building costs $40 per square foot, town houses $50 per square foot, and single-family detached structures about $60 per square foot. The council found that floor area minimum requirements exceeding the health and safety standards are the single most important factor in housing unit price, and it has recommended their elimination.[15]

For single-family homes, 45 percent of developing communities prescribed minimum floor areas and one-quarter of them exceeded 1,000 square feet.[16] Half of the CURA high-growth suburbs specified minimum floor sizes of between 960 square feet and 1,100 square feet for single-family homes—well above the the state building code requirements.[17]

In multifamily developments, floor area minimums rarely fell below 700 square feet for two-bedroom apartments or 800 square feet for three-bedroom apartments. Since 1977, four communities dropped and ten added floor area requirement for multifamily housing.[18] Seven out of ten high-growth cities set minimum floor area requirements for multifamily construction. Floor space requirements for apartments in Edina and Maple Grove were equivalent to many cities' minimums for single-family homes.[19]

A single garage adds $7,000 to the cost of a home; a double garage, $9,000. A garage requirement for multifamily housing adds 10 percent to the unit cost.[20] Thirty-nine percent of the State Planning communities had a two-car garage requirement for single-family homes. Eighty-eight percent of these communities added this requirement after 1977. Four of the ten high-growth communities required that a two-car garage be built at the same time as the house, while the remaining communities required lot widths large enough to accommodate such garages. Five of the ten cities required at least one garage space per multifamily unit. The Met Council has recommended removing garage requirements for multifamily housing.

Three CURA cities required a conditional use permit for any multifamily development. Obtaining a special permit increases the cost of development through permit fees, the time to gain approval, and the risk that any additional conditions imposed could further raise costs through site plan review. The city of Minnetonka is more restrictive than most—no land is initially zoned multifamily. Thus, before multifamily construction can occur, land must be rezoned by the city council from a single-family to a multiple-family district.[21] Some cities argue that a special use permit for multifamily housing allows a city the opportunity to waive density requirements. However, the quid pro quo for such a waiver, such as underground parking or more expensive exteriors, often eliminates the cost savings.[22]

Seven of ten CURA high-growth communities reduced the amount of land that the cities had designated for multifamily development. In all, these communities "downzoned" 530 acres from high-density to low-density housing. Lakeville alone down-zoned over 350 acres.[23]

Manufactured housing is one of the most affordable types of housing. Excluding lot and foundation costs, a 1,300-square-foot home can be purchased for about $38,000. This price includes drywall construction, ceramic tile, woodwork, and cabinetry similar to those in traditional site-built homes. Nearly half (48 percent) of the developing suburbs exclude manufactured housing, and half of those that permit it do so only as a conditional use, on the presumption that it will not be allowed.[24] Six out of ten CURA high-growth cities allow mobile homes.[25]

Two other factors were cited for further inquiry: fees and development schedules. The Metropolitan Council identified twenty-five building construction fees and sixteen zoning and planning fees that Twin Cities communities assess on builders. The most commonly assessed fees are for building permits, building plan checks, conditional use permits, and park dedication.[26] In the high-growth cities, development fees range from $1,250 to more than $5,000. Park dedication fees alone varied from $384 in Coon Rapids to $900 in Eden Prairie. Many developing communities are seeking broader impact fees that will allow them to assess the environmental and social effects of growth.[27] In general, the more exclusive the suburb, the higher the fee.

In terms of development schedules, developers typically go through three stages to obtain project approval: preapplication meetings, preparation and review of the preliminary plat, and review and approval of the final plat. State law permits a 120-day review period for the preliminary plat (including the public hearing) and sets a 60-day limit for approval of the final plat. Review periods for subdivisions can add up to six months to the process. The time developers spend in pre-plat meetings and preparation of the preliminary plat, which is not included in these limits, can add several more months to the process.[28]

Concurrently with city reviews, watershed district reviews are conducted by the Department of Natural Resources, and the Board of Water and Soil Resources (if wetlands are involved), the Waste Control Commission, and the Pollution Control Agency. If required, an environmental assessment worksheet or environmental impact statement must also be completed before final approval of the subdivision.[29]

All told, the review period for subdivision approval can take anywhere from two months to twelve months across the metropolitan area. Prolonged review periods or unexpected delays are more burdensome to many developers than fees or other local requirements. Particularly troublesome are review periods that leave land idle for months during the winter—all the while accruing property taxes, interest payments, and depreciation on equipment that raise finished costs.[30] The bottom line is that time costs money, and the buyer pays.

Fiscal Disparities

Restrictive zoning not only fosters low-density land use patterns but is also a major force in growing fiscal or tax base disparities among metropolitan communities. When the property tax is a basic revenue source for local governments with land-planning powers, fiscal zoning occurs as jurisdictions compete for property wealth. Through fiscal zoning, cities deliberately develop predominantly expensive homes and commercial industrial (CI) properties with low service needs and limit less costly housing and entry to the community by the people who normally buy it.[31] In this way, these communities attempt to limit social need and the demand on tax base that it can engender. Taxes are further curtailed by spreading controlled needs over a broad, rich property tax base.

The dynamics of fiscal zoning creates three sets of mutually reinforcing relationships. First, the residentially exclusive suburbs with low tax rates continue to attract more and more businesses, whose presence continually lowers the overall tax rate. Because of low social needs, cities can concentrate on providing a few high-quality local services. School districts in these cities thrive by educating a pool of upper-middle-class students off a rich tax base with low tax rates.

A second reinforcing relationship involves cities where increasing social needs lead to both declining consumer demographics and increased taxes. Both factors are large negatives in terms of business location and retention. In general, core cities and school districts spend a great deal on an unsuccessful effort toward socioeconomic stability as their tax base evaporates.

The third relationship concerns the developing suburbs that lose the battle of fiscal zoning. For lack of business or executive housing, these communities must pay for their schools, police, parks, curbs, and gutters with fewer resources. To keep taxes from exploding, they are forced to abandon long-range thinking and build the lower valued homes and multifamily units rejected by wealthier suburbs. As a council member from a northern suburban community confessed, "To pay the bills, we build whatever is left. Hell, we'll build anything. . . ." Further, in a futile attempt to remain competitive in tax terms, working-class communities suppress local expenditures on public services. Today's working-class suburbs thus become tomorrow's declining suburbs.

The increase of property wealth in outer suburbs and the stagnancy or decline of value in the central city and in inner suburbs represents, in part, an intraregional transfer of tax base. As such, the loss of value in older poorer communities is one of the costs of economic polarization and urban sprawl. Regions spend billions of dollars building infrastructure such as schools, freeways, and sewers, which add enormous value to outer-ring land. To the extent that these public expenditures serve to transfer value, they are wasted. Adding to this dysfunction, the infrastructure of new cities is often paid for by taxes and fees levied on residents and businesses in older parts of the region.

Central City

In 1988–93, the Minneapolis central business district lost 15 percent of its commercial value, partly because too much office space was built in the early 1980s. At the same time, polarization caused by the concentration of poverty and the dynamics of gentrification combined to cause a split in residential property valuations. Core and transitional neighborhoods lost value, and most city neighborhoods, with stagnant values, failed to keep pace with inflation. In contrast, residential property values in certain gentrifying neighborhoods rose more rapidly than in some exclusive suburbs. Ghetto neighborhoods such as Phillips and Sumner-Glenwood lost one-fifth of their residential value. Transitional neighborhoods such as Lyndale, Hawthorne, Central, and Harrison lost about 10 percent of their residential value over five years. Gainers among gentrifying neighborhoods included: Kenwood (50 percent), Linden Hills (29 percent), Lynnhurst (30 percent), and Fulton (24 percent).

The Region

Large residential tax base disparities from community to community in the Twin Cities are compounded by disparities in commercial industrial (CI) location because in Minnesota CI property is taxed at a significantly higher rate. The southern and western developing suburbs, with $30,000 of CI per household, have three times the CI base of the working-class suburbs, and one-third more than the other subregions. The southern and western developing cities of Eden Prairie and Minnetonka together have about the same commercial industrial base as the city of Saint Paul ($1.5 billion), but only one-third as many residents and virtually no poor people requiring costly services.

The central cities and inner suburbs saw about a 72 percent increase in total property valuation over the decade, about 31 percent below the metro average increase. The weakest increases in the region occurred in Saint Paul (50 percent) and inner-ring suburbs such as Columbia Heights (51 percent), Robbinsdale (52 percent), Crystal (56 percent), Saint Anthony (60 percent), New Hope (62 percent), and Fridley (63 percent).

On the commercial-industrial side, the central cities, with 146 percent growth (mostly in downtown Minneapolis) were stronger than the inner ring (116 percent). The growing mid-developing and east metro suburbs, both with small commercial industrial bases, saw an increase of about 170 percent. The southern and western developing suburbs, the subregion with the richest commercial base, experienced the region's largest commercial growth (240 percent). CI growth was nothing short of phenomenal in some southern and western cities in the Twin Cities region: 856 percent in Chanhassen (with almost 40 percent of its tax base in tax increment financing districts), 583 percent in Eden Prairie, and 369 percent in Maple Grove.

Effective Net Tax Capacity

Minnesota's fiscal disparities system (see the discussion that follows) shares 40 percent of the post-1971 growth of commercial industrial property among the 187 cities, 49 school districts, and 7 counties of the Twin Cities metropolitan area. The pooled money is distributed to cities on the basis of the comparative commercial industrial wealth. In general, property tax–base sharing moves a large amount of tax base from the southern and western developing suburbs and other commercially rich suburbs to the rest of the region. In 1996, the revenues distributed through the re-

gional pool amount to over $367 million. However, even after this realloca-
tion, disparities in property wealth remain enormous (map 4-1).

Effective net tax capacity (ENTC) reflects the potential revenue
from a city's property tax base after the fiscal disparities contribution or
distribution (map 4-2). The central cities, inner-ring, and working-class
suburbs all had an ENTC of approximately $1,800 per household. The
east metro with $2,407 per household and southern and western develop-
ing suburbs with $2,749 had, respectively, 25 percent and 30 percent
more tax base per household than the rest of the region.

Regionally, then, there is a mismatch between housing available and
needed by individuals, and between tax base available and resources
needed by communities. There is also a mismatch between affordable
housing and available jobs.

5

From "Spatial Mismatch" to Urban Sprawl

Twenty-five years ago John Kain, an economist at Harvard, observed that a "spatial mismatch" was taking place between affordable housing and available jobs.[1] Though still controversial, this theory is widely accepted today, because it describes so well the living and working conditions in many American metropolitan areas, including the Twin Cities. This mismatch (reflected in traffic congestion) influences and is influenced by the construction of highways, sewers, and other regional infrastructure leading to the outer metropolitan edges. All of these factors, unshaped by a regional plan, add up to urban sprawl as people move outward.

American cities are undergoing transformations from production centers for goods into information-processing centers, as Kain foresaw. Blue-collar, manufacturing jobs, once the economic backbone of cities, have either vanished or moved—to the suburbs or overseas. Despite low population growth in center cities, work-seeking residents still outnumber the low-skilled manufacturing jobs available there. Many neighborhood retail businesses serving the middle class have also relocated to the suburbs.[2]

But it is not just a problem of numbers. Job content and workers' education are also mismatched in center cities. Jobs with high educational demands are on the rise, but the average worker's educational achievements are declining. It is mainly in the suburbs and exurbs that the pool of jobs for unskilled workers is growing, not in the center city.[3] This exodus of low-skilled jobs to the suburbs disproportionately affects center-city poor people, especially minorities, whose choice of housing in growth areas is limited by income and often by local land use restrictions.[4]

All outward indications point to a large "mismatch" in the Twin Cities, although no rigorous "mismatch" studies have been undertaken (map 5-1). The raw numbers show rising central-city unemployment and massive new job creation in the southern and western suburbs. Commuting patterns and growing congestion on the roads into the employment basins of the southern and western suburbs further suggest a mismatch between jobs and affordable housing.

Job Creation: Lopsided at Best

The inner ring, with 26 percent of the region's population, captured 19 percent of all new jobs created in 1980–92. Half of these 45,000 new jobs were in Brooklyn Park, an inner-ring (but still-developing) suburb, and at Fort Snelling, a military base with an adjacent state park. The declining, older inner-ring suburbs represented a halo of job loss surrounding the central cities.[5]

The mid-developing suburbs (11 percent of the region) gained 10 percent of the region's new jobs. These suburbs gained a total of 25,000 jobs, about as many jobs as the single southwestern developing city of Eden Prairie. Almost half of this increase occurred in two clusters of growth in Blaine, Andover, and Ham Lake to the north and Inver Grove Heights to the south.

The southern and western developing suburbs, with 27 percent of the region's population, gained 61 percent of the region's new jobs. These suburbs alone created 147,000 jobs over the period, a 71 percent increase in total jobs over the previous decade. Three suburbs, with only 7 percent of the region's population, accounted for 26 percent of its new jobs: Eden Prairie (23,151), Minnetonka (20,522), and Plymouth (19,030).

Finally, the east developing suburbs, with 6 percent of the region's population, gained 8 percent of all new jobs in the Twin Cities, but only about 12 percent as many as were created in the southern and western developing suburbs. With 19,000 new jobs, all of east metro saw as much growth as southwestern developing Plymouth alone. Only Woodbury, a fast-growing residential community in the east developing suburbs, gained more than 4,000 jobs over the period.

A thousand jobs with benefits (and many more without) go unfilled in Eden Prairie, Chaska, and Chanhassen for want of workers, according to the executive director of the Eden Prairie Chamber of Commerce, Lisa Sisinni.[6] Every year, about sixty southern and western metro employers, together with the Southwest Community Transit and the local chambers of commerce, hold a jobs fair trying to entice low-skilled central-city workers to southern and western Twin Cities jobs sites. Daily, the reverse commute system operated by Loring-Nicollet-Bethlehem, a Minneapolis nonprofit, and by the Hennepin County Work Readiness program buses more than 1,000 workers from the central cities to the southern and western suburbs. Fast-food restaurants in the southern and western suburbs pay $1.00 to $2.00 an hour more than the same restaurants in downtown Minneapolis for identical jobs, indicating a shortage of low-skilled labor in this subregion. Recognizing the mismatch between the location of new jobs and the residences of workers needed to fill them, the southern and western chambers of commerce and the southern and western suburban transit services have repeatedly asked the Minnesota legislature to support large reverse-commute programs. They have argued that such programs are vital to the region's economy.

The correlation between employment and affordable housing can be seen in Dakota County, which has the only large subsidized housing program in the southern and western developing suburbs. Residents of housing managed by the Dakota County Housing and Redevelopment Authority are four times more likely to be employed than residents of subsidized housing in central cities.

Jobs and Property Values

Job growth and appreciation in real estate and commercial-industrial value are closely related. Between 1980 and 1992, the central cities of Minneapolis and Saint Paul showed a 1 percent increase in jobs, while unemployment grew rapidly. Both cities saw huge reinvestment in their central business districts. The Minneapolis business center saw a large job increase, while Saint Paul's lost jobs over the period. The industrial areas of both cities—Northeast, Camden, and Longfellow in Minneapolis and Summit, Buffaloe-Phalen, and West Seventh in Saint Paul—all lost a substantial percentage of jobs. Over a five-year period in the late 1980s, assessed residential property value stagnated or slightly declined in virtually every Minneapolis neighborhood surrounding these industrial areas.

At the same time, many Minneapolis neighborhoods in extreme poverty lost one-fifth and transitional poverty neighborhoods one-tenth of their assessed residential value.[7] In contrast, the gentrifying southwestern parts of both cities saw a greater than 40 percent increase in jobs. The southwest neighborhoods of Minneapolis experienced growth in residential property value ranging from 18 percent to 33 percent.[8]

Infrastructure: Tickets to the "Good Life"

For most U.S. regions, freeways, sewers, and infrastructure in general are tickets to economic development—and new tax base. Cities fight intensely for new infrastructure at metropolitan meetings and in the state legislature, and these battles are the only real metropolitan activity in most regions. Favored-quarter suburban governments and their development interests usually rule the metropolitan planning organizations, formed at the insistence of the federal government to distribute federal highway funds in metropolitan areas. These organizations, together with academics and good-government forces, are the main promoters of "regionalism" in most parts of the United States.

Highways to Growth

Transportation construction usually responds to congestion, and highways are no exception.[9] Highways leading into the southern and western suburbs (home of the Twin Cities' most spectacular recent growth) are the most congested, and the southern and western metro area is receiving the most highway improvement funding.[10]

Highway planning in the Twin Cities metropolitan area is done by the Met Council's Transportation Advisory Board in conjunction with the Minnesota Department of Transportation (MnDot). All highway projects around the Twin Cities must receive Met Council approval (see appendix).[11]

Of the $1.087 billion spent on metropolitan highway construction around the Twin Cities, $830 million (75 percent) went into roads serving the southern and western developing suburbs over the last decade. Major projects included Trunk Highway (TH) 77 bridges, walls, and surfacing ($37 million); Interstate (I) 394 bridges, walls, and surfacing ($136 million), and $300 million more in 1990–92; and the I–494 Minnesota River crossing ($153 million). Contingent on the passage of a significant funding package proposed by the commissioner of transportation, another $1.85 billion will be spent to expand capacity in the I–35W and I–494 corridors, also serving the southern and western developing suburbs.[12] Plans are also active to greatly expand the capacity of TH–212 in Eden Prairie, Chanhassen, and Chaska; County Road (CR) 18 and TH–101 in Shakopee and Chaska; and CR–32 in Eagan and Inver Grove Heights. The Metropolitan Council has also recommended improvements on CR–18 between I–494 and TH–101 in Scott County. A few transportation improvements are slated for the northern suburbs, but the two major southern and western interstate projects could easily exhaust all the available construction funds for the next decade.

The Twin Cities' freeway capacity, which is far larger than average, contributes to its ranking as the metropolitan area with the third lowest density in the nation, its greater-than-average dependence on automobiles, and an increasingly underused transit system.[13] Of the 20 largest U.S. urban centers, the Twin Cities ranked nineteenth in terms of freeway congestion in 1988.[14] (Many of the automobiles that clog highways at rush hour are driven by people who cannot afford to live close to their jobs; fair housing, including barrier removal, would go far toward reducing freeway congestion.[15]) Of the 24 largest U.S. urban areas, the Twin Cities had the second shortest average commuting time in 1990 at 20.5 minutes.[16] Most of MnDot transportation dollars have gone and will continue to go to the southern and western developing suburbs—which, owing to the proximity of residence and employment, already have the shortest commuting times in the region (map 5-2).[17]

Massive regional subsidies for highway construction distort the transportation market place, prevent it from reflecting the real economic cost of low-density sprawl and highway congestion, and foster a low-density, consumptive pattern of resource use. Automobiles pay $0.02 to $0.03 per vehicle mile to drive on the region's most congested arterials; the real cost, including constant maintenance, is closer to $0.49. Appropriate pricing, accomplished through a computerized toll system, would return the real costs to sprawl and massive highway construction and could encourage transit use and more economical development patterns.[18]

Recent advancement in federal transportation policy allows gas tax revenues to be used intermodally, or interchangeably, for roads or transit, but the Minnesota Constitution retains an explicit dedication of gas tax proceeds to "highway purposes."[19] Though the region's transit needs are arguably greater than the need for new roads, legal restrictions therefore prevent transit from gaining the full benefit of the new federal flexibility. Political reality further dictates that money provided for public works that create construction jobs is seldom returned unspent. Although federal resources could help solve transit and congestion problems, state law prevents the use of this money and makes it likely that it will be spent making present problems even worse. In the meantime, the continual increase in highway capacity intensifies the mismatch between the location of jobs and workers and the overall socioeconomic polarization occurring between central-city and outer-ring communities.[20]

Sewers: Skeletal New Cities

Waste water treatment infrastructure—sewers and treatment plants—form the skeletons of new cities. The Met Council builds and operates the regional treatment plants and main interceptors, or large regional sewer pipes. Since the early 1970s, the Met Council has spent well over $1 billion on sewer capital costs in the seven-county metropolitan area. In 1995, the Council's sewer capital budget totaled $224 million. This budget included many multiyear projects with long-term debt service. Its 1995 capital expenditures were thus broken down into $74.8 million in pre-1994 expenditures, $29 million in 1994 expenditures, $63.2 million in projected 1995 expenditures, and $57.1 million in expenditures for 1996 and beyond.[21] In 1995, the council approved a long-term capital improvment program that projected capital spending for 1996 to 2000 of $384.72 million, for 2001 to 2005 of $321.71 million, and for 2000 to 2015 of $1.207 billion.[22] Local governments, developers, and citizens also spend huge sums building trunk lines connecting new and growing subdivisions into the regional framework.

Like highway funds, most regional sewer capital resources, outside of the central metro treatment plant, have gone to the southern and western developing suburbs. Many of the large regional projects being undertaken in the south and west metro areas include the Empire wastewater treatment plant expansion with a total project cost of $15 million, the Elm Creek Interceptor coming in at $39 million, Chaska treatment plant phasing at $21 million, and solids processing at the Blue Lake and Seneca plants at $48 million. All told, there are more than $150 million worth of ongoing capital projects in the southern and western suburbs.[23]

Sewer operations and capital costs are financed on a uniform regional basis, with all regional sewer users paying the same basic fee. When the Met Council floats bonds to build new sewer capacity, all sewer users in the metropolitan area therefore pay to service that debt. This pricing system means that fully developed older communities subsidize the developing communities where new sewer capacity is introduced to serve lower-density patterns of development (map 5-3).[24]

Central cities and inner suburbs pay the largest subsidies. On average, the central cities pay over $6 million more in fees each year than they incur in costs. Yet while the average Minneapolis household subsidizes the system by $19 a year and the average Saint Paul household by $25 a year, the average household in inner-ring Falcon Heights and South Saint Paul subsidizes the system by $33 a year.[25] Households in the growing southern and western suburbs receive subsidies of between $10 and $136 per household annually. Some of the largest subsidies go to wealthy cities like Apple Valley ($65), Eden Prairie ($41), Farmington ($100), and Rosemount ($166).

Besides being inequitable, this pattern of allocating and financing infrastructure puts an end to any semblance of orderly regional development.

Land Use and Sprawl

The massive oversupply of developmental infrastructure in restrictively zoned communities has created land use patterns across the United States that are particularly low density, economically inefficient, and environmentally dangerous. In 1990, of the 25 largest metropolitan areas in the country, the Twin Cities, with 1,956 persons per square mile, had the third-lowest population density, after Atlanta, Georgia, and Kansas City, Missouri.[26] Between 1970 and 1984, the population of the metropolitan area grew by 9.7 percent, while the percentage of land used for urban purposes increased by 25.1 percent. Between 1982 and 1987, 86,832 acres of farmland (136 square miles) in the Twin Cities were lost to metropolitan development.[27]

By 1990, 131,488 acres—nearly one-quarter of the urban area served by sewers—remained undeveloped. Yet between 1987 and 1991 at the request of cities and developers the Metropolitan Council provided sewer access for another 18,000 acres, instead of redirecting new growth into areas with adequate sewer capacity (map 5-3). Constructing the new sewers at public expense, on land previously as zoned very low density, greatly increased the value of this land for its owners. Sixty percent of these exceptions to the Metropolitan Urban Service Area went to the southern and western developing suburbs (10,490 acres), 23 percent to the east developing suburbs (4,069 acres), and 14 percent to the mid-developing suburbs (2,465 acres).[28]

Only a small subset of the central-city neighborhoods are developed at densities above 3,000 persons per square mile. The city's peripheral neighborhoods and most of the first-ring suburbs have between 1,000 and 3,000 people per square mile. Most of the census tracts that developed in the 1970s and 1980s had about 500 people per square mile.[29]

During the 1980s, the number of housing units in all the developing subregions increased uniformly by approximately 50 percent. The southern and western suburbs added 78,737, or about half of the new regional housing units. The most construction in this subregion occurred in Eagan (11,244 new units or 156 percent), Eden Prairie (9,695 units or 169 percent), Plymouth (8,577 units or 77 percent), and Minnetonka (6,888 units or 52 percent). The mid-developing suburbs added about 28,120 new units. Only Coon Rapids, with 7,363 new units, came close to the south and west metro area's pace of housing development (68 percent). The east developing suburbs produced 13,745 new units, with Woodbury at 4,066 new units (117 percent) by far the largest builder. The inner suburbs added 31,145 units (a 15 percent increase) and the central cities 10,448 (a 4 percent increase).

In 1980, there were 26,250 surplus housing units in the region. By 1990, after the construction of a record-breaking 162,235 more units, the housing surplus reached 44,164 units, or about 5 percent. This surplus was equal to 15 percent of the housing units in the central cities. By 1990, in many distressed neighborhoods in Minneapolis the vacancy rate was increasing.

The lack of a regional planning policy and growth of infrastructure ever outward sap the strength of the Twin Cities and contribute to polarization. Nothing short of a metropolitan approach will suffice to break these patterns, to stabilize the central cities and older suburbs, and to create equity throughout the region.

6

Metropolitan Solutions

The forces of polarization—the push of concentrated poverty and the pull of concentrated resources—operate throughout metropolitan regions. Because the dynamics are regional, only a regional approach can change them. There is little that communities acting on their own can do to affect these trends.

Fragmented regional communities cumulatively concentrate the social and economic needs of the region on the weak resource base of the central cities and inner suburbs, those least able to resist. As their costs increase and their resources decline, these communities are surrounded by aggressively competing communities with lower social costs and greater resources. In this environment, they can do little fundamentally to stabilize themselves. They become, as David Rusk has said, "the poorhouse of the region . . . the residual category for those without choices."[1] By the same token, as long as parts of a region can enjoy the benefits of a regional economy—its markets, transportation systems, and labor force—but exclude many of the region's social costs and responsibilities, resources and households with broad economic choices will naturally flow there. When the older communities are taxed to fund the massive supporting infrastructure for this new, more exclusive development, they are further enervated, the process accelerates, and injustice increases. As polarization continues, the concentration of poverty creates waves of socioeconomic decline that roll outward astonishingly fast. Disposable cities mark their passage. Fragmented land use patterns and competition for tax base by all developing fringe communities lead to wasteful, low-density overdevelopment—John Adams's (and H. Ross Perot's) "giant sucking sound" that drains further resources from the built community. Hence, the fragmentation of the metropolis, fueled by spending on regional infrastructure, institutionalizes polarization and squanders the value of built assets and natural resources. Who pays? We all do.

To stabilize the core, the forces of polarization must be broken. Reforms are needed in several closely related areas: housing and reinvestment, property tax-base sharing, schools, land use and infrastructure planning, transportation and transit, and welfare. The first three reforms are directed at deconcentrating poverty, providing resource equity, and beginning the physical rebuilding to bring back the middle class and restore the private economy. The second group of reforms are reinforcements. To lead and administer these reforms, a voter-elected metropolitan council of some sort is very important.

The Dynamics of Deconcentration

Concentrated poverty creates a series of problems vastly greater than the sum of its parts—problems so immense that no plausible level of public and private expenditure can solve them in place. Concentration and the attendant social isolation contribute to titanic levels of crime in core neighborhoods and increased aggregate metropolitan crime. They foster an oppositional culture that rejects middle-class norms and disdains the traditional value placed by the broader society on education and work. Concentrated cores of poverty send out waves of surrounding property devaluation, middle-class flight, and general disinvestment, which together with high urban taxes, lack of available land, and endemic environmental problems make market-based investment extraordinarily difficult. The poor track record of enterprise zone programs in areas of concentration attests not so much to poor programs or administration, but to the intractable nature of concentrated poverty and its effects.[2] As David Rusk observes, "Bad neighborhoods defeat good programs."[3]

Concentration dilutes political support for responsive programs. As people with problems of all types become concentrated in a few legislative or congressional districts, their very concentration isolates them from middle-class districts. The pathologies of these neighborhoods make up half of what most Americans see on the nightly television news, which gives them enormous significance in state and national politics. As violence escalates in these isolated neighborhoods, as individual crimes receiving saturation-style reporting become more horrible, and as community development and in-place strategies fail to stem the violence or the expansion of distressed areas, these neighborhoods become a powerful symbol conservatives use to draw frightened, defensive, lower-middle-income and middle-income voters into their ranks. The existence and expansion of these neighborhoods then become an argument against compassion and intervention, and ultimately against government. The endless debates about crime and welfare spending that dominate our election cycles are about these neighborhoods. (No matter that the hated Aid to Families with Dependent Children is less than 3 percent of both state and national budgets, a tiny fraction of such items as social security, medicare, or K-12 education.) And in an increasingly segregated society, divisions in our society widen dramatically when the only experience that the middle class has with people of color are crime-dominated TV news reports or rare drives through depressed, dangerous neighborhoods. Over time, middle-class politicians and their constituencies stop relating to residents of poor neighborhoods. Today, attacking these neighborhoods and the government programs that would try to help them has become one of the central ways both parties garner swing votes.[4]

As the cores become politically isolated from middle-class sensibilities and sympathies, they cease to function internally on a political level. Socioeconomically distressed areas are transient places with minimal voter turnout, where it is difficult to develop a sense of community or political power.[5] In older cities, elected officials in one-party districts, free from a watchful electoral oversight, are unaccountable and therefore prone to corruption.

The Liberal-Conservative Debate

Responding to the issue of core stability, traditional liberals and conservatives take quite different approaches. Liberals concentrate on bringing in outside resources to promote enrichment programs in the city, conservatives on cutting off government funds and regulations and letting the discipline of necessity restore order. Although they agree on little else, both major approaches attempt to solve the core problems in place by turning disadvantaged residents into more successful (and more middle-class) people. However, neither strategy seriously considers the effects of socioeconomic and racial segregation on creating, intensifying, or perpetuating poverty, or the concentration effects of needy people on the stability of core communities. Nor does either take into account evidence that deconcentrating poverty has powerful effects in terms of providing access and opportunity to poor people and in stabilizing older metropolitan centers. Finally, neither contemplates efforts to bring back the middle class or persuade young, stable families to settle in the older parts of the region where poverty is concentrated.

Truth straddles the center line in the liberal-conservative debate. The liberals are correct that a laissez-faire approach, under the present governmental fragmentation, will lead to far more desperate problems and that their specific programs often empower individuals, who in turn leave poor neighborhoods. The conservatives are correct that existing programs have failed to turn the metropolitan tide in inner cities. However, both sides are tragically wrong in their shared perspective, implicit or explicit, that the problems of the central city and older suburbs—concentrated poverty—can be solved in place.

The Liberals: "Community Development"

At some point after Lyndon Johnson's War on Poverty, as the backlash from civil rights began to resonate in working-class communities and suburban fair housing became untenable and as separatist elements in the African-American communities gained prominence, liberals moved away from integrative strategies. The standard liberal approach toward stopping the spiraling decline of inner cities evolved into a compromise strategy called "community development."[6] Conservatives preferred this strategy to moving the poor into their communities. Liberals could support it because it meant new resources and programs. Over time, community development became a loosely connected series of programs in job training, economic development, housing rehabilitation, and consciousness raising designed to reinvigorate and empower both poor individuals and distressed communities.[7]

In central cities such as Minneapolis-Saint Paul, a large part of community development consists of repairing or adding additional low-income units in the poorest part of the city and regional economy. In a fragmented region, where poor residents are undeniably the sole responsibility of older communities, this is humane and necessary. The buildings are blighted, and people need places to live. However, in a regional context, by centering affordable housing in the most desperate neighborhoods, it moves against the grain of a long-term strategy to establish access to opportunity for people and stability for core communities.

After twenty years, even the largest and most successful Community Development Corporation (CDC) initiatives in the country have not changed the basic downward spiral of poor, segregated neighborhoods. In the areas where the country's leading CDCs were operating, despite large CDC investment, family and individual poverty rates and median household income have moved further from metropolitan norms, and the communities have grown more segregated.[8] One of the CDCs studied by David Rusk was the Twin Cities' Project for Pride in Living, operating directly in the middle of the extreme-poverty area that is the fourth–fastest expanding in the United States. In these neighborhoods, the crime rate increased by 50 to 70 percent, property values frequently declined by 10 to 25 percent over a five-year period, and racial and social segregation increased dramatically. At the same time, local business was leaving, as symbolized by a massive, empty Sears store a few blocks away. In the Twin Cities, $91 million is spent annually on metropolitan employment and training programs, $4.5 million of it from foundations and corporate gifts. The metropolitan unemployment rate has declined over the decade but has increased in the most distressed areas of the Twin Cities. Perhaps more disturbing, many of these programs do not evaluate their success in individual terms, and there is no large-scale measure of their effectiveness.[9]

The Conservatives: Discipline, Deregulation, and Incentives

Conservatives argue that the increasing severity of urban problems is largely *the product* of welfare and community development initiatives.[10] In their view, welfare creates a dysfunctional dependency that begets laziness, isolation from middle-class values, and (ultimately) extreme social disorder. Community development, say the conservatives, is a series of expensive programs that create make-work temporary employment, renovate buildings only to have them neglected later, and generally do little or nothing to reverse the basic forces of core decline.[11] To bolster their case, conservatives cite endemic mismanagement and fraud relating to welfare and community development initiatives. Conservatives further maintain that the chief accomplishment of community development is the creation of a poverty bureaucracy that maintains public and private funding for failed programs and protects these programs from evaluation and reform.

To conservatives, the answers are simple. First, dismantle welfare programs, specifically those that reward unmarried women for having children; the morality of necessity will then return people to work or to celibacy.[12] Second, end the expensive failed experiment of community development; third, lower regulation and taxes that impede the city's redevelopment and the market will make appropriate decisions to restore prosperity. Finally, to the extent the government becomes involved, it should do so through enterprise zones or other government tax incentives to businesses, who are responsible, rather than through community development agencies or local residents, who are not.

A Regional Approach

The conservatives have in recent years generally prevailed in the policy debate. Welfare benefits and enrollments have been declining. The national welfare bill signed in the summer of 1996 represents an even larger victory for the conservatives. As the tax base of central cities erodes, federal programs evaporate. As foundations become overburdened, community development initiatives are themselves being dismantled. There is little base in the middle- and working-class suburbs for programs geared toward all poor central-city constituencies. Enterprise zones and tax incentives are used extensively—abusively, say some. However, as with the community development process, the tide is not turning. Poor neighborhoods are expanding. Even when the cost of doing business in central cities falls well below what it would be in the favored suburban quarter, businesses do not return, and the market has not lifted these areas out of harm's way.

Most people believe that a middle-class presence is necessary for healthy, stable communities. The middle class sets social norms, participates in the community, provides tax base, and through its presence supports *and demands* an appropriate level of public and private services. However, transforming dense clusters of poor people into members of the middle class is extraordinarily difficult through either liberal empowerment or conservative discipline-type strategies. First, poverty has to be deconcentrated.[13]

Deconcentration operates on two levels. For individuals, it opens access to opportunity in the form of jobs, unstressed schools, and adequate local services. It undermines negative influences on individual achievement, exercised by oppositional culture from within and socioeconomic and racial prejudice from outside influences. For a community, deconcentration breaks poverty down into pieces that smaller decentralized programs can conquer. By alleviating social and fiscal stress, deconcentration stabilizes community decline.

Deconcentration, Fair Housing, and Reinvestment

To allow the pull of fair housing to draw individuals from the core in search of opportunity, a corresponding push of redevelopment must begin in the city and the inner suburbs. A small amount of pull in terms of affordable housing continually achieved at the edge of a metropolitan area can make a huge difference. In a study of forty of the nation's largest cities, Anthony Downs found that if 5 percent of the new development in the 1980s were set aside for subsidized housing, this would allow 12.7 percent of the inner-city households in distressed neighborhoods to move to developing, job-rich communities. In thirteen of these areas, the share would have exceeded 30 percent.[14] Around Atlanta, a fast-growing region with a comparatively small central city, if 5 percent of the new units at the developing edge during the 1980s had been subsidized, 82 percent of poor residents of central-city distressed neighborhoods could have moved to job-rich communities. Over several decades, progress could be considerable if a region steadily insisted on it.

As affordable housing becomes available at the region's periphery, the expansion of the urban and suburban distressed areas will slow and ultimately stop. Consistent metropolitan fair housing will dilute the concentration of poor children in core schools and allow a return to legally unchallengeable "neighborhood" schools and will reduce crime, disinvestment, and loss of property value. At this point, the natural amenities of the central cities (strong housing stock, parks, cultural activities, entertainment, services, and regional centrality) will assist revitalization.

A Two-Pronged Program

Fair or affordable housing can be tackled in two steps: by passing barrier-reduction legislation and by establishing a metropolitan fund for housing and redevelopment.

Barrier reduction. Barrier reduction is the logical first step, because irrational barriers frustrate any effort to create affordable housing in affluent suburbs and waste any available governmental resources. Removing discriminatory, nonmarket-oriented barriers costs nothing, can make a big difference in the availability of affordable housing, and is philosophically difficult for opponents to attack. It is a *deregulatory* step that the building community can support, actively or passively. This industry has long argued that regulatory barriers such as large lot sizes, prohibitions on multifamily housing, and assorted fees hurt the natural marketplace for affordable housing. A barrier-reduction strategy is also a way to build an early relationship with an important private sector element on land use.

In this light, a study by the U.S. Department of Housing and Urban Development (HUD), *Not in My Back Yard,* is extremely useful not only because it presents compelling information but also because Jack Kemp (a well-known conservative who became the 1996 Republican vice presidential candidate) commissioned and endorsed it while secretary of HUD in the Bush administration.[15] The HUD task force systematically identified barriers to affordable housing in developing communities and assessed their dramatically wasteful impact on builders and the U.S. economy.

The legislation should require communities to reduce nonmarket-oriented obstacles in terms of zoning codes and development agreements and practices, subject to review by a regional agency such as the Metropolitan Planning Organization or a state agency (see the appendix, page 173). *In exchange*, the community will receive resources it wants, such as federal, state, or regional subsidies for highways, sewers, and schools. This law would not supersede local authority but would make large state and metropolitan grants conditional on compliance with regional housing policy. Growing communities could choose to preserve their rugged independence, but to receive state and communal subsidies they would have to deregulate their housing markets by reducing barriers to affordable housing.

Metro Fund. The metropolitan fund for housing and redevelopment, with resources from property tax base–sharing (see below), would provide for increasing housing opportunities in the suburbs and help the market rebuild the core. This funding system is arguably an elegant, self-correcting solution. The largest beneficiaries of regional infrastructure investment would be the largest contributors—the wealthiest cities, with the smallest social needs. This solution not only provides resources in a progressive manner but, by regionalizing any windfalls from exclusive zoning, also undermines incentives that support fiscal zoning. Such a fund is likely to be one of the few sources of financing that is sufficiently large and stable to sustain an effective reinvestment pool.

Two additional measures that are relatively inexpensive are worthy of consideration: a regional system of testing for housing discrimination by race and class and housing counseling for poor city families. The testing system could alert the community to poorly understood housing market problems that perpetuate regional disparities. The evidence it provides can be helpful in terms of further action. Counseling poor people about any housing available at the periphery could also help the marketplace work.

"Not in My Backyard"

Needless to say, opposition to fair housing can be intense, both from wealthy suburban opponents and from centers of political power within the poorest parts of the city as well.

Segregation. In some older metropolitan areas with far more intense segregation and racial polarization than in the Twin Cities, objections to regional fair housing have surfaced in the battle between African-

American political and civil rights leaders. Douglas Massey, in *American Apartheid,* details how Congressman William Dawson fought efforts by Robert Taylor and Martin Luther King Jr. to desegregate public housing in Chicago. Dawson, Chicago's first African-American congressional representative, wanted to maintain his political base and connections with the white power structure. King and Taylor, the first African-American chair of the Chicago Public Housing Authority, wanted to end the horrible conditions in Chicago public housing, which they believed were intrinsically related to racial segregation.[16] A similar controversy almost killed the Gautreaux housing program in its first year (see chapter 2). In addition, in older, more polarized metropolitan areas confronting school desegregation lawsuits, the African-American political leadership has sometimes fought hard against initiatives by the National Association for the Advancement of Colored People (NAACP) seeking interdistrict busing remedies.[17]

Large African-American populations in cities make the election of African-American public officials possible, according to some African-American political leaders.[18] They consider African-American officials role models and more effective advocates of African-American issues than whites. This basic appeal is bolstered by the hiring practices of African-American–led city departments. At best, they argue, integrationist strategies are paternalistic in their doubts that African-Americans can govern themselves; at worst, they are a plot to dilute the African-American power base and prevent the election of African-American officials.

In response, integrationist civil rights groups like the NAACP argue that regional fair housing efforts are not about dispersing the African-American community and destroying an African-American power base, but about allowing individuals to choose whether to stay in poor central-city neighborhoods or seek out opportunity wherever it may be. They state that although electing African-American officials is desirable, it is not worth the price of forced racial segregation and concentrated poverty and their attendant individual and community harms. It is ultimately more important to create an open society that will provide individuals with access to opportunity and break down destructive prejudice. In such a society, multiethnic constituencies will elect an African-American mayor not because of his or her skin color, but based on character. Civil rights leaders frequently point to Sharon Sayles Belton of Minneapolis and Norman Rice of Seattle, African-American mayors in majority-white cities, as role models.

In highly practical terms, integrationists argue that by the time African-Americans gain political control over a segregated city, that city is in the advanced stages of concentrated poverty and socioeconomic decline. David Rusk has made the analogy that this situation would be as if the white captain passed the *Titanic*'s wheel to the African-American engineman as he himself headed for the lifeboat. True, the engineman is now the captain, but his ship is doomed.[19]

Finally, civil rights advocates note that though some African-American political leaders support status quo levels of segregation, their constituents do not. Many African-Americans want to live in integrated neighborhoods. Although some African-Americans are uncomfortable in virtually all-white neighborhoods, they also express strong distaste for neighborhoods that are entirely African-American. Their ideal neighborhood has a racial composition approximately 50 percent African-American.[20] Similarly, in the Twin Cities the African-American households that can afford to make choices—the African-American middle class—overwhelmingly decide to live in integrated neighborhoods. Almost half live in the suburbs. In this light, Minneapolis residents rated "least desirable" the most racially segregated African-American neighborhoods in Minneapolis.[21]

Housing poor people. Some seemingly altruistic opponents say that poor people need to live in the city to be near public transit and social services; dispersing them only makes their lives more difficult and exposes them to suburban prejudice. Fair housing does not, however, force anyone to live anywhere. It simply lets people choose where to live—to leave poor, often violent city neighborhoods or to stay there. It allows them to seek opportunity in an economically expanding area with unstressed schools or to remain where they are.

In affluent suburbs, government-subsidized housing for poor people (granted through Section 8 certificates) does meet with enormous resistance. Most suburban low-income housing (both market-rate and subsidized) is therefore located in declining inner suburbia, not in affluent communities. The inner suburbs often do not choose to create low-income housing; they are the least able to resist it. Individuals who move from the inner city to the inner suburbs often leave a high-density poor area with transit and services for a low-density inner-suburban area with neither. Often these areas have less economic opportunity than the central cities. However, the vacancy rates and waiting lists for affordable housing in the inner suburbs suggest that people prefer them to poor central-city neighborhoods. A choice to live in declining inner suburbia usually results from a cost-benefit analysis and a trade-off between safety and school opportunity and the availability of transit and other services.

The low-income housing experience is different in economically expanding suburbs and declining inner suburbs. Expanding suburbs offer many more employment opportunities and much stronger schools. In Chicago's Gautreaux program, movers were far more likely to have jobs than those who remained in the central city.[22] In the 390 low-income units in Dakota County, one of the Twin Cities' only job-rich areas with low-income housing, more than half the residents are employed, compared with 15 percent in the city.[23] In both cases, children from low-income households were far more likely to attend successful schools than their counterparts in the older suburbs or the central cities. As for transit, an employed person can usually afford some sort of car for travel to whatever services are needed. In Dakota County, 93 percent of employed residents have cars; in the central city, where mass transit is far better, 65 percent of employed residents had them.

People of color may well encounter racism if they move to all-white suburbs.[24] In this light, African-American families (for example, those in the *Gautreaux* case) that move to overwhelmingly white suburbs remain uncomfortable about the lack of racial diversity but "put up with white people" to gain access to opportunity for themselves and their children.[25] In any case, overt acts of racism dissipate rapidly as people get to know their neighbors.[26] On a societal level, integration and social interaction is one of the only ways to overcome racism.

More traditional objections to fair housing focus on two basic themes: that cities and townships, as independent local units of government, have autonomous land-planning powers that must not be interfered with. In response, a properly drafted fair housing bill does not supersede local authority. It merely conditions large state and metropolitan grants for local government aid, roads, and sewers on compliance with regional housing policy (see chapter 5). But it could be argued that discriminatory housing practices force low-income housing on the older parts of the region. Every time the wealthy suburbs say "no," the central city and inner suburbs have to say "yes" twice. In this light, the wealthy developing suburbs have no right to concentrate affordable housing on the city.

Property Tax Base Sharing

The link between basic local services and local property wealth fosters socioeconomic polarization and sprawling, inefficient land use. Property tax base sharing severs this link by creating equity in the provision of public services; breaking the mismatch between social needs and property tax base resources; undermining local fiscal incentives supporting exclusive zoning and sprawl; decreasing incentives for intrametropolitan competition for tax base; and making regional land use policies possible. Basic public services such as police and firefighters, local infrastructure, parks, and (particularly) local schools should be equal throughout the metropolitan area. People of moderate means should not have inferior public services because they cannot afford to live in property-rich communities.

School spending illustrates the need for equity. Even with Minnesota's school equity system, low spending in the northern low–tax capacity suburbs of the Twin Cities, coupled with the increasing challenges of single parentage and poverty, is a likely contributor to high drop-out rates and low college attendance levels. Equity is also critical in the central cities, where need multiplies exponentially as local tax base evaporates and state and federal support for urban programs declines.

In almost every part of the United States, wherever social needs are growing, the tax base is uncertain or declining; wherever the tax base is solid, social needs are stable or declining. In the Twin Cities in the early 1990s, for example, Saint Paul has had to raise taxes dramatically but, as a result of huge and fast-increasing social responsibilities, it has also had to cut services. At the same time, dramatic tax base increases have allowed exclusive suburbs like Minnetonka and Plymouth, with their small and declining social needs, to reduce taxes and maintain high service levels. Regionalizing the tax base would make growing property wealth available for growing social needs throughout the Twin Cities region.

Any community that can increase its tax base and limit its local social responsibilities and costs by exclusive zoning will use it. The great disparities on a metropolitan level in tax base per household show the strength of local fiscal incentives for exclusionary zoning. For example, developing communities may make explicit decisions to build only houses priced above $150,000 that "pay their way."[27] Low-density development is an intrinsic part of this fiscal zoning, because requiring large lots is one of the only ways to ensure that expensive housing will be built. Regional sharing of taxes on expensive homes would weaken local fiscal incentives to create exclusive housing markets.

Besides promoting low-density development patterns, a fragmented metropolitan tax base fosters unnecessary outward movement. Unnecessary outward movement occurs when more new housing is built on the metropolitan fringe than new households are formed in the region, and housing vacancies accumulate at the core.[28] The push of decline in the core community and its attendant fiscal crisis and the pull of rapidly growing communities that need tax base to pay for infrastructure fuel this type of sprawl as new households choose to locate in relatively problem-free communities.

In the Twin Cities, the exodus from Brooklyn Center, a declining inner suburb, to Maple Grove, a residentially exclusive growing suburb, typifies these trends. As Brooklyn Center declines, the number of poor children in its schools increases, crime grows, and residential values become increasingly uncertain. As the push of these factors gains momentum, residents are moving into Maple Grove and other northwestern developing suburbs. The Brookdale shopping center, an important part of the Brooklyn Center's commercial-industrial base, is also in financial trouble. Under deteriorating demographics, the shopping center is losing tenants and customers to a new mall in Maple Grove but is becoming a popular hangout for poor youth. Brooklyn Center thus must face its fast-growing social needs with a crippled tax base and a highly public symbol of decline. The community will have to raise taxes or cut services at the very time good services are most needed to shore up the city.[29] People and businesses pushed out of fiscally strapped Brooklyn Center are pulled into Maple Grove on a fiscally fueled housing boom.

As new communities develop, they take on large debts for the concentrated development of streets, sewers, parks, and schools. Tremendous pressure builds on these local governments to spread the costs of debt service through growth when debt falls due and property tax increases seem inevitable. This is how tax base fragmentation encourages sprawl.

Low-density sprawl is also encouraged by building communities at densities that cannot be served by public transit and with infrastructure costs that the existing tax base cannot sustain.[30] The same local fiscal pressures that encourage low-density development to enrich tax base contribute to unnecessary low-density sprawl.

Tax base sharing eases the fiscal crisis in declining communities, allowing them to shore up decline. It also relieves pressure on growing communities to spread local debt costs through growth and erodes fiscal incentives encouraging low-density sprawl. As the local property tax base becomes less dependent on growth, communities can exercise a regional perspective in terms of land use. They will be able to consider measures that will benefit the region as a whole such as urban growth boundaries, mixed-use development, greater density, and more efficient use of regional infrastructure.

In itself, intrametropolitan competition for tax base harms the entire region, not just the city that loses. When cities engage in bidding wars for businesses that have already chosen to locate in a region, public monies are used to improve one community's fiscal position and services at the expense of another's well being. Businesses can take advantage of this competition to shed social responsibilities. By threatening to leave, they can force troubled communities to pay them to stay. The widespread use of tax increment financing has reinforced this trend, allowing cities to compete (some would say gamble) for tax base not only with their own resources but also with those of the local school district, county, and state without the input of these jurisdictions.

A Beginning: The Fiscal Disparities System

Minnesota already has a partial tax base–sharing system created by a moderate Republican legislature as a less dramatic alternative to regional disparity than consolidation or annexation. Under the fiscal disparities system, each city contributes to a regional pool 40 percent of the growth of its commercial industrial tax base acquired after 1971. Annually, the pool amounts to about $367 million, about 20 percent of the regional tax base. Money is distributed from this pool on the basis of inverse net commercial tax capacity. Fiscal disparities reduce tax base disparities on a regional level from 50 to 1 to roughly 12 to 1. For cities with populations above 9,000, commercial industrial tax base disparities are reduced from 18 to 1 to 5 to 1.[31]

This system makes regional competition marginally fairer, but actual disparities remain high and fiscal zoning and competition for tax base intense. A more comprehensive sharing system, which included a larger percentage of commercial industrial tax base and some of the high-valued home tax base, would be able to reach the broader aims of reducing competition for tax base and undermining the incentives behind fiscal zoning. More often than not, the winners of intrametropolitan competition remain the developing, high–tax capacity areas with room to expand, few social problems, and comparatively low taxes. The losers are low–tax capacity, fully developed areas with many social problems and high taxes. The affluent expanding suburbs grow increasingly stronger, shutting out the overleveraged suburbs, saddled with the debts of an unfair social burden.

Two other distributional inequities can arise. Cities with a higher than average commercial base, but with low-valued homes and increasing social need, contribute tax base. At the same time, cities with mainly high-valued homes and large per household tax bases that have eschewed commercial development receive money from the system.

Barrier Reduction, Housing, and Redevelopment

In addition to a housing barrier-reduction bill, a properly managed housing and redevelopment fund and a regional redevelopment master plan need to be established.

Passage of a housing barrier–reduction bill would encourage the construction of a variety of market-rate housing in affluent communities, providing choices for households earning approximately 30 to 50 percent of the metropolitan median income. For people earning this, however, the market by itself will not provide opportunities.

At this point, outside resources will be needed to underwrite low-income housing and to create a plan to revitalize the city and inner suburbs. A housing and development fund should therefore be created. Its spending should be governed by the following rules:

Resources must be used to provide the maximum number of opportunities for the poorest families. Existing units in recipient communities should be used whenever possible. If new dwellings must be built, government money should leverage private efforts with strict income guidelines. A voucher-based system to allow rental portability should be emphasized, using rent enhancement when it is more cost effective than building.

Affordable suburban housing opportunities should be scattered as broadly as possible throughout the recipient community. Dispersal will forestall any miniconcentrations of poverty. Clustered affordable housing aggravates social problems, is likely to impair local property values, stigmatizes tenants, and physically isolates them from community life.

A Context: Regional Redevelopment Master Plan

All these activities should take place within the context of a regional redevelopment master plan for the long-term, coordinated revitalization of the city and the older suburbs. Such a plan should be approved by an elected metropolitan council or, in its absence, by the legislature. This plan should proceed under the following rules:

Core communities and planning areas within communities must coordinate their plans. Uncoordinated deconcentration and revitalization efforts could easily derail metropolitan progress. For example, each year the troubled northern inner suburbs request state and federal funds to demolish thousands of blighted apartment units filled with poor people. If they succeed, this rapid subregional deconcentration, in the absence of a coordinated supply of affordable housing scattered throughout stable growing areas, could reconcentrate poverty in adjacent suburbs or in north Minneapolis, destroying the revitalization plans of those communities.

Redevelopme...t efforts should build on socioeconomic strength. Redevelopment should be targeted to areas adjacent to stable neighborhoods. The market-based momentum created by gentrification and renewal already occurring should be used to best advantage. Neighborhoods surrounded on all sides by poverty are prone to economic reversal and are unlikely to attract middle-class and business investment.

Locally strong examples of this strategy come from the University of Minnesota Design Center for the American Urban Landscape. The center has taken two distressed neighborhoods, one in Minneapolis and the other in Saint Paul, and created plans reconnecting them to stable parts of these cities. In one case, a submerged creek would be exposed to the air and its ecological functions and habitat restored, and it would be connected to the city's parkway system. In the other, a lost wetland was restored, thus providing attractive natural space around which to redevelop true mixed-income communities.[32]

Resources must be concentrated in target areas until stability is achieved. The political process tends to divide resources broadly to achieve political support, but there will never be enough money to attack all problematic areas at once. If a master plan can be agreed to, with every community receiving resources at a certain date, however, it might be feasible. A little revitalization across a large number of planning areas is unlikely to make significant progress. Once stability is achieved in a targeted area, an adjacent area will be targeted along with a long-term metropolitan plan. If a long-term, predictable pattern of redevelopment is established and effective, the marketplace will anticipate and leverage governmental action.

Governmental resources must be maximized. Every effort should be made to preserve remediable, architecturally significant structures, but structures that are not significant or economically salvageable should be removed.

Gentrification and renewal may occur spontaneously in transitional areas that have preservation-grade housing stock adjacent to stable areas. Nevertheless, the city and older suburbs have huge surpluses of unsal-

89

vageable housing stock, "urban solid waste."[33] Some of this housing is so neglected that it cannot be economically restored. Other housing types, particularly small bungalows in interior suburbs, are no longer marketable to families that want more amenities. Layouts of streets and open space are also inadequate in many older communities. Without public investment, unwanted housing stock will remain empty or become a magnet for low-income individuals from other jurisdictions.

Direct governmental efforts should be limited. Government should focus on clearing marketable parcels, rezoning to achieve mixed income neighborhoods, cleaning up polluted business sites, and providing urban parks. In terms of rezoning, market-based middle-class preferences for housing types must receive great deference.

Schools

Because a metropolitan housing solution and a comprehensive metropolitan reinvestment plan will address concentrations of poverty, they are vital to the stability of central-city and inner-suburban schools. Busing is a second-rate solution to a housing problem. In the absence of affordable housing regionwide, however, busing lawsuits would be filed as the only way to prevent poverty from becoming concentrated in overstressed schools. A strong metropolitan housing program would ultimately make school busing unnecessary to achieve racial desegregation.

Sidetrack Strategies for School Stability

"If you just fix the schools so the middle class will be comfortable, the city will stabilize," reform advocates often say. This claim would be true if anyone knew how to fix monolithically poor schools. School reformers, like reform advocates for cities, rarely take into account the effects of concentrated poverty on schools—effects that are fundamental to how attractive these schools appear to the middle class.

Three broad fix-it approaches have been proposed to stabilize local schools. The first is the traditional approach of spending more money to strengthen programs that improve poor children's educational opportunity. The second involves internal educational restructuring to make the schools more autonomous and competitive. The third approach seeks to return central cities like Minneapolis with school desegregation to a system of neighborhood schools as a way of bringing back the middle class. However, it is extremely unlikely that any of these reforms, if made in the face of rapidly concentrating poverty, either by themselves or in combination, will have any significant effect on stabilizing school populations in the long term.

Traditional solutions. Because central cities and inner suburbs depend on declining school tax base, raising the resources necessary to deal with the effects of concentrated poverty is difficult. As central cities become poor and dominated by minority students, they become increasingly hard to fend for in the rough and tumble of legislative politics. Very seldom do affluent suburbanites find it in their hearts to devote new money to school systems for poor minority students. More often than not, these systems become prize political targets for conservative legislators seeking headlines. Sadly, to obtain financial aid from wealthy suburbs, some central cities have used the threat of a metropolitan desegregation lawsuit as a leverage point. This approach worked for Chicago, Atlanta, and other big cities. It worked for Minneapolis and Saint Paul in 1988, and they are considering another such effort.

In this ugly conspiracy between wealthy suburban and central city school districts, implying "we'll keep them here if you send us money" in effect bargains away the rights of children to increase the school systems' financial resources. The central cities get money to deal with their "special problems," and the region avoids the confrontation of integration. This "solution" never works because the middle class flees concentrated poverty as well as segregation. Even when significantly above average funds are spent on majority poor, minority schools, middle-class families will not move back to them.

Central cities and inner suburbs undeniably face far greater challenges than the rest of the metropolitan school districts and need more money per pupil. In fact, they are already the highest spending group of school districts in the Twin Cities. Programs targeted at poor children do make a difference, but money and programs cannot, by themselves, solve the problems related to concentrated poverty. When all of a school's students have serious problems, when virtually no one is succeeding, when they are cut off from mainstream society, making schools function is extraordinarily difficult.[34] Flight accelerates, test scores continue to decline, and drop-out rates rise in a pattern far more related to the concentration of poverty than any other factor. Increasing expenditures and programs may slow these desperate trends, but concentrated poverty overwhelms many of their positive effects.

Internal restructuring. Giving local schools wider autonomy and forcing them to compete for pupils is a solution put forward by the School Choice movement, begun in the 1980s in Minnesota. Despite the scant evidence that the approach will work, the movement is gaining a following across the nation.[35] In the Twin Cities, lack of comparable metropolitan testing data until recently has made it impossible to evaluate. In the meantime, the School Choice system should not be used to help middle-class families opt out of schools with economic and racial diversity, thus further segregating metropolitan schools.

Neighborhood schools. Some school reformers claim that the return to neighborhood schools is a panacea that will solve virtually all the problems of city schools. In so doing, they maintain that ending school busing will stop the flight and return middle-class families to the cities. They also argue that busing has not improved the lives or education of minority children and prevents the development of neighborhood schools, which encourage stronger communities and parental participation. It is just not that simple.

With busing, Minneapolis lost 40 percent of its white preschoolers during the 1980s. Without busing, Saint Paul lost 31 percent; the inner-ring suburbs, all with neighborhood schools, were close behind Saint Paul. Because school systems without busing also lost large numbers of white preschoolers, busing cannot be the sole cause of white flight. Much of the white preschool flight from the central-city systems occurred in neighborhoods ranged around the expanding poverty cores. As distance widened between neighborhoods and this core, the intensity of flight diminished. Some gentrifying neighborhoods gained white preschoolers.

Yet apart from the expanding cores of poverty, significant (if less intense) flight persisted in both cities' gentrifying and middle-income neighborhoods. In middle-income Minneapolis neighborhoods, this may well have been because of the sudden mass importation of poor minority students from other parts of the city. Seemingly overnight, poor and minority students became more than one-third of the student body in affluent parts of the city. Although these levels are small in a citywide context, residents of middle-class neighborhoods had the economic means to move quickly and quietly to southern and western developing suburbs without school poverty or diversity—and with lower taxes.

Although the slightly greater volume of white flight in Minneapolis than in Saint Paul may have been prompted by busing, it could just as well reflect the greater severity of poverty, economic depression, and crime in Minneapolis's core. It may also reflect white parents' racial preconceptions in that non-Asian minorities make up 45 percent of the student body in Minneapolis schools, compared with 25 percent in Saint Paul and still less in the inner suburbs.

In the end, a return to neighborhood schools in central cities would not stop white flight, which seems to be largely related to the expanding geographic cores of poverty. Neighborhood schools would have some stabilizing effect in middle-income or affluent neighborhoods far removed from the core—but only until poverty touched their borders. Stability would last only as long as growing crime, property devaluation, or taxation did not override the lure of socially desirable, close-to-home schools. However, this stability would be achieved only at the price of allowing some schools to become all poor and segregated, a devastating educational experience for the children who attend them.

As with almost every other important regional issue, the busing-versus-neighborhood-schools controversy has played itself out in larger, older metropolitan areas around the United States. Different choices have produced extremely different outcomes in terms of white middle-class flight.

In 1981, Los Angeles became the first large American city to dissolve a mandatory busing plan, yet between 1981 and 1988, the city lost more than one-third of its white students. Similarly, during the 1980s, Oklahoma City, Dallas, and Norfolk, Virginia, all ended school busing and returned to neighborhood schools. All continued to lose white students, and an intensely segregated group of African-American schools emerged with severe educational problems.[36] The largest white flight in the nation during the 1980s occurred in two large suburban systems with neighborhood schools—those outside of Washington, D.C., and Atlanta.[37] Similarly, Chicago, which had a neighborhood school plan with a limited voluntary magnet program, lost one-third of its white students during the 1980s. Finally, Atlanta, New York, and Baltimore, which chose neighborhood schools over busing, had some of the largest losses of white students of any central city districts in the nation.[38]

In contrast to opponents' claims, important scholarly research shows that students attending desegregated schools were more likely to attend selective colleges, to major in scientific and math-related fields, to find work in growth sectors of the economy with predominately white workers, and to live in integrated neighborhoods as adults. In other words, students attending integrated schools had a better chance of making it across the color line in metropolitan society on a number of socioeconomic dimensions. Integration does not end racial inequalities, but at least it makes it possible to have access to more competitive schools and preparation for a multiracial college, job market, and society.[39]

In terms of community building, neighborhood schools can undoubtedly be important institutions for pulling neighborhoods and communities together. Middle-class parents participate in neighborhood schools, especially through periodically scheduled parent-teacher association activities. However, fewer and fewer middle-class parents can become involved in the school's daily activities, because both parents are income earners in many middle-class households in the 1990s.

For poor parents, it is a different story. Despite extensive outreach programs in the Twin Cities, poor parents rarely participate in school activities, partly because they cannot maintain residence for more than a few months. Their transience in a neighborhood makes it almost impossible to build relationships with teachers and schools. In addition, poor residents are often overwhelmed by drug addiction, turbulent relationships, long work hours with low pay, and general despair. The recent Minneapolis Quality Schools initiative made extraordinary efforts to contact poor parents about school reform but had little success either locating these parents or eliciting their opinions of the schools.[40]

In the absence of strong progress on metropolitan housing, demands for metropolitan school busing to achieve desegregation will be unceasing. Without affordable housing, civil rights advocates will argue that only school desegregation will allow poor children access to a competitive educational experience.

In Minneapolis, Saint Paul, or any of the internally segregated suburban systems, however, single district desegregation in the absence of other reforms is counterproductive, because it accelerates the flight to areas without busing. Until affordable housing or a broader school solution by legislation or litigation comes about, cities like Minneapolis that are trying to desegregate by themselves may have to limit the number of poor and minority students in middle-class neighborhoods to the metropolitan averages for these categories, or some other number where middle-class stability can be maintained. This will vent some pressure impelling flight from middle-class schools and neighborhoods. At the same time, it will recognize metropolitanwide responsibilities. Without this stopgap solution, the city will desegregate virtually every middle-class family out of the city into jurisdictions that do not acknowledge regional responsibilities. This will leave an all-poor, all-minority school system that will further isolate the city socioeconomically and politically. Such a decision, however, should only be made in the context of a committed effort by the city or the state to seek a broader metropolitan resolution.

In the last analysis, the region needs socioeconomically mixed schools to stabilize core communities. This stability is a necessary but insufficient condition for improving schools and does not preclude other types of educational reform. This should be achieved through housing.

A side-track strategy aimed at returning to neighborhood schools without other regional reforms such as fair housing will have little effect on city stability or the problems of the city schools as a whole. As schools gradually solve their immediate stability problems, the region should continue to pursue reforms that raise the levels of academic achievement not just for the college bound but for labor market entrants.

Land Use, Infrastructure, and Transportation

Further polarization within the region will be hard to stop as long as the Twin Cities and other communities continue to sprawl into unplanned patterns of low-density suburban development. Older areas, saddled with old infrastructure and housing, high taxes, social disorder, and industrial pollution, will have great difficulty competing with the heavily subsidized, socially exclusive periphery. These wasteful patterns also unnecessarily threaten groundwater, sensitive environmental habitats, and highly productive farmland.

Land Use Reform

Metropolitan land use reform is best built on a framework of community-wide planning goals; locally developed land use plans addressing these goals; and review of these plans by a regional entity, an adjudication process, and periodic effectiveness evaluation by an independent entity.[41]

Regional goals. Ideally a regional entity promulgates a statement of planning goals applicable to all communities in the region. The goals then encompass the development of a regional growth boundary, affordable housing (including overall density goals), and coherence with regional plans for transportation, sewerage, parks, and school infrastructure. Any local plans and policies inconsistent with these goals are challengeable in court or in special forums created for such adjudication. In conjunction with these reforms, building standards and maximum turnaround time for local development decisions are then made uniform. These reforms help builders make long-term plans to maximize their resources and foster patterns of regionwide sustainable development.

In terms of the development of a regional or urban growth boundary, the region is required to plan for growth at present absorption rates and to draw a line around itself that would accommodate such growth over a set period of time, perhaps twenty years. Growth is deflected from sensitive environmental areas and highly productive farmland and toward areas where urban services are present or could most easily be provided.

In the early 1970s under the leadership of moderate Republican Governor Tom McCall, Oregon instituted the nation's most thoughtful, comprehensive land use planning system. Oregon requires each city to develop an urban growth boundary, a concept similar to the Twin Cities' Metropolitan Urban Service Area (MUSA) line.

The density and affordable housing goals could reinforce the barrier-reduction component of the fair housing bill, as was discussed previously. In Oregon, the housing rules promulgated under this goal require Portland's metropolitan cities to allow for a construction mix that includes at least 50 percent multifamily development and allows development at certain minimum target densities. In the city of Portland, the target density is ten units per buildable acre; in most Portland suburbs, it is six to eight units.[42]

In Washington County, Oregon, the most affluent of the Portland region's three metropolitan counties, 11,110 multifamily units approved in five years nearly equaled the 13,893 units that were planned to be built over twenty years under the pre-housing rule plans. Multiple family housing now makes up 54 percent of new development.[43] Before the housing rule, average lots sizes were 13,000 square feet. Since the rule, two-thirds of the homes are built on lots smaller than 9,000 square feet.[44] Without the growth boundary and housing rule, the same number of housing units would have consumed an additional 1,500 acres of land.[45] Because of the density savings already realized, there will be space for 14,000 additional units within the Portland urban growth boundary. While the price of land has gone up within Portland's urban growth boundary, the housing rule has lowered the cost of housing on a regional basis, and Portland's average housing costs are lower than those of comparable West Coast cities. Seventy-seven percent of the region's households can afford to rent a median-priced two-bedroom apartment, and 67 percent can afford mortgage payments on a median-priced two-bedroom home.[46]

Increasing building density and housing-type diversity makes mass transit economically and physically possible. Density also saves local infrastructure costs for building new highways and sewer extensions.

Local land use plans. If local governments are to be required to develop a comprehensive land use plan that addresses the regional goals, citizen participation should be required in formulating these plans. Planning and revision would remain in the hands of local governments, which helps preserve local autonomy, but within the context of a broader regional framework.

Regional-level review. The regional entity would be empowered to review all local plans to ensure consistency with regional goals and suggest revisions of any inconsistencies. This entity would have the power to withhold approval from local plans, which prevents the municipality from receiving beneficial services such as regional roads, sewers, or other aid from state and federal governments. The same regional entity coordinates local transportation, utility regulation, environmental protection, and activities of other governmental units that have a regional significance. This ensures that all actions of state agencies within the region are consistent with regional plans, local plans, and other agency decisions.

Transportation is particularly important in this regard. Land use policy needs to govern decisions about new infrastructure. All land use and infrastructural decisions must be coordinated in a way that maximizes the use of existing roads, sewerage, and other infrastructure. Today, in transportation planning, congestion and demand (perhaps also political power) are the main criteria for providing new infrastructure. This means that a growing community receives new sewers or roads even if an adjacent community has excess—paid for—capacity. Infrastructure-on-demand, costless for the new community, perpetuates leapfrogging, low-density patterns at the periphery, and the entire metropolitan region pays. Moreover, affordable housing near new jobs can relieve commuter congestion on regional roads.

Adjudication process. An adjudication process needs to be set up to settle disputes between the local governments and the regional agency and between developers and local governments. A special court, or a quasi-judicial administrative agency, would then be designed to do this, without resorting to state and federal courts. It thus allows localities to develop an expertise in these matters and be more efficient, cost less, and render faster decisions than the courts.

Independent review. Finally, an independent entity, not the regional structure, periodically would evaluate the effectiveness of the coordinated plan.

In the end, such a system would not involve a prohibition on growth or even growth control, but a system of sustainable, planned growth. It would recognize new housing needs of a growing regional population, and also the necessity for anticipating and planning growth. Through planning, the region maximizes the use of existing public infrastructure, reduces stress on highways and sewers, allows individuals access to opportunity in communities where it is plentiful, reduces regulation and its costs for the building industry, and stabilizes the region's core communities.

Transportation and Transit Reform

Transportation reform—highway construction and mass transit—is closely connected to land use reform. In Minnesota and some other states, statutory or state constitutional provisions prevent gas tax proceeds, or other funding sources for transportation, from being used for transit inside metropolitan areas. In addition to coordinating with transit and land use as discussed above, such restrictions should be repealed, and a stable regional fund for mass transit should be created from the gas tax.

Major roads and sewers should not be extended to undeveloped parts of the region while excess capacity exists elsewhere. Further, infill development and redevelopment of underutilized neighborhoods in the city and older suburbs that have paid-for infrastructure should be given priority over new development that destroys forest and farmland at the periphery.

The foregoing shows rather emphatically that infrastructure and development must pay their true cost. The Mohring and Anderson study of highway transportation and the Luce, Lukermann, and Mohring sewer study (discussed in chapter 5) are simply the local manifestations of dozens of studies in other regions of the United States. All of them show that the present system of infrastructure construction—particularly highway infrastructure—results in huge subsidies that move from the center of the region outward. In addition, the communities that practice fiscal zoning create huge externalities in terms of congestion, businesses without labor, and people without jobs that must be paid for by the public at large, through either higher product costs or taxes. The human externalities associated with concentrated poverty are beyond calculation. In fact, the list of improperly priced commodities and services is outlined in every other chapter in this book and is truly almost without limit.

At the outset, the notion that freeways should be priced appropriately through tolls or taxes seems compelling. New suburban highway capacity is best priced through a toll system. Those that use them most—the communities most dependent on them—should pay their full share of the cost. The same holds true for sewers and school infrastructure when financed on a broader than local level.

Welfare Reform

To give individuals a sense of self-respect and access to opportunity, welfare reform and job creation must ideally be carried out simultaneously in core poverty neighborhoods. Welfare should allow and encourage people long isolated from a normal work routine to make a transition back into a productive schedule of activity. Jobs are also necessary to stabilize violent communities where boredom and isolation breed crime. Jobs projects should be targeted for local renewal. This process relieves physical distress and helps to restore a sense of hope and order to dysfunctional neighborhoods.

In conjunction with deconcentrating low-income housing, social service providers (particularly the counties) must be more flexible in providing services on the suburban level. Concentrating welfare services in the core further concentrates poverty. While service providers may argue that decentralizing services will increase their costs because deconcentrating services will deconcentrate poverty, it is therefore likely to reduce the severity of social problems. The services provided are more likely to have a meaningful effect when reinforced by functional middle-class communities.

Metropolitan Structural Reform

In the early 1970s, moderate Republicans in Minnesota and Oregon created the nation's only metro councils. In Oregon, the council was elected; in Minnesota, appointed by the governor. For any metropolitan area with demographics like those of the Twin Cities, coordinated new housing, tax base sharing, reinvestment, land planning, and transportation and transit reform are imperative for improving equity and bringing stability to the region. Strong regional majorities will be able to endorse these reforms, though controversial and powerfully resisted. These reforms cannot be accomplished by automatic formulas like fiscal disparities. Neither can their control be left to appointed individuals whose power derives from other elected officials. Elected officials are needed. This does not mean that reform should be deferred until an elected structure is in place. It does mean that, in the long run, these reforms will be far more effective with an accountable, legitimate regional coordinating structure.

Central control versus local autonomy in federated systems has always been a fundamental political dilemma in American political history.[47] Today, 70 percent of the nation lives in metropolitan areas that are destabilizing and polarizing to one degree or another. The only real solutions involve a new metropolitan compact—to plan a common future, share benefits and responsibilities, reinvest together in older areas, protect forests and farmland, conquer social prejudice, and in general foster sustainable, interdependent regions. How will this be accomplished? By building the structure of an elected federated metropolitan union and tying the grant of metropolitan resources to compliance with metropolitan objectives.

The Power of Metropolitanism

In *Cities without Suburbs*, David Rusk showed that areas that had created metropolitan governments by annexation or consolidation were less segregated by race and class, more fiscally sound, and economically healthier. Rusk studied 165 metropolitan areas with populations of more than 200,000. He compared cities that were *elastic,* which grew by annexing suburbs and other developing parts of their metropolitan areas, to those that were *inelastic,* whose borders remained fixed. The *zero-elastic* cities, which did not grow at all, had an average of 120 cities and 45 school districts in their regions; the *hyperelastic* cities, which captured the most territory, had an average of 23 cities and 12 school districts.

Rusk found that the more elastic a city was, and the less fragmented its region, the less likely were great fiscal disparities between communities and the more likely were central cities to remain financially and socially healthy. Specifically, he found that elastic cities had median incomes much closer to those of their suburbs, tended to grow in terms of both population and tax base, and had much better bond ratings. But, most important, Rusk found that elastic regions were much less racially segregated than the inelastic, fragmented regions: "Smaller jurisdictions are typically organized to promote and protect uniformity rather than promote diversity. Conversely, areas characterized by geographically large, multipowered governments and more unified school systems tend to promote racial and economic integration and achieve greater social mobility."[48]

The Taeuber or dissimilarity index is a well-known measure of racial segregation. It measures *evenness,* the proportion of a minority population that would have to move to produce an absolute proportional distribution of that minority across all census tracts in a metropolitan area. The most inelastic regions had a dissimilarity index of .72 for Afri-

can-Americans and .57 for Hispanics, the hyperelastic regions .57 for African-Americans and .37 for Hispanics. In terms of schools, the zero-elastic regions had a .71 segregation index for African-Americans and .59 for
Hispanics, the hyperelastic regions .47 for African-Americans and .38 for
Hispanics.

Rusk repeated this experiment with seven pairs of metropolitan areas
matched in most respects, except that one of each pair was elastic and the
other rigid. These pairs had roughly the same population and proportions
of poor and minority citizens and the same number of new home buyers.
In each case, the inelastic region was far more segregated than the elastic
region for both African-Americans and Hispanics. Rusk also found that
the elastic areas tended to adjust better to economic times, have far better
bond ratings, a higher percentage of the suburban income, and a smaller
share of the region's poverty.

In his research Rusk discovered that there were in effect twenty-
three "metropolitan governments" in the country. To Rusk, a metropolitan government had 50 percent or more of the regional population and a
central-city had a median income that was 90 percent of the suburban average or greater. Five of his metropolitan governments were the consolidated city-county governments of Nashville-Davidson, Tennessee;
Indianapolis-Marion, Indiana; Lexington-Fayette, Kentucky; Jackson-
ville-Duval, Florida, and Columbus-Muskogee, Georgia. The rest maintained their dominance by aggressive annexation policies.[49] In general,
Rusk found these areas to be less segregated and more economically
healthy than more fragmented but otherwise comparable regions.

Popular Elections—Why?

In Portland, Oregon, politicians win and lose major elections on growth
management issues. Most voters in the Twin Cities and most other parts
of the nation are completely unaware of the vital importance of these issues to their daily lives. Popular election of regional officials publicizes
the issues and invites people to think regionally about common problems
and solutions, but the issue is more basic than that. An elected official's
power derives from voters. The official has power within the legal reach
of the office and the tolerance of those voters. The stronger the politician's leadership, the broader discretion becomes. Elected officials tend
to test the limits of their authority vis-à-vis other units of government.
Similarly, because elected officials defend their prerogatives, competing
governments are less likely to usurp power from elected bodies than from
appointed bodies.

Appointed power derives from the appointing authority. A strong appointing authority can tightly circumscribe the appointee's duties and decisions. The appointing authority is less likely to view the appointee as a thoughtful, discretionary agent of the general good than as a representative of well-defined interests. Appointed officials often avoid confrontations with the appointing authority.

Differences in the operating styles and accomplishments of the two regional entities derive in part from the sources of their governing power, the Twin Cities' appointed Metropolitan Council and Oregon's elected Metropolitan Council. Oregon's regional government has been more willing than the Twin Cities' appointed Metropolitan Council to exercise its powers vis-à-vis competing authorities.

Oregon and Minnesota both have strong land use laws with growth boundaries. In Oregon, the elected governing body has better enforced these laws. In twenty years, Oregon has permitted 2,000 acres of exceptions to its boundary. In Minnesota, the Twin Cities' Met Council, with its weak derivative power, has avoided confrontation and has never brought a lawsuit to enforce its land planning act (see the appendix, page 173).[50] Between 1987 and 1991, the Twin Cities allowed seventy-eight exceptions to the boundary, and 18,000 acres of forest and farmland were added.

Some people in the Twin Cities object to the idea of electing regional officials on the grounds that it would add "another layer of government," with a parochial outlook, in a region that already has too much local government. In the political climate of the 1990s, the term "another layer of government" has a rhetorical force akin to "no new taxes" or "mindless bureaucrats." Implicit in this argument is the assumption that an elected metropolitan council would cause further regional bickering and paralysis. Electing Met Council members would hardly create another level of government, however. The Met Council and most regional metropolitan planning organizations (MPOs) have been in existence for more than a quarter of a century. Direct elections would simply make their members legitimate and publicly accountable, like Portland's council members. The governmental entity with the most potential for redressing regional polarization should not be the weakest and least accountable.

As for the parochialism of elected officials versus the allegedly broader perspective of appointed officials toward the common good, this debate over the Twin Cities' metropolitan government has raged for years. On one side lies the danger of pork barrel politics that precludes any efficient action for the common good; on the other, lack of legitimacy and accountability, and insulation from real human needs. The framers of the American Constitution (and of most democratic institutions since) decided that lack of accountability poses the greater danger. They believed that any governmental body entrusted with important decisions, great discretion, and significant taxing and spending powers should be elected. Winston Churchill correctly recognized that, despite its deep problems, democracy was better than alternative forms of government.

The appointive process does not ensure regionalism or leadership, nor are elected officials all venal and parochial. The track record of regional visionaries appointed to the Twin Cities Met Council has been singularly unimpressive. Moreover, most of the region believes that the council's apparent unity and collegiality reflects not regional consensus, but a profoundly shared parochialism focused on the development of the southern and western developing suburbs. In the Twin Cities region, council appointments have been uneven and increasingly weak, and there is no systemic way to ensure that they will be better in the future. Regional issues are too important to be relegated to the hope that effective council members will be designated by the governor or other appointing authority.

At the heart of this debate is the assumption that there is a consensus-based "regional perspective." Most people could probably agree on some amorphous statement about "efficient use of resources," "long-term strategies," and "the common good," but beyond this—perhaps even before—the consensus shatters. To the Twin Cities northern suburbs, the fiscal disparities system is an inadequate step toward regional fairness. To the southern suburbs, the system is unconstitutional, and they challenged it all the way to the U.S. Supreme Court.[51] To the central cities, freeway expansions sap their middle-class and business vitality. To the developing suburbs, freeways are a right, necessary to the free movement of people and goods. The common good and the regional perspective—like truth, beauty, and justice—do not exist in some ideal form. In the end, the closest approximation comes from a fair contest of ideas, values, and perspectives decided by the elected representatives of the people. In the interim, however, progress can be made toward solving regional problems, issue by issue, by building self-interest based coalitions—"metropolitics."

7

Metropolitics: Regional Coalition Building

This chapter, which details the political nuts and bolts of regional coalition building and legislative politics, is written in the first person. Because this is very much a personal story, it would have been hard to write it any other way, and I hope the reader will indulge my shift in narrative style.

* * *

"Metropolitics" began with studies, sewers, and maps and moved on through mayoral associations, the Minnesota State Legislature, and the governor's office. Issue by issue, bill by bill, the coalition was forged. Today it spans the central cities, inner suburbs, and low–tax base developing suburbs, hundreds of metropolitan churches, environmentalists, civic groups such as the League of Women Voters and the Citizens League, and the Twin Cities metro area's communities of color. It is strong and continues to gain influence and credibility.

Because school statistics gave the most dramatic early warning of social and economic change in the suburbs, I began to collect statistics on the region by city and school district units during 1991 and 1992. Local property wealth was a substantial resource for the financing of local services and of deep interest to cities and school districts, so I was also interested in the property tax base. What I found revealed a remarkable pattern of inner-suburban decline and regional polarization. The inner-suburban school enrollment was growing poorer and more diverse, with small and stagnant property tax resources. Newer suburbs to the south and west had low levels of poverty and less diversity, with large, fast-growing tax bases. From countless discussions with planners, I learned that most of the region's new infrastructure seemed to be going to support the southwestern suburban development boom. Yet the Twin Cities Metropolitan Council and the Minnesota Department of Transportation both told me that data collection practices did not support my conclusions. They gave me broad unsupported assurances that all growing areas received infrastructure equally. In the light of my research, I remained unconvinced.

The 1991–92 Legislative Session: From Maps to Bills

My first step in the ensuing legislative history was to draft a bill requiring the Met Council to do a comprehensive study of the economic health of the city and the first ring of "fully developed," older suburbs. In what the committee chairman said was a first, I testified in the Senate myself on behalf of the companion bill, because its Senate author was too busy. The Fully Developed Area Study, initially opposed by the council, produced two reports that began to shed light on regional polarization.[1] These reports largely confirmed the social and economic decline of the inner suburbs but offered few solutions.

The Metropolitan Infrastructure Stability Act

In January 1992, I introduced the Metropolitan Infrastructure Stability Act, a bill that required subregional pricing of sewer infrastructure.[2] Before 1987, the Met Council had "priced" sewer infrastructure so that developing areas paid a higher share of the cost of new sewers to support their growth. In 1987, the legislature imposed a uniform pricing system through which the whole region shared the cost of new sewer capacity. This move seemed to have originated outside the council, because its staff had opposed these changes. Staffers argued that it was unfair for the older areas of the Twin Cities region to pay for this capacity and that spreading the costs of sewers made the possibility of more urban sprawl too easy. My bill was drafted by Minnesota House Research in consultation with a Met Council attorney and with the help of several of the council's planning staff members. In short, the Metropolitan Infrastructure Stability Act would have overturned the uniform regional debt-service fee and made the growing areas pay a larger part of the cost of new sewer capacity. This looked like a perfect issue to begin building a coalition between the central cities and older suburban communities. It seemed manageable in scope and did not involve race or class issues, and the status quo was hard to defend in terms of policy.

In a sequence of events that became predictable, this bill was immediately and strongly opposed by the Builders Association of the Twin Cities, several powerful developers, real estate agents, and growing cities. House leaders soon let me know that builders and real estate agents were among the largest contributors to the political process and warned me to step back. The Met Council moved quickly from a neutral position on the bill to outright opposition. After the session ended, one developer of expensive homes invited me to lunch and told me that he and several other developers had written large personal checks to hire additional lobbyists to kill the bill and that they would continue to do so.

In committee, I presented the bill as part of a way to stabilize the city and declining inner suburbs. My statistics showed the social and economic weakening of the older inner suburbs; it also showed that virtually all new sewer construction—$50 million to $80 million a year—was going to the southern and western suburbs.

The northern inner suburbs looked like natural allies of this bill. The North Metro Mayors Association, a group of seventeen northern low–tax capacity suburbs, was divided between severely declining inner-suburban areas and growing middle-income areas. Because some of the growing areas that were members of the association wanted sewers at regional expense, they had to oppose the bill, though they were in many ways sympathetic to its broader aims. Nonetheless, in the course of this struggle, we learned to acknowledge our common interests and began to think about working together. The North Metro Mayors Association would later become one of the most staunch supporters of a regional agenda.

Two of the most vigorous opponents of the bill were a South Minneapolis state senator and a city council member. Both were on the Met Council when it created the uniform financing system. The state senator had testified in favor of it before the legislature in 1987.[3] In many long conversations with them, I never understood why these officials supported this system. The state senator would later sponsor a bill to reform sewer financing to allow appropriate pricing in 1996.

Next, the executive director of the Metropolitan Waste Control Commission, Gordon "Gordy" Voss, and Anoka County commissioner Paul McCarron, a former member of the Waste Control Commission, lobbied intensely to defeat the bill. Both were powerful former legislative committee chairs from the northern suburbs—smart, savvy, and tenacious. Voss argued that without the regional pricing, growing areas would be unable to meet costly environmental regulations. In contradiction to this, in other committees he argued that the proposed change would make no difference and that the bill was a waste of time. Voss and McCarron, with the assistance of the large and growing cohort of real estate developers, quickly killed the bill in the Senate. The bill's author never got a hearing.

In this seemingly hopeless battle, Irv Anderson, chair of the Local Government Committee and soon to be Speaker of the House, took an interest in the bill at my urging. He understood its equities. As added motivation, in 1980 when Anderson first ran for Speaker, Gordy Voss, then a state representative, was instrumental in a controversial internal Democratic coup that resulted in another House member's becoming Speaker. The bill received a hearing in Anderson's committee and, on a rapidly gaveled voice vote, was sent straight to the floor of the House, avoiding damaging potential referrals to other committees.

Had the bill passed, it could have significantly increased sewer fees for residents of developing suburbs. As it moved to the floor of the House, the bill gathered opponents—six or more lobbyists from the building industry, lobbyists from the real estate industry, growing cities, and labor unions—in addition to Voss, McCarron, and the South Minneapolis state senator and the council member. Although the bill was dead in the Senate, its opponents were still afraid it would be amended to one of the large omnibus bills on the floor in a long, late-night session.

As the forces opposed to the bill grew more powerful, in exchange for withdrawing the bill the Met Council and the Waste Control Commission agreed to finance a $400,000 infrastructure study of freeway and sewer financing to be done independently at the University of Minnesota. This compromise resulted in two significant studies that provided detailed evidence of both the historical pattern of infrastructure subsidies and the virtues of pricing infrastructure regionally.[4] These studies showed conclusively that, after the central cities, the northern suburbs were the largest subsidizers of the southwestern suburban infrastructure expansion.

This debate taught me several lessons. Builders and real estate agents, partly because of the amount of money they gave to both political parties, were some of the fiercest opponents in the legislative process. Without Irv Anderson's help, the bill probably would have died in committee. The political world of the northern suburbs was also more complicated than I had thought. Though seemingly sympathetic on many issues, these suburbs had their own alliances, which had to be considered. Clearly, the pattern of regional polarization was not well understood and was difficult to explain. Without significant preparation and communication, not even my colleagues in Minneapolis could be relied on to support regional reform policies.

The Regional Fair Housing Coalition

After the 1991–92 session, I began to concentrate on building an alliance with the northern suburbs for regional reform. The seventeen northern suburbs of the North Metro Mayors Association had twenty-six House seats, which, together with the eighteen from the central cities, would create a regional majority voting block. If other inner-suburban and low–tax base areas could be persuaded to join, we would have a decisive majority. Concurrently, through endless discussions and debates with policymakers and academics, the steps necessary to redress this growing regional polarization began to crystallize around legislation for strong regional housing, tax base sharing, land use planning, and reform of governmental structures. Meeting with the northern suburban city officials, we discussed their areas' rapidly growing social needs and broached the possibility of building an alliance around any or all of those issues.

Color maps, which powerfully and simply conveyed complex patterns and trends, were critical to these discussions. In late 1992, with $750 of my own money, I bought a Datanet Mapping package, a rather primitive type of geographic information system (GIS) software. Speaker Dee Long assigned me a staff member one day a week who helped collect and interpret census and agency data over the summer of 1992. By early 1993, I had developed a series of GIS maps that illustrated the region's changing demographics.[5] My maps and presentations of the pattern of regional polarization soon found a receptive audience throughout the region: I made more than seventy speeches in 1993 and more than 100 in 1994. Local officials especially liked the maps showing placement of new regional infrastructure, locations of new jobs, fiscal disparity between communities, and patterns of tax base polarization. Soon I could not keep up with requests for my maps and gave them to the State Planning Agency to be reproduced and distributed. By late 1993, the State of Minnesota had sold 5,000 copies of the first set of regional demographic maps.

Because of the political unpopularity of city issues and the socioeconomic and racial divisiveness of metropolitan policies, getting maximum visible support in the suburbs was critical. For regionalism to succeed, it had to become a suburban issue. At first, the suburbs (no matter how badly off) saw no reason to join in a political alliance with the central cities. Foreign to their worldview, the very idea smacked of a sort of political degradation. In addition, some suburban city officials did not want to publicly acknowledge any problems. An extensive series of meetings began—first with individual officials, then in larger groups—using maps and presenting arguments for regional reforms that demonstrated the self-interest these suburbs had in regionalism.[6] Guiding many of my meetings and providing important advice and counsel was William Barnhart, a lobbyist for the city of Minneapolis who had long cultivated suburban support on many important city issues. Barnhart had a strong knowledge of the suburban community and its elected officials and the workings of regional government (particularly the fiscal system) and was well respected. Phil Cohen, a lobbyist for the North Metro Mayors Association, was Barnhart's suburban counterpart. Cohen, a former mayor of Brooklyn Center, an inner-ring suburb, had strong contacts in both Democratic and Republican legislative circles. He, like Barnhart, intimately understood the legal and political world of roads, housing, land use, and regionalism. Without Cohen, approaching the North Metro Mayors Association would never have been possible.

North Metro Mayors Association: Inner Suburbs, Low Tax Base

Most inner-suburban city officials understood the inevitable deepening of their cities' problems. None of the cities that were members of the North Metro Mayors Association had enough property tax base to adequately support community services. After the fiscal disparities distribution, they still had one-third less tax capacity per household than the southwest and east developing suburbs. Believing in the axiom that economic development followed major public infrastructure expenditures, the association had become disgruntled about the disproportionate metropolitan freeway designation and sewer spending in the southwestern quadrant.

The North Metro Mayors Association exists as an organization to win approval for northern highway projects and sewer projects, to preserve the present fiscal disparities system or increase local government aid payments to its member suburbs, and to acquire new programs and resources in response to the explosive growth of social needs in the northern inner-suburban area. However, troubling cross-currents disturbed this seeming consensus.

In member city Brooklyn Park, an angry group of citizens that some called the Legion of Doom began to exercise their political influence, throwing out longtime elected officials and protesting low-income housing and problematic apartment buildings in their communities. In this time of upheaval, a strong antiestablishment candidate, professional wrestler Jesse "The Body" Ventura, became mayor of Brooklyn Park. Though less visible and not yet dominant in these aging suburbs, this same sentiment was present in many inner-ring neighborhoods—a source of growing instability not necessarily compatible with the complexities of a regional movement. However, while this group grabbed attention, the northern suburbs had strong, competent officials who continued to go about doing their jobs. Elwyn Tinklenberg, a former minister and powerful public speaker, president of the North Metro Mayors Association, strongly understood the potential for the growing alliance and provided powerful, eloquent testimony in legislative hearings. His city manager, Don Poss, a skilled legislative craftsman who was respected in the northern part of the region, was also instrumental in building support. Joseph Strauss, the executive director of the North Metro Mayors Association—a former elected official with strong ties to organized labor and a highly capable public relations strategist—worked behind the scenes to build a strong and sinuous base for regionalism in the north.

In January 1993, the North Metro Mayors Association called a large public meeting of all the north suburban city, school district, and county-elected officials and other community leaders. The meeting focused on demographics and the outline of regional reform in terms of housing, transportation reform, fiscal equity, and structural reform. Afterward, the North Metro Mayors Association and its member cities endorsed the outline of regional reform and would later endorse all of the specific bills of the Metropolitan Community Stability Act (see below). Even Mayor Ventura was in favor of the agenda. This support gave enormous momentum to metropolitan reform and helped persuade other suburban communities to join us.

With this first strong public show of support, we set about drafting a detailed legislative agenda for the 1993 session. Expanding the tax base–sharing system was discussed and rejected. Although the suburbs that were members of the North Metro Mayors Association wanted a broader tax base–sharing system, they depended heavily on fiscal disparities revenue and had recently headed off a strong attack by the western suburbs, Hennepin County, and Minneapolis (which had become a short-term contributor). The North Metro Mayors Association wanted to test the strength of a regional alliance before putting the fiscal disparities system at issue again. Without an expansion of tax base sharing, they would not think about substantive land use reform that could hinder the ability of the northern developing suburbs to gain tax base. Nor were they interested initially in expanding the Met Council's power.

On the positive side, they would enthusiastically support transit and transportation reform, particularly if it could help them get better transit service and a completed Highway 610, a project for which they had been fighting for twenty years. Most important, the North Metro Mayors Association was interested in any housing reform that would shift some of the burden of providing affordable housing onto the affluent western suburbs. In their view, this was an important defensive strategy to preserve their residential stability.

The association's strong, almost immediate support for regional fair housing surprised me. I was also worried that the media might portray regional fair housing as an effort to make *all* the suburbs build *more* affordable housing. If such was the case, groups like the Legion of Doom could blow our coalition apart before we could accomplish anything. I decided to forge ahead, but to make sure the media understood the depth of suburban support and the reasons behind it. Specifically, it was important that citizens in deeply distressed communities like Brooklyn Park understand that the housing bill would ultimately ease their affordable housing burden rather than increase it.

Support from Low-Income, Minority, and Good-Government Groups

Once the North Metro Mayors Association had signaled its strong support for regional housing reform, building a strong base for regional fair housing in the central cities became the next imperative. Because fair housing initiatives were so divisive in older regions, we had approached local community development groups early on. We hoped to head off any anxiety about loss of city-dedicated housing resources or the massed political power of disenfranchised groups. By engaging these groups early on regarding the issues surrounding fair housing and in the design of a local bill, we avoided much mistrust.

This venture had two strong suits. Solution and design of the proposal came from the bottom up, not the top down. It was a legislative solution with broad community input, not a litigation-based court decision lacking grassroots input. In addition, metropolitan reforms were not presented as alternatives competing for resources and power but as complementary methods that would *gradually* reduce the overwhelming nature of central-city problems and provide resources for community development through metropolitan tax base sharing.

More meetings were held in fall 1992 and winter 1993 at the offices of the Urban Coalition, which represented the interests of low-income and minority communities. Its research arm independently came to the conclusion that the regional dynamics of concentrated poverty had to be more widely understood. We simultaneously contacted the Legal Aid Society, which was just beginning a lawsuit against the Minneapolis Public Housing Authority and associated entities.[7] Good-government groups were also important in building a coalition for fair housing and other regional reforms.

At the Urban Coalition meetings, a great deal of time was spent on demographics and the implications of growing regional polarization for low-income communities in the central cities. Confirming the suspicions of many activists, members presented real evidence of the huge societal expenditures going to build exclusive communities on the metropolitan fringes, in a development pattern that had severe detrimental effects on central-city neighborhoods. This group dealt methodically with the implications of the housing and other metropolitan reform bills for low-income communities and community development groups. Community development groups then moved to support the multifaceted regional reform agenda (and specifically the fair housing bill) to complement continued community development efforts within the central cities.

The Legal Aid Society suit initially threatened a remedy largely within the city borders of Minneapolis. After discussion and internal debate, Legal Aid and its plaintiffs moved toward a metropolitan-level solution. In the process, the stand Minneapolis took toward the lawsuit changed from hostility to support. Thereafter, Minneapolis and the Legal Aid Society, as coplaintiffs, cross-claimed (sued) the Met Council to enforce the council's dormant housing Policy 13/39 as part of the remedy (see section on housing in the appendix on page 174).[8]

The first draft of the Comprehensive Choice Housing bill was produced jointly in a series of meetings between community development groups and the Legal Aid Society. Now, more than three years since the housing bill was first introduced, these groups—potential opponents—have become strong allies. Their support and understanding of low-income communities have been invaluable both in drafting the bill and in maintaining vital connections to affected parts of the metro region.

The League of Women Voters embraced the regional initiative immediately and enthusiastically. It had recently studied school desegregation and had come to the conclusion that desegregated housing was the best long-term solution to segregated schools.[9]

The Citizens League (the group that had led the initial regional reforms of the 1960s and 1970s) was far more cautious and would not testify in favor of the housing bill in 1993, despite its endorsements of similar positions in the past. During the 1980s the league, which had been the leading proponent of important regional reform, had gradually taken an increasingly ineffectual, defensive position in which many of the initial accomplishments secured in the 1960s and 1970s had been seriously eroded. Instead of supporting the housing bill, the league opted for a public study committee on fair housing. This committee, with a larger participation than any other study committee in Citizens League history, was careful to represent (and arguably to overrepresent) the interests of developers, real estate agents, and western suburban communities. Finally, on May 27, 1994, almost a month after the housing bill had been vetoed for the second time, the league announced support for a metropolitan fair housing bill similar to the bills we had advanced.[10] Ultimately, the support of the Citizens League was important in terms of acceptance of a renewed regional fair housing agenda by moderates in the more affluent suburbs.

The 1993 Legislative Session:
The Metropolitan Community Stability Act

In the 1993 legislative session, six regional reform bills were introduced for fair housing, metropolitan structural reform, reinvestment, land use planning, transportation and transit, and welfare. A tax base–sharing bill was discussed but was not introduced until 1994. The Metropolitan Infrastructure Stability Act was frequently attacked as reflecting too narrow a regional agenda and unlikely to significantly affect regional trends. In contrast, a comprehensive approach was initially well received.[11] The bills were collectively called the Metropolitan Community Stability Act (MCSA).

The legislative session was an enormous success. All of the bills received a hearing, and all but the reinvestment bill were voted on. The housing, transportation, and land use bills passed both houses of the state legislature. Although the 1993 session flamed out in a major veto on housing and a minor one on transportation, significant parts of the land use planning bill were signed into law. Most important, legislative success with these initiatives, particularly the tough central issue of housing, signaled the basis of a strong city-suburban regional reform coalition. This stunned many pundits who did not believe a substantive regional agenda could be revived. Moreover, the press was interested, and the editorial boards of both metropolitan papers strongly supported the initiatives. The northern suburbs had seen that our coalition could hang together, and they were energized by our success.

The session also signaled strong and mounting southwestern Republican opposition to the agenda and growing anger toward me as the leader of this agenda. The transportation bill, which had no substantive opposition, may have been vetoed simply to send a signal.

Comprehensive Choice Housing Act

The centerpiece of the three bills that formed the deconcentration-reinvestment leg of the MCSA was the Comprehensive Choice Housing Act (the housing bill), and our coalition spent most of its energies on it.[12] The housing bill was the product of dozens of meetings with the North Metro Mayors Association, the Association of Metropolitan Municipalities, an umbrella group of seventy cities representing 90 percent of the region's population, the Met Council, and dozens of interest groups. Through an administrative hearing process, the bill directed the Met Council to give each metropolitan community a goal to meet its fair share of the unmet need for affordable housing in the Twin Cities area. Three categories of need were specified in the bill's goals: at 30 percent, 50 percent, and 80 percent of the metropolitan median household income. In formulating community goals, the council gave each community credit for the affordable housing it already had and took into account factors including the local creation of entry-level jobs and the community's stage of development. For example, the goals for Chanhassen, Maple Grove, and Lakeville—communities with huge entry-level job creation and considerable land open to development—would be different from those set for affluent and restrictive communities such as North Oaks or Sunfish Lake, which had few entry-level jobs and were fully developed.

The housing bill did not apply in any way to a community that had reached its goal, as was likely in the central cities and older suburbs. For a community that had not reached its goal, three requirements were imposed: to *reduce unreasonable barriers* to affordable housing in its zoning codes, development agreements, and development practices; to *comply with the efforts of public or private developers* whose projects would help the city achieve its goal; and to *ensure that the affordable housing added remained affordable*. This last requirement addresses a common subterfuge: building affordable housing but later turning it into expensive units at market rates.

Several significant penalties apply to any community that does not reduce barriers, comply with existing opportunities, and maintain affordable rents. It loses its local government aid—namely, revenue sharing payments from the state government. In addition, unless half the communities are in compliance in a "sector" slated for new roads or sewers, construction cannot go forward.[13] Finally, noncompliant communities cannot use tax increment financing, a favorite local government tax-abatement tool for economic development.

Because of the severity of these penalties, the final community goals would be set by a neutral administrative law judge. The North Metro Mayors Association and the Association of Metropolitan Municipalities would not endorse the bill without this provision. It allowed cities and interested parties due process rights concerning final goalsetting.

Because of the goals portion, opponents of the housing bill often called it a "quota bill"—in American political parlance, an affirmative action racial goal with penalties if the goal is not achieved. This criticism is inaccurate. The housing goals are not quotas that must be achieved, but a demarcation line that decides which communities should engage in barrier reduction. Penalties are assessed if a community *does not remove barriers;* nothing requires communities to achieve goals. The goals (such as they are) are economic rather than racial. This was an unspoken part of our compact. We would concentrate on affordable housing and not mention race in any of the bills.

Though essentially a barrier-reduction measure, the housing bill also required the Met Council, within its authority and resources, to "facilitate, coordinate, and cause" the development of affordable housing in "inverse proportion" to the communities' past record on housing. This meant that to the extent that resources became available, the council should concentrate first on the communities that had the worst records on affordable housing. This reassured those communities that were more open and that had not met their goals that the council would not take the path of least resistance by concentrating its efforts on them. The inverse proportion or the "worst go first" rule, drafted by Don Poss (the city manager of Blaine, a northern city with a low tax base) was essential to maintain the support of the North Metro Mayors Association.

The bill also encouraged the council to use a housing counseling service to help inform poor citizens about affordable housing in the suburbs. The *Gautreaux* case and other suburban experiences had shown the benefits of providing information about suburban housing opportunities.

The political support for the MCSA came entirely from legislators who believed that their districts would tangibly benefit—immediately or quite soon—from the policies set forth in the MCSA. In practical terms, this meant the central cities, the inner suburbs, and the low–tax capacity suburbs. Of the forty-five representatives from these regions, all but six were Democrats in 1993.[14] From the outset, the debates surrounding the bills became almost unavoidably partisan.

The politics of self-interest were particularly apparent in the housing bill, where the decisive suburban political support was largely defensive in character. Civil rights and access to opportunity were an important part of the housing bill's rationale. But most suburban members—and city members, for that matter—supported fair housing, largely to protect their communities from an "unfair" burden of low-income housing and from future neighborhood decline. These members were resigned to the fact that their communities had poor people. They believed that the high–tax capacity developing suburbs must also accept their fair share of poor residents and their accompanying social costs. Otherwise, their older communities would be overburdened by social needs, and decline would accelerate. As one representative put it, "Every time that guy's city says 'No' to some poor family, my city has to say 'Yes' twice."

In a strenuous effort to achieve some measure of bipartisan support, all of the Republican coalition members from the inner and low–tax capacity suburbs were sought out as coauthors. All considered, but ultimately rejected, this possibility. From the outset, it was recognized that the housing bill had the potential to shake traditional Republican notions of local home rule and independence. However, in discussions with the inner-suburban and low–tax capacity Republicans, only one totally opposed action on these grounds. The most common substantive request was to remove the penalties from the housing bill. Yet several Republican members voiced no substantive objections to the bill. At several points, we offered to remove the penalties or make any other changes in the bill in exchange for support. When faced with this offer, the Republican members always demurred. In the end, although they did not totally oppose fair housing, we could not come up with any changes that would secure any Republican support.

The Republican opposition to the housing bill in the older suburbs had less to do with the specifics of the housing bill than the fact that a clear majority of the metro Republican caucus strongly opposed the concept of fair housing. It was simply too difficult for these Republican members to oppose their normal allies on so controversial an issue. To the extent these members did not carefully examine the equities, it was easier to accept their allies' negative characterizations of the bill over the positive ones of a traditional political foe.

Especially persistent efforts were made to secure the support of Representative Charlie Weaver of Anoka, whose father had been the author of the original fiscal disparities legislation twenty-five years before.

Weaver fully understood that Anoka schools were beginning to show signs of socioeconomic change. Anoka also had considerably more than its fair share of affordable housing; it was a large recipient of fiscal disparities revenue (and potentially of any conceivable tax base–sharing program); and, as a charter member of the North Metro Mayors Association, it was foursquare in support of the MCSA and its housing component.

The reason Weaver gave for refusing authorship was that his support of the housing bill would lead to erosion of the present fiscal disparities system and of efforts to make school aid formulas more equitable. Weaver was one of the only Republican members representing areas with low tax wealth who vocally supported these measures. With the vast majority of Republican members strongly opposed to any form of tax base sharing or broadened school aids, he was sometimes a controversial member of his caucus.

Weaver's argument, however, was based on the notion that somehow his neutrality would preserve Republican support necessary to maintain or enhance these programs. But there was *no* high–tax capacity Republican support, or even acquiescence, in these programs. Throughout the fair housing controversy, the attacks by Republicans from high–tax capacity districts on these programs and their votes against them continued unabated.

The fair housing bill caught the Met Council between a rock and a hard place. During the 1970s the council had established a housing and redevelopment authority, and through its housing policy 13/39 it had for a time tied the allocation of regional resources to the progress a requesting community made regarding affordable housing (see appendix). On the one hand, the Comprehensive Choice Housing Act (the housing bill) expanded the council's power in an area where it had always sought to widen its authority; on the other hand, its members were Republican appointees connected with a legislative Republican caucus strongly opposed to fair-housing issues. Initially, we sought the Met Council's input on the housing bill and made dozens of individual changes for council staff in 1992–93. By the time the bill was introduced, it was as much the council's as our own, and the council supported it.

After the bill's introduction, as Republican opposition mounted, the council changed its position and opposed the housing bill. Severely criticized for this about-face by the editorial board of the *Minneapolis Star Tribune*, the council again reversed its position and supported the bill.[15] The Minnesota Housing Finance Agency (MHFA) reviewed the bill carefully, offered several suggestions that were incorporated, and never took a formal position on the bill.

Amid increasing controversy, the pro-housing forces attempted to establish direct communications with the governor's office concerning the housing bill. Early on, the governor's office had informed us that it would follow the Met Council's lead. We made particular efforts to contact the governor's deputy chief of staff, Curt Johnson. Johnson had been a community college official in Inver Grove Heights, where he saw first-hand the needs of low–tax base suburbia. At some point, he made the leap from this job to the Citizens League, a historically powerful proponent of regional planning. Johnson would later become a coauthor, with Neal Peirce, of the book *Citistates*, a strong call for a more powerful commitment to regionalism. On the road in national speaking engagements with Peirce, Johnson's views sounded compatible with the "metropolitics" I have proposed in this book. In local politics, however, that compatibility seemed to disappear.[16]

Throughout the debate, Johnson kept the pro-housing and metropolitan reform forces at arm's length and did not return telephone calls. At the same time, he condemned this coalition as bad politicians and poor policymakers in numerous conversations with reporters and editorial boards.[17] At this point, he began referring to the bill's "quotas" and sometimes called the housing bill a "quota bill."[18] This was particularly hurtful coming from the former head of the Citizens League. The bill's supporters had hoped that if political circumstances made it difficult for Johnson to join them, he could provide counsel, or at least maintain neutrality. Instead, his actions made our approach to moderate Republicans (who looked to Johnson for guidance) quite difficult. It was not until 1995 that we finally convinced several of these moderates to support the fiscal parts of the regional agenda.

Early in the 1993 session, the Republican members from southwestern suburban areas made clear to the governor that if he did not veto the housing bill, they would no longer sustain his veto power in the legislature. Without the threat of a veto in an overwhelmingly Democratic legislature, the governor's power would be severely curtailed.

Of immediate concern to the governor was a campaign finance reform bill that contained provisions to limit gubernatorial campaign contributions substantially. Despite the popularity of these provisions, Arne Carlson, a governor with great fund-raising capabilities, strongly opposed them. In a tumultuous closed meeting, the Republican legislative leadership told Carlson that if he signed the housing bill, they would not sustain a veto of the campaign finance bill. After this meeting, the governor's opposition to the housing bill crystallized, and his office refused to negotiate. On April 23, 1993, shortly after the governor's meeting with the Republican caucus, he outlined his objections to the housing bill in a letter urging me to withdraw it.[19] He stated he would then appoint a blue-ribbon committee to seek a compromise over the interim for the next session.

Governor Carlson substantively objected to the bill because the term "barriers" was ill defined. In fact, the housing bill defined barriers as including "zoning requirements, development agreements, and development practices" that unreasonably impede the development of moderate- and low-income housing. This definition was agreed on after lengthy negotiations with the North Metro Mayors Association and the Association of Metropolitan Municipalities. The city and suburban representatives who drafted this language (in concert with the governor's appointees at the Met Council) believed that it provided sufficient legislative guidance in terms of barrier removal. They wanted more specific delineation of the term by a neutral administrative law judge in the rulemaking process. It was unlikely that any process could produce a better definition supported by so broad a coalition of city governments. I informed the governor that we would be willing to negotiate further.[20]

The governor also asserted that the bill ignored the "single most obstructive barrier to low-income housing—land cost." But the bill directly addressed these issues by seeking to curtail unduly restrictive, large-lot zoning provisions and encourage higher-density multifamily development. The governor's office had been repeatedly told that any suggestions that the governor supported would be incorporated, and I reiterated this offer.

In addition, the governor objected to the bill as an affront to local prerogatives. The North Metro Mayors Association and the Association of Metropolitan Municipalities (organizations whose function is to protect these prerogatives) disagreed. Further, the governor had recently directed the council to study the consolidation of local governments. It was therefore difficult to reconcile his interest in consolidation with his respect for local prerogatives. Again, I offered to negotiate on this point.

Governor Carlson stated that the Local Government Aid (LGA) and Homestead Agricultural Credit Aid (HACA) penalties were outside the Met Council's charter, that the council was unequipped to use such power, and that such an exercise could result in gross injustice to cities. In response, his concern for local prerogatives again exceeded the concern expressed by the North Metro Mayors Association and the Association of Metropolitan Municipalities. Moreover, the agencies in his administration charged with policy in this area—the Met Council and the Minnesota

Housing Finance Agency—had not raised any concerns about these powers. The governor could offer no specific precedent or authority that would prevent the council from exercising such powers.[21] However, we offered to delete the penalties.

The governor countered that the bill had too many penalties and not enough incentives.[22] I informed him that pro-housing forces had offered a package of incentives in the negotiating process but that his office rejected these incentives. The council, negotiating on his behalf, was quite emphatic that the Carlson administration would support no new spending in this area. I told the governor that virtually any incentive he approved would be included. After this exchange, the governor's office cut off all contact with me and the pro-housing forces. Dozens of calls to Tom Weaver (Representative Charlie Weaver's brother, and one of the governor's chief lobbyists) and Curt Johnson were not returned. The debate on the House and Senate floors became nasty and acrimonious. Representative H. Todd Van Dellen (Republican–Plymouth) argued strenuously in opposition: "The suburbs exist for a reason. They give people something to shoot for."[23] The bill passed 79 to 51, 11 votes short of an override.

All House Democratic members voted for the bill, except for four representing the southwest and east developing suburbs. The only Republican member voting in favor represented Saint Louis Park, an inner-ring community. The rural Democratic members followed the lead of their metro counterparts, as did the rural Republican members.

In the Minnesota Senate, because of the governor's veto threat, the housing bill was amended in its entirety into the omnibus tax bill. The Democratic leaders in the Senate did not think the governor would veto the entire tax bill that financed all of state government simply because he opposed the housing bill. They were wrong. On the Senate floor, Edward Oliver of Deephaven, in the southwest developing suburban area, repeatedly stated that the bill was "social engineering" that usurped local powers.[24] A sarcastic senator asked him whether the 22,000-square-foot lot size requirements practiced by one of Oliver's communities were "social engineering." Thereafter, a motion to delete the housing provisions from the tax bill failed by a single vote.

When the tax bill came up in the conference committee late one night in May 1993, Commissioner Morrie Anderson of the Department of Finance represented the Carlson administration. Doug Johnson, Senate tax chair, and Ann Rest, House tax chair, were the lead conferees. Anderson announced that the housing provision was a "veto item." Both

Johnson and Rest repeatedly tried to find some compromise to prevent the governor from vetoing the entire tax bill. As they offered each option (including the removal of all penalties), the only reply, repeated over and over, was an ominous, mechanical "That is a veto item." The housing provisions were finally extracted at 2:30 a.m. when it became clear that no compromise was possible.

The housing bill was again brought up and was amended on the floor of both bodies to meet all of Governor Carlson's objections stated in his letter of April 23, 1993. Specifically, all penalties were removed, and mechanisms were created both to define barriers to affordable housing more fully and to identify incentives for producing such housing. Further, based on an oral request from Tom Weaver, the requirement of Administrative Procedure Act rulemaking was eliminated from the bill. The toothless housing bill was now essentially a "request" (without penalties) to communities to remove their housing barriers. The bill passed by slightly larger margins and was promptly vetoed on May 23.[25] In his veto message, perhaps because the pro-housing forces had responded to each of his original objections, the governor raised a series of entirely new ones.[26]

Although this bill was vetoed, tremendous energy and awareness had been raised in a very short time. The endurance of a coalition on this difficult issue was itself an important step forward, and the forces behind the bill were dedicated to the pursuit of housing reform. We realized that the going would be tough, but we believed that we could only achieve ultimate success by continuing to put the issue before the public.

Metro Structural Reform: Reviving the Met Council

After years of threats to its powers from the governor, the legislature, and other units of government, the Metropolitan Council found its continued existence in doubt at the beginning of the 1991 legislative session. In what became an annual rite, amendments to eliminate the Met Council were offered to the appropriations bill; by 1991, they were coming perilously close to passage. Governor Carlson told the council to improve its performance or it would be abolished. What he meant by improving performance was far from clear. Initially, he suggested that the council's function was to consolidate local governments. This idea was quickly abandoned.

These dynamics were abruptly reversed by early 1993, when several proposals were introduced to strengthen the council.[27] The impetus came from groups that saw a reinvigorated elected council as an instrument of reform and others that simply wanted to preserve an institution that had constituencies. I introduced a bill for popular election of council members, who would elect their chair.[28] The chair would then appoint the heads of the regional commissions from among the council members. But Phil Carruthers from Brooklyn Center, who was soon to be house majority leader, took a different tack. He introduced a bill abolishing the regional agencies and placing their functions under the present Met Council. He also provided for a stronger chair, the "regional administrator."[29] In a sense, the first approach moved toward the beginnings of an elected regional government; the other made the council a more powerful executive agency.[30]

Both proposals met with significant opposition, but the question of direct election of members proved the more controversial. Implicitly, members believed that popular elections would strengthen and empower the Met Council. Proponents of a strong regional presence favored election; those who preferred a weaker regional entity were opposed. Most legislators from the central cities and inner and low–tax capacity suburbs generally supported the idea of an elected council, with two powerful exceptions: Senator Larry Pogemiller of Minneapolis and Representative Tom Osthoff of Saint Paul. The southwestern and east developing suburbs were opposed, and rural members were uneasy about election of members. Some Democratic members from the east developing suburbs, who had opposed the housing bill, supported an elected Met Council. I think this was because they, like the moderate Republicans, wanted to acknowledge and support some part of the growing wave of regional reform.

In the 1993 session, the Minnesota House heard both bills. The elected council bill passed the Local Government Committee and the Government Operations Committee but was killed by a successful motion by Representative Osthoff to refer it to the General Legislation Committee, where it was not heard. The Carruthers bill also failed to clear the necessary committees by the House deadlines. The Senate author of both bills, Ted Mondale, was unable to get a hearing for either one.[31]

Land Use and the Politics of Sustainable Development

Under the Metropolitan Council Act (MCA) of 1967, the council was directed to develop a comprehensive plan to guide growth in the region— the Metropolitan Development Guide (MDG). Over the years, the MDG has evolved chapters on ten specific areas: health, airports, housing, recreational open space, transportation, solid waste management, sewage disposal, surface water management, water use and availability, and law and justice. Each chapter represents a comprehensive statement of the policies and objectives that should control the region's development in a particular area.

The Regional Blueprint that replaced the Metropolitan Development Investment Framework (MDIF) attempts to give systematic coherence to all the council's plans in other chapters of its development guide.[32] It does this by establishing an overall policy for supporting development with major regional facilities such as sewers and highways, and sets forth a general direction for future development patterns in the metropolitan area.

The blueprint contains procedures for guiding decisions about regional investment and development proposals submitted to it for review; preparing reports on the region's fiscal health and the degree to which the council's decisions reflect its policies; helping to ensure that council policies are carried out through the actions of the regional commissions; and resolving issues resulting from changes in a community's expectation about its growth.

The council's powers under the Metropolitan Development Guide were augmented by the Metropolitan Land Planning Act of 1976 (MLPA).[33] The act required all metropolitan cities to submit "comprehensive plans" to the Met Council. The plans had to be consistent with the growth projections and infrastructure planning of the council in its Metropolitan Development and Investment Framework (MDIF). There are four Metropolitan "systems," or policy areas over which the council has strong regional authority by statute: transportation, airports, wastewater treatment, and open space. Under the Land Planning Act, a local government unit's comprehensive plan must contain a local land use plan, a transportation plan, and a community facilities plan.[34]

The Land Planning Act allows the council to require a local community to "modify a comprehensive plan or any part thereof which may have a *substantial impact* on or contain a *substantial departure* from metropolitan systems plans."[35] Though these terms are fairly broad and open ended, the Met Council has narrowly construed its authority. Under a system of self-imposed restraint, the council will require a plan amendment only when the local comprehensive plan imposes a burden on a metropolitan system that "threatens its capacity"—a fairly cataclysmic event.[36] Consequently, the council has rarely used its authority to shape regional planning, and the Twin Cities region continued to develop in an exceedingly low-density, restrictive, fragmented pattern. The Metropolitan Agricultural Preserves Act of 1980 gave specific legislative approval for the council's concept of a metropolitan urban service area.[37] The MUSA line was the boundary beyond which the council would not provide urban services (such as sewer lines) and within which metropolitan growth was to be directed.

Of all the vital issues for metropolitan stability, land use planning proved the most difficult around which to develop a constituency. Though unencumbered by the racial and class baggage of housing or tax-base sharing, land use planning—in difficult economic times, and facing the opposition of builders and labor unions—lacked a natural legislative constituency. It was constantly in danger of becoming a "wine and cheese" issue for liberal elites and not-in-my-backyarders (NIMBYs).

Developing the issue of head-to-head competition between fully developed and developing areas for tax base, jobs, and the middle class rapidly brought along those in the central cities and older suburbs. When development patterns and their effects are explained carefully to these jurisdictions, their representatives can support sustainable development and infrastructure pricing. When the issue of farmland protection comes into play, rural support for such programs is also considerable.

The low–tax capacity developing suburbs, however, were desperate for tax base. When these cities—with few resources and the worst-funded schools in the region—said they needed to increase their tax base to pay for services, it was hard to argue with them. Fiscal zoning and large-lot exclusive development promise too much of a windfall (real or perceived) to be ignored by developing communities. As long as cities get costless infrastructure, they will build on large lots in the belief that it will maximize their tax base and reinforce desired social characteristics in their community.

Ethos or enthusiasm on this point differs slightly between the high–tax capacity and low–tax capacity developing suburbs. The high–tax capacity suburbs like the world the way it is. For both social and fiscal reasons, they want to build only expensive homes. The low–tax capacity suburbs, in a fragmented and competitive metropolitan housing market, want the option of exclusivity for social reasons, as well as to increase their tax base. As a practical matter, most city officials in low–tax capacity districts recognize that the expensive housing market is not within their reach and that they often end up building vast tracts of inexpensive working-class housing simply to pay for local infrastructure and services. When they build this housing, they know that someday people who are comparatively disadvantaged will live in it, because they have seen this same pattern in communities closer to the city core. To pay today's bills, however, they must go on building such housing.

When offered increased resources from a broadened fiscal-disparities pool, these communities would prefer resources gained in this way to
those gained by building themselves into future problems. In exchange
for more regional money, they will support sustainable development.
Broadening the metropolitan fiscal-disparities pool can thus increase potential support for metropolitan land planning from 50 to 60 percent of a
metropolitan area representatives.

The high–tax capacity areas, on the other hand, are home to some of
the strongest environmentalists and some of the region's most powerful
NIMBYs, working to protect much of the most beautiful open spaces in
the area. Their financial and social resources often allow them to mount
awesome opposition to local development decisions. However, if they are
properly engaged, local preservation groups can generate sufficient enthusiasm in wealthy areas to dampen (if not dispel) overt local governmental opposition to land planning. Covert local government opposition
is probably impossible to dispel from these areas.

In the 1993 session, I introduced the Metropolitan Land Use Planning Act, a comprehensive metropolitan land use reform bill that
strengthened the regional land planning act.[38] The bill, drafted by the
Land Stewardship Project, a nonprofit group supporting regional land use
decisions, tightened the concept of Metropolitan Urban Service Area
(MUSA) lines in several ways. MUSA expansion would occur only when
the region (not an individual city) had no undeveloped land. MUSA extensions could not be granted unless city comprehensive plans satisfied
all the guidelines in the Metropolitan Development Guide, not just the regional road, sewer, airport, or park plans—the four systems tests. As I
discussed, the Met Council could reject a city's comprehensive plan if it
failed to be in concurrence with these four systems tests. MUSA exceptions could be rejected only if they interfered with the overall metropolitan plan for these four systems—that is, by requiring greater regional
efforts in terms of sewers, roads, airports, or parks. Adding the other
guideline areas of the Metropolitan Development Guide (affordable housing, for one) would broaden the criteria for deciding whether a MUSA
exception would assist the region's overall development. Only growth
projections made by the Met Council, not local cities, would be used to
justify MUSA expansions.

The Land Planning Act added an agricultural policy chapter to
the Development Guide providing actual policy guidance to preserve
farmland. It also allowed farms of more than forty acres to initiate themselves in the Metro Agricultural Preserves Act's program without local
approval.

In terms of enforcement, the Land Planning Act provided explicit authority for both the Met Council and interested citizens to sue to ensure that the Development Guide was followed.[39] It reversed the so-called "Merriam Amendment," which had given local zoning laws precedence over comprehensive plans.

Finally, the Land Planning Act protected metropolitan farmers from assessments for storm sewers, public roads, and other public works. Municipalities often placed storm sewers and public roads across farms within the Metro Agricultural Preserves program and then assessed the farmers for these "improvements." The resulting assessments (by the frontage foot) were so large that farmers often were forced to subdivide their land for residential development to raise money to pay the assessments.[40]

In substance, we managed to pass only the provision that protected farmers from storm sewer and public road assessments. The other provisions were rapidly stripped from the bill under intense opposition from cities, developers, real estate agents, labor unions, and builders. This bill passed and was signed into law.

Transportation Reform: The Politics of Fair Roads

My transportation planning bill required the state transportation department to develop plans to help stabilize the region's fully developed core. It also required the council to assess whether transit reform would relieve traffic congestion better than capacity expansion. The council also had to evaluate the impact of each highway expansion (in conjunction with existing housing and land use practices) on the economic isolation of poor residents from economic opportunities in the developing area.[41] Supported by MnDot, the Met Council, and virtually every imaginable interest group, the bill passed by a wide margin. It was ultimately vetoed because the Republican members from the southwestern suburbs feared that it might lead to some restrictions on highway expansion or suburban development or to enactment of fair housing legislation of some kind. Some said that this bill was found guilty by association with the housing bill.

Welfare Reform: The Politics of Politics

In the area of welfare, we started with a bill to revise work readiness—a program serving single, able-bodied adults, and the least expensive area where reform action could be taken.[42] Day care costs for single mothers initially made reform of aid to families with dependent children (AFDC) too expensive to contemplate. In 1993 the work readiness system gave applicants $203 a month for six months, with no real strings attached. We proposed to raise the stipend to $408 a month in return for twenty hours of work a week at minimum-wage jobs that would rehabilitate depressed neighbori..ods. The net cost was more than $25 million for the first biennium.

Welfare rights and community development organizations met the bill with strong protests head on.[43] However, it was enormously popular among the middle-class suburban legislators. The bill passed unanimously into the omnibus health and human services act, but the program was not funded in the appropriations process. The work readiness program was abolished in the 1995 legislative session.

Summer 1993: Civil Unrest

The 1993 session had ended in a tumultuous veto of the fair housing bill. However, the debate—one directed at the solar plexus of American politics—had truly drawn the region's attention to the issue of affordable housing. Over the summer, a NIMBY outcry in an affluent suburb (one of a dozen or more each year in the metropolitan area) suddenly drew the interest of the whole region as that suburb's actions were roundly condemned in the press and in the chorus of media opinion. Meanwhile, the Met Council and the governor's office struggled to come to terms with the cry for regional reform, and specifically for fair housing. The ice that had enveloped this issue was beginning to melt, although the process of finding a bipartisan solution was just beginning.

To prevent the construction of a market-rate apartment complex, an angry crowd in Maple Grove, a community in the northern corner of the southwestern developing suburbs, staged a near-riot in late summer 1993.[44] Hoyt Development had proposed construction of a ninety-five-unit building with two-bedroom apartments renting for $550 a month and three-bedrooms for $650 a month. These were hardly low-income units, and the city planning commission had unanimously approved the project.[45] Shortly before it came before the entire city council for approval, a group of citizens began to pass out fliers announcing that a low-income housing project was going up and that citizens should attend the city council meeting to oppose it.

On November 15, 1993, the city council was faced with 200 people in its chambers who opposed the upcoming development. In a moblike atmosphere, cheerleaders from the local high school were crying; Minneapolis police officers, who were residents of Maple Grove, were heard to say that the poor people should be kept in one place so that the officers "could keep track of them."[46] The city rejected the apartment development. The metropolitan newspapers, primed by the legislative housing debate, covered the story carefully, and the editorial boards of both metropolitan newspapers condemned Maple Grove's action.[47] After weeks of intense public pressure, the project was reconsidered by the city council and approved.[48] The council said it was forced to do this because of a pending zoning lawsuit by the developer. However, even the city of Maple Grove had been swayed by the intensity of public opinion.

In the wake of these disturbances, Governor Carlson appointed a blue-ribbon housing commission in late fall. Our committee included legislators, southwestern suburban officials, bankers, and central-city builders of low-income housing. Operating by consensus, the commission took testimony but refused to consider any controversial proposals. It did, however, produce a background paper, surveying fifty-seven metro communities. Its findings are detailed in the Barriers section of this book.[49]

Unrelated to the housing disturbance, over the 1993–94 interim the legislature and the governor jointly appointed the State Advisory Council on Metropolitan Governance, cochaired by Senator Carol Flynn and me. This advisory committee, set up by statute in the waning days of the 1993 session, was composed of half gubernatorial and half bipartisan legislative appointees. The group included James Hetland (the first and strongest chair of the council appointed by the moderate Republican governor Harold Levander) and Wayne Popham, one of the early key Republican legislators involved with regionalism. In the advisory council hearings, the metropolitan counties proposed a regional council of government and greatly enhanced powers for the counties. This plan, which would have weakened the Met Council, was not well received by the advisory council or the metropolitan press.[50] Following closely on the heels of the Carruthers proposal of 1993 to consolidate the agencies, the advisory council unanimously recommended the abolition of the regional agencies and narrowly recommended the election of council members.[51]

The 1994 Legislative Session: Housing and Regional Structural Reform

The 1994 legislative session signaled a rapidly growing public awareness of the regional housing issue. As press coverage dramatically increased, the editorial boards of both papers demanded progress, and the metropolitan church community began to get deeply involved and to support the issue. By session's end, hundreds of church congregations and other groups with religious affiliations were directly involved in support of regional fair-housing and equity legislation. Even the now stodgy Citizens League, pressed by growing public debate, came out in direct support of a strong regional fair housing bill. Although the session ended in another bitter veto, enormous pressure was building for movement in the 1995 session.

The 1994 session also witnessed the most dramatic structural reform of the Met Council since its inception in 1967. The Metropolitan Reorganization Act, signed into law by the governor, moved the council from a $40-million-a-year regional planning agency, with loose supervisory control over regional agencies, to a $600-million-a-year regional government directly operating regional sewers and transit systems. This reform would make the Twin Cities Met Council the largest and most powerful regional government in the United States, perhaps in North America. The crowning piece of this reform—direct election of the Met Council members—failed by only one vote in the House. Preliminary skirmishes on tax base sharing also provided strong evidence that enhancing the regional tax base–sharing pool was a viable concept and prepared the stage for major tax base–sharing legislation in 1995. Finally, the session saw the introduction of a statewide land use plan, modeled on Oregon's.

The Metropolitan Poverty Reduction Act

In early 1994, after the Maple Grove housing controversy was splashed all over the front pages of area newspapers, Republican House members from the southwestern developing suburbs introduced the Metropolitan Poverty Reduction Act.[52] Though substantively not significant, the Poverty Reduction Act did represent a considerable change in rhetoric. Where the Republican position on affordable suburban housing had once been "nothing, no time, never," the Poverty Reduction Act represented a symbolic acceptance of suburban affordable-housing policy and regional responsibility for the problems of the city and older suburbs.

The bill began with a major reform of the state's troubled workers' compensation system and reiterated the provisions of the governor's welfare reform plan. The Republicans argued that the workers' compensation system was expensive, hurt business, and kept poor people out of work, thus destabilizing central-city neighborhoods. They maintained that a dramatic state cut in benefits (the central part of their bill) would lead to new business and job opportunities for the poorest Minnesotans.[53] The welfare proposal generally sought to cut benefits and encourage self-sufficiency; whatever its merits, it was popular on a bipartisan basis.

On the fair housing issue, the Poverty Reduction Act proposed reducing the building materials tax on low-income-housing projects and recommended a pilot project for affordable housing (at 50 percent of the median income) in Eden Prairie, a city that was already planning to act independently on housing-related issues. Whether this pilot was part of what Eden Prairie had planned was never clear. The act also sought to improve regional coordination of existing programs and funding sources for affordable housing, and, in a related area, to improve the region's reverse-commute program. None of these initiatives included any funding or assurance of it from the governor's office.

The pro-housing forces praised the modest step forward represented by the Poverty Reduction Act and supported all provisions of the bill except the workers' compensation reforms. It was our hope that the Poverty Reduction Act could lead to a workable compromise.

Workers' compensation reform has become one of the most divisive, entrenched political issues in Minnesota. For a generation, the Democrats (with the encouragement of labor unions) and Republicans (with the encouragement of chambers of commerce) have engaged in a political war on workers' compensation. Both sides have taken rigid, litmus-test positions that have barred flexible, effective reform. Because organized labor had already condemned the governor's proposal, on its introduction the bill was referred to the House Labor Committee. Committee chairman Pat Beard, a union official and steel worker, refused to hear it until the workers' compensation provisions were extracted.

Pro-housing forces might have accepted substantial workers' compensation reform to achieve a substantive housing bill, but they were not powerful enough within the Democratic caucus to negotiate to accept the Chamber of Commerce position on the issue, which called for large benefit cuts. At the same time, the Republican authors would not support even their own weak housing positions unless the governor's program of workers' compensation reform was enacted in full. Given that the Republican housing reforms were modest and unfunded and tied to a rigid, massive, arguably unrelated reform of the workers' compensation system, it is fair to say that the Republican position (though representing a rhetorical change) was still not substantive.

Comprehensive Choice Housing

With the hope that some compromise solution might present itself, the housing bill was reintroduced.[54] As its chief author, I announced my willingness to compromise daily. The bill proceeded through both houses and to the floor, again on a party-line vote. The Republican forces would not compromise at all; it was either the Poverty Reduction Act in its entirety or nothing.

Nonetheless, support for the housing bill increased during the 1994 session. The Association of Metropolitan Municipalities supported the bill in its final form. By the time the bill came to the House floor, 175 church congregations, the League of Women Voters, and a variety of community organizations supported it. In 1993, the *Star Tribune*'s editorial board had endorsed the bill eight times, and the editorial board of the *Pioneer Press* had called three times for a housing bill of some kind.[55] The governor's office, throughout the session, refused to return phone calls or to discuss the bill in any way. Curt Johnson was again unavailable to pro-housing forces, although he continued to denounce in print the divisive nature of our effort. The Met Council testified against the bill.[56] Pro-housing forces desperately tried to achieve some compromise and, in that hope, unilaterally stripped out the bill's penalties.[57]

What was most notable in the 1994 session was the church community's coming on board with the issue. The packed auditoriums at housing hearings were full of priests, ministers, rabbis, and other clerics, many from the affluent western suburbs. This effort was led by the Metropolitan Interfaith Coalition for Affordable Housing (MICAH), the first church-based organization to take interest in the bill. The lead witnesses in each hearing were religious officials in clerical garb. These churches and synagogues had an enormously positive impact on the tone of the hearings, which became much less nasty and more substantive.

As public pressure mounted, instead of discussing the bill, the governor's office and legislative opponents of the bills from both parties began a series of harsh personal attacks against me. They argued that the only reason bills were not being signed and compromise was not possible was that I was the author, and my strategy was too divisive. After this argument gained some currency, the church community and ultimately the metropolitan press reacted against these attacks.[58] We continued to offer virtually any sort of compromise; there was no response. Once again I unilaterally withdrew the penalties. In the end, the bill passed 79 to 54. The governor promptly vetoed it.[59]

In his veto message, Governor Carlson's rhetoric had hardened. He objected to the bill because he said it contained "quotas."[60] During the legislative session this rhetoric had escalated among the Republican forces and was, we believed, a sound bite designed to foster misunderstanding and divisiveness.[61] The bill was not a quota bill in the sense that it enforced affirmative housing goals with penalties. Instead, it asked for barrier reduction, without penalties, in communities that had a poor record on affordable housing issues.

Governor Carlson said he objected to the housing bill because it amounted to a platform for penalties to be imposed later on cities. He had frequently objected to penalties in the housing bill, stating that most communities would consensually eliminate barriers, once these barriers were identified. The penalties had been dropped to secure his approval, but the governor seemed to be playing a no-win game.

He further objected to the bill because it did not get at the causes of poverty. However, the bill would have helped poor people get to jobs in the southwestern suburbs—communities with 100,000 new entry-level jobs but little affordable housing. By preventing concentrations of poverty, the bill would also help to prevent many of the poverty-associated pathologies to which conservatives have long objected.

The governor also argued that Chapter 577, a Republican bill to study barriers to central-city redevelopment, would solve all the problems that the housing bill was designed to attack. Alternatively, he argued that the Poverty Reduction Act would solve these problems. Chapter 577, a short bill that assessed central-city redevelopment issues, may have had some independent merit but was almost totally irrelevant to the housing issue central to this controversy. The Poverty Reduction Act, as I have discussed, had little if any substance.

About a month after the housing bill was vetoed, the Citizens League released a report declaring that housing was an extremely important regional issue and announced its support of elevating housing to become the fifth regional system (that is, a regional comprehensive plan could be rejected if it lacked adequate provision for affordable housing).[62] In the 1960s and 1970s, the Citizens League had led the regional debate. In the 1990s, it was the last major interest group to support regional reform initiatives. In addition, the report concluded that it was appropriate to withhold construction of freeways and sewers from communities that refused to allow affordable housing. In the aftermath, the Met Council announced plans to support a housing-system approach and to place 100 certificates for low-income housing in the suburbs.[63] The proposal to create a housing system was defeated in the council's Community Development Committee.[64] The new certificates never materialized.

Regional Structural Reform: A Swelling Wave

In 1994 the most significant accomplishment of the reborn regional movement occurred through the passage of the Metropolitan Reorganization Act.[65] This bill, which came from the State Advisory Council on Metropolitan Governance, created a directly elected Metropolitan Council; abolished the Metropolitan Waste Control Commission, the Regional Transit Board, and the Metropolitan Transit Commission; and put the functions of these three entities directly under the Met Council's aegis. The council retained its advisory role on operations of the Metropolitan Airports Commission (MAC). This legislation transformed the council from a planning body with loose supervisory control into an operational agency with a budget of more than $500 million and supervisory control over the $300 million MAC budget. After Hennepin County, the Met Council was Minnesota's second-largest unit of government in terms of budget, and perhaps its most significant in terms of authority.

During the 1980s, at almost every session, the legislature had cut the Met Council's formal power and political status.[66] In 1991, the council was on its way to being abolished. The Reorganization Act created the most powerful regional government in the nation. How did this turnaround happen?

The real force behind the Reorganization Act was the growing wave of regional reform. In essence, with their church and other religious communities and civic associations up in arms, moderate Republicans wanted to do something in response to the clamor for regional reform, and they preferred the organizational initiatives over those involving housing or equity. In this light, consolidation of agencies (which moderates had opposed only one legislative session earlier, calling it the creation of a regional supergovernment) was now praised as a bold effort to streamline government. The reorganization also benefited from publicity about recent minor administrative scandals at the transit and waste control commissions. Yet though the moderate Republicans would support consolidation, they would not support election of council members.

The reorganization bill moved first in the Senate, where the provisions for an elected council were stripped out by a motion from Minneapolis senator Larry Pogemiller. In the House (where I was the bill's author), the bill moved narrowly through the Local Government committee but was stalled in the Transportation Committee, where Chair Tom Osthoff refused to hear it.

A parliamentary maneuver dislodged the bill from Osthoff's committee. When the bill passed the Senate and returned to the House, the House Rules provided that the Speaker could refer the bill "to the appropriate committee."[67] In the history of the House, the Speaker had always referred a passed Senate bill to the committee where its companion lay. However, I argued that "appropriate committee" meant any committee with jurisdiction over the bill. After consultation with the chief clerk, the Speaker, at my urging, referred the bill to the Government Operations Committee, where the provisions relating to transportation and transit reform were stripped out, effectively snatching the bill from Osthoff's grasp. Enraged, Osthoff, a member of the Government Operations Committee, attempted to defeat the bill there.[68] The bill narrowly passed out of committee and was referred to the General Elections Committee, where it passed to the House floor by one vote.

The metropolitan counties also were strongly opposed to an elected council. Led by Hennepin County, the Association of Metropolitan Counties (AMC) made defeating the elected council one of its highest priorities and spent tens of thousands of public dollars to do it. The AMC enlisted the statewide county association, and together they began a vigorous propaganda campaign to erode rural support for an elected council. Outstate county commissioners (from outside the Twin Cities) lobbied rural members, telling them that if the metropolitan area were to unite under one elected government, it would stop state aid from flowing to rural Minnesota. The counties' intense effort cost us at least ten votes in the House.

On another front, although the Association of Metropolitan Municipalities supported a strong elected council, it opposed the abolition of the regional agencies and ended up weakly opposing the bill. Only the Citizens League and the metropolitan newspapers fully supported the Advisory Council bill.

Our primary argument for election of council members was that the council makes important decisions and has significant spending and taxing powers. The Met Council, even before the Reorganization Act, made the decisions on where to put billions of dollars of freeways and sewers; whether the region needed a new airport, and where it would be built; and which areas of the region are served by transit, and how well. It also had significant power over local land use decisions and housing policies, as well as review authority over all public or private projects of "metropolitan significance."

After the reorganization, an appointed council would have under its direct operational authority the council planning staff ($40 million annual budget), the operation of metropolitan transit ($300 million), and waste control ($250 million)—a combined yearly budget of more than $600 million. These operations are financed by state grants, user fees, *and $100 million of property taxes levied annually by the council.* This new jurisdiction, added to its previous powers, would make the Met Council the second most powerful government entity in the state.

In deciding infrastructure investments of this magnitude involving freeways, sewers, and airports, the Met Council and its coordinate agencies effectively choose which parts of the region will grow and which will not. In this light, airport decisions have huge ramifications not only for the surrounding communities but also for the entire region's economic well-being. As the council actively or passively shapes the region's cities, it has a large impact on people's lives. In terms of freeway and transit access, land use planning, and fair housing, it makes fundamental decisions affecting a community's desirability and access to its resources.

In America, we argued, any governmental entity making decisions with such dramatic effects on communities and individuals is elected. From the time of Locke to the Boston Tea Party to the Declaration of Independence, a central theme of American democracy has been that only elected officials may exercise the power to levy significant taxes.

Though few argued that these decisions are insignificant, some opponents claimed that state law so tightly circumscribes the Met Council's authority to use revenue from the property tax levy that it is not equivalent to taxes levied by local governments. We responded that, although the proceeds of the council's levy may be exhausted by state mandates, this same pattern (namely, a state grant of taxing authority fully dedicated to carry out state mandates) occurs with cities and especially counties.

The central cities, the inner suburbs, and the northern suburbs—most areas of the Twin Cities region—have asserted that they have little input in Met Council decisions and that the council unfairly favors the development interests of the southwestern suburbs. Because this majority in regional communities feels isolated from the council's decisionmaking process, we also argued, the council should be elected. Increasingly, these disaffected subregions ignore council authority, want to diminish council power, and refuse to cede any further power to the present council. These attitudes would not exist if these subregions had elected representatives on the council.

The lack of Met Council legitimacy became apparent in the negotiations surrounding the regional reinvestment bill (see below). The coali-

tion of communities supporting reinvestment rapidly gained sufficient po
litical support to fund a regional initiative. This consensus evaporated
when the coalition had to designate an entity to administer the fund. The
Met Council, by function the logical choice, was immediately rejected because of perceived bias. Although these communities would have given
such authority to an elected council, after much debate they delegated it
to the Minnesota Housing Finance Agency, because it was headed by a
government employee who they believed was fair. This decision greatly
weakened the reinvestment bill.

The opt-out transit experience also illustrates the need for legitimacy
and accountability. Here the southwestern and eastern developing communities seceded from the regional transit system because, they argued,
the appointed bureaucratic transit commission was insulated from the
needs of their communities. If elected representatives from their area supervised regional transit, the communities that opted out would have had
difficulty making this argument.

If the Met Council were elected, we argued, the legislature's numerous actions limiting council powers would probably not have occurred.
Despite all the mismanagement by cities and counties, in not one instance
did the Minnesota state legislature remove a comparable power from
them. In an unwritten rule, elected bodies do not easily interfere with the
recognized authority of other elected bodies.

In response, opponents argued that, given the Met Council's role in
providing infrastructure, developers would contribute heavily to Met
Council candidates and therefore have undue influence on council decisions. We responded by giving the proposed bill for an elected Met Council the strongest public financing system yet proposed in Minnesota: $100
contribution limits from political action committees (PACs) or individuals, reporting of all contributions above $50, and low total-spending lim-
its. We argued that Portland, Oregon (which has had an elected council
for decades), has stronger growth management than the Twin Cities and
fewer real estate developers as council members. In this light, we argued,
the presence of developers on the council has always been highly significant. Under an election system, council members' occupations and
sources of contributions would be subject to close public scrutiny.

Opponents also argued that the district size was too large (132,000
voters), would require too much money to run, and would produce
elected officials who were more powerful than legislators. We replied
that these districts were about the size of a Hennepin County commissioner's seat, which each represent about 125,000 voters. We believed the
size workable but made clear that it was negotiable.

Probably the most damaging argument against the elected council was that a strong regional government (read: an elected Met Council) would hurt rural Minnesota. In the 1994 session, the rural counties lobbied strongly against an elected Met Council.[69] The force of this argument was that a unified metropolitan region would strengthen the hand of the Twin Cities in the increasingly hostile conflict between metro and rural areas in Minnesota over state resources. The lobbyists and rural county commissioners told their legislators that a vote for an elected council would make them part of the metro conspiracy to stop the flow of resources to rural areas.

We responded that none of the metropolitan bills had anything to do with outstate Minnesota. To the extent that they had any relevance, they served as a principle for more equitable statewide local government and school aid programs. Finally, in Oregon (the only other state with an elected regional government) the mere existence of elected officials had no effect on the ever-present battle between metro and rural areas over resources.

As the massive reform bill came to the floor, a proposal to delete the elected council provisions failed by a vote of 65 to 64. The bill itself failed final passage by one vote.[70] By bipartisan agreement, it was brought up again and (sans elected provisions) sent to conference. The conference committee compromise abolished the Regional Transit Board, the Metropolitan Transit Commission, and the Waste Control Commission and folded their powers into the new Metropolitan Council. The role of the regional administrator was also enhanced. This bill passed roundly, with the moderate Republicans on board.[71] But the conservatives remained staunchly opposed.

Tax Base Sharing and Reinvestment

Central cities and older suburbs with aging infrastructure, blighted housing, brownfields, and other polluted business properties requested a regional reinvestment fund, which was also important to capture support from community development groups in the central cities. The Metropolitan Reinvestment Act was introduced as an answer, but as political support fell away, it was displaced by the Housing Disparities Bill.

The proposed reinvestment act was funded by a system of tax base sharing modeled on fiscal disparities.[72] Instead of placing part of the value of commercial industrial growth into a regional pool and redistributing it as shared tax base, each city was required to contribute to the reinvestment pool the portion of its tax base that came from the increment of value on homes valued above $150,000 each. In other words, all cities would keep the tax base on all homes up to the value of $150,000; the value above that would go into the regional pool.

In fiscal year 1994, this mechanism would have created a metropolitan reinvestment fund of $113 million with a highly differential contribution rate. The central cities, inner-ring, and mid-developing suburbs, because they had few expensive homes, would contribute a relatively small part of their tax base to the pool. Because the region's high-valued homes were clustered in the southwest and east developing suburbs, these communities would contribute more heavily. Nevertheless, after the contribution, the southwest and east developing suburbs would still have a far greater tax capacity per household than the other groups of suburbs.

Because of the dysfunctional status of the appointed Met Council at that time, the fund was to be administered by the Minnesota Housing Finance Agency. Under the bill, one-third of the resources would remain in suburbs that had not met their housing goals under the Comprehensive Choice Housing bill. Either they could keep the fund and provide the housing locally or the MHFA would administer their contribution. Two-thirds of the money could be used by cities that had met their goals to redevelop and reinvest. These communities could apply to the MHFA for grants for deconcentration and reinvestment uses consistent with the goals previously described.[73] Specifically, the grants could be used for public parks, environmental cleanup, and removal of blighted structures.

Introduced late in the short 1994 session, the Metropolitan Reinvestment Act was widely praised by academics and good-government groups and immediately endorsed by the Minneapolis papers. Owing to poor preparation, its political support rapidly fell apart. Predictably, the southwestern and east developing suburbs protested violently, and the Republican governor promised a veto. However, Saint Paul and the northern suburbs (which would contribute a very small percentage of their base and would be likely candidates to receive far greater resources in return) opposed the bill. Their stated opposition stemmed from the lack of a *guarantee* that they would get back more resources than they contributed. It is more likely, however, that they preferred to receive their distribution from the reinvestment pool as straight tax base sharing, with no strings attached.

As political support eroded, the Reinvestment Act evolved into the Housing Disparities Act. The Housing Disparities Act took the Reinvestment Act pool and placed it in direct tax base sharing. This move greatly increased the size of the fiscal disparities pool. This measure was at once enormously popular in the central city and in inner-ring and mid-developing suburbs. Under the terms of the Housing Disparities Act, 24 percent of the region (by population) contributed $113 million to the remaining 76 percent.

By any measure, such a bill was an easy one to pass, and the Housing Disparities Act began to gather the momentum of a rodeo bull in a steel chute. Facing a certain veto, Senate leadership ultimately killed the Housing Disparities Act in exchange for committee votes on a controversial nuclear waste disposal bill. However, Senate leadership strongly approved of the bill and promised that it would be back in the next session. It is striking that the Housing Disparities Bill marked the first time since the 1970s that a form of tax base sharing had been modeled in order to build a political coalition. The lopsided majority of winners also convinced the North Metro Mayors Association that tax base sharing would be a viable strategy for 1995.

Land Use: A Trial Balloon

In 1994 I introduced a statewide land-planning bill based on Oregon's system.[74] Because this was a short session in the House, however, and great energy was being spent on housing, tax base sharing, and Metropolitan Council structural reform, we did not seriously attempt to move the bill. Instead, we used it to begin the discussion of statewide land use planning. Land use planning generally found a far more receptive political climate within the metropolitan area than in outstate Minnesota.[75]

In the latter part of the 1994 session, during the debates on tax base sharing, we began to see a powerful synergy between tax base sharing and land use planning. In 1993 our allies on housing and tax base sharing in the low–tax capacity developing suburbs had refused to consider land use reform. This time, discussions about combining tax base sharing and land use began to crystallize. These discussions formed the basis for a new combined land use–tax base sharing bill for the 1995 session.

Civic Regionalism and Conservative Surge

Over the summer of 1994, the Alliance for Metropolitan Stability was formed and received funding support for staffing from local foundations. It included the church and other religious groups mentioned previously, land use and environmental groups seeking to protect forest and farmland at the metro periphery, inner-city poverty groups, and city neighborhood groups.[76] The founding organizations of the alliance identified the need for a coordinated educational campaign to expand the base of organizational and public support for regional solutions such as affordable housing, tax base sharing, land use planning, and urban reinvestment. The alliance functions as a central coordinating organization and clearinghouse for the disparate groups involved in these issues.

Since the fall of 1994, the alliance has recruited new organizations and has developed principles that reflect the wider interests of this expanding coalition. In response to growing regional inequities, members of the alliance adopted certain goals:

—To ensure that metropolitan government is an entity that is representative, is accountable, and has the necessary power to further the purposes of community, stability, equity, and renewal;

—To reduce barriers to affordable housing where they exist, making housing available in all communities to diverse racial and income groups;

—To target economic development to low-income people and low-income communities;

—To promote land use planning that balances growth with conservation and creates opportunities for greater economic equity and social justice;

—To modify financing and tax structures to create greater tax base equity;

—To develop and fund a reliable transportation system that promotes access to job and housing choice while placing greater emphasis on cycling, walking, carpooling, and mass transit; and

—To promote high-quality, fully funded, integrated schools throughout the metropolitan area.

The alliance's leader was an able community-based organizer, Frank Hornstein, who had cut his teeth on regional environmental issues. Russ Adams took over in 1995, after Hornstein moved to found the Jewish Metropolitan Organizing Project, a member of the alliance.

In 1994, the Saint Paul Ecumenical Alliance of Congregation (SPEAC), a liberal Saul Alinsky–type organizing entity; the Metropolitan Interfaith Coalition for Affordable Housing (MICAH, an affordable-housing group that was suburban, church based, and more conservative); and the Office for Social Justice (OSJ, the large social justice arm of the Catholic Church) all began a series of meetings throughout the region at individual churches. SPEAC, under the leadership of Pamela Twiss and Paul Marincel (as well as other young, idealistic central-city organizers) generated large, high-energy meetings in poor central-city neighborhood churches. These meetings were filled with the old-style spirit of the civil rights movement. Ron Krietemeyer, Kathy Tomlin, and Jay Schmitt of the Office for Social Justice brought the message out to hundreds of churches in the city and suburbs. Congregation after congregation endorsed the plan followed by bishop after bishop. In 1994, Archbishop John Roach issued a major statement declaring that regional fair housing, equity, and land use planning were serious moral issues in the late twentieth century.[77] MICAH, under the quiet leadership of Mike Anderson, worked behind the scenes to line up suburban clergy and local citizens. In 1995, setting the stage for a major legislative push, these groups organized a peaceful march from Saint Luke's Catholic Church to Governor Carlson's residence. The cumulative effect was powerful.

In 1995 and 1996, the regional churches (under the leadership of the Office for Social Justice for the Archdiocese of Minneapolis and Saint Paul as well as eight other major religious groups) organized an event called the Metro Future Sabbath.[78] Hundreds of churches and synagogues throughout the seven-county metropolitan area held meetings on the polarization of the regional community. The purpose of these events was to call for a renewed commitment to "rebuild the city and to revive and strengthen the urban core of the metropolitan area." The organizers came equipped with packets summarizing regional trends, a description of legislative activity in response, and a specific call to action to the communities involved. They generated tremendous support and involvement and were instrumental in the final passage of the housing compromise in 1995.

In September 1994, the Met Council approved a revision of the Metropolitan Development Investment Framework, now called the Regional Blueprint. The council approved language to accomplish much of what the original housing bill had attempted.[79] Specifically, it stated that the council would "give priority for regional infrastructure investments or expenditures of public dollars to communities that have implemented plans to provide their share of the region's low- and moderate-income and life-cycle housing opportunities."[80]

The Republican surge of 1994 did not skip Minnesota. After electing Paul Wellstone (the nation's most liberal U.S. Senator) in 1990, it elected Rod Grams, one of the nation's most conservative politicians, in 1994. In addition, for reasons unrelated to regional reform, Governor Arne Carlson defeated his Democratic opponent. This event effectively postponed sweeping regional reforms for at least four years.

The election brought a large change in the composition of the Minnesota House (the Minnesota Senate was not up for election in 1994). The Democratic party lost 13 seats, plus two special elections during the session, bringing the balance to 69 Democratic members and 65 Republican members. Of eight seats lost in the suburbs, six were in inner and low–tax capacity suburbs and in high–tax capacity areas. The seven defeated rural Democrats generally had supported metropolitan reform; the new Republicans probably would not. Because passing a bill required 68 affirmative votes, and because three or four Democratic members from suburban areas could not support metropolitan reform, each bill would fail if it did not have several Republican votes.

The 1995 Legislative Session:
Tax Base Sharing and Livable Communities

In 1995, the electoral change and the introduction of a fair-housing compromise by moderate Republicans led to the opening of a significant second front on regional tax base sharing. The session would end with a vetoed bill on tax base sharing and a modest housing compromise that would set the stage for further progress. By mid-1995, regional reform legislation of one sort or another was in the newspaper almost every day and soon on television and talk radio as well, with mixed results. The community of interest supporting regional reform, particularly the churches and religious groups, grew dramatically.

In the previous two legislative sessions, I had spent most of my time on housing issues and regional structural reform. In 1995 moderate Republicans approached Senator Ted Mondale with a serious housing compromise proposal. The advent of these negotiations preempted this area of policy. We did not think bringing forward a strong housing bill would be productive until we saw what would happen here. However, we made clear that if nothing happened, comprehensive choice housing would be back. Ironically, with the loss of so many moderate Democrats in the northern suburbs in the 1994 election, passing a strong fair-housing bill would probably have been difficult anyway.

So I turned my energy in the 1995 session toward passing a pure tax base–sharing bill. Tax base sharing is a powerful tool for building regional alliances. Most other regional issues, such as fair housing and land use planning, are long term. Structural reform is theoretical. However, tax base sharing means (for most of the region) what everyone always promises in American politics but almost never can deliver: immediate lower taxes and better services. This combination builds firm coalitions quickly.

The Politics of the Original Fiscal Disparities Bill

The passage of the original fiscal disparities bill was highly controversial. The author of the bill was Charles R. Weaver Sr., a Republican from the low–tax base satellite city of Anoka. Weaver had heretofore been suspicious of the growing wave of metropolitanism. He believed its sewer and land-planning components threatened the ability of the low–tax base northern suburbs to develop property wealth. In 1969, he introduced the first fiscal disparities bill, a product of the local Citizens League. It passed the Minnesota House, but the Senate refused to take it up. In 1971, the bill was again brought forth and met with strenuous objection from the southern and western suburbs. Representative Graw of Bloomington stated, "This is not a fiscal disparities bill, it is a share the wealth bill." His colleague Representative Ticen of Bloomington called the bill a plot.

On March 31, 1971, the bill passed the House again, this time by 90 to 42—24 fewer votes than two years before. It was supported by a coalition of "central-city," "poor"-suburban, and outstate legislators and opposed by "rich"-suburban representatives and scattered outstate reinforcements.[81] Because Charlie Weaver was a Republican, the Republicans from northern suburban low–tax base areas, as well as metro Democrats, voted with him, as did many rural Republicans with whom Weaver had built personal relationships. However, Weaver never gained the support of the Republicans from property-wealthy southern suburban areas. Under the bill, the two-thirds of the region that won new tax base, Republicans and Democrats alike, supported Weaver; the one-third that did not opposed him.[82]

In the Senate, where opponents sensed a stronger chance of defeating the bill, representatives from the southern suburbs fought it violently. Jerry Minea, chairman of the legislative committee of the Dakota County Development Association, called the bill "community socialism" and said such bills "are like Robin Hood—they take from the progressive communities such as Dakota County and give to the so-called backward ones."[83] He continued, "We would be feeding our weaker communities with the product of the work of others. . . . Why should those who wish to work be forced to share with those who won't or can't help themselves?"[84] Eagan town board chairman John Klein stated, "The fiscal disparities law will destroy the state. The seven metro counties will lose potential, people will be unemployed and children will be sent outside their communities to go to school." Klein added, "It was all a plot for one large metropolitan government which is nothing more than 'creeping communism.'"[85] Inver Grove Heights mayor George Cameron denounced the proposal, asking "How can metro government take 40 percent of what we have and give it to those who can't operate on 100 percent?" and repeating Cameron's assertion that the bill was "communistic."[86]

Senator Howard Knutson of Dakota County believed the bill was good long-term policy for the region and became one of its authors. He was immediately denounced by Dakota County commissioner Pat Scully, who said, "[Knutson] is out to hurt the taxpayers of this county. . . . and [doesn't] have the interests of this county at heart, that's for damn sure."[87] There would never again be a prominent "loser" in favor of tax base sharing.

The bill squeaked out of a special Senate fiscal disparities subcommittee of the Metropolitan Affairs Committee by a single vote. It was subsequently killed in a procedural motion on the Senate floor. During a special legislative session called that summer to solve a school-funding deadlock, the bill was brought up again and battled its way to the Senate floor, where it passed by a single vote after another bitter debate. Seventy-five percent of the suburban senators voted against the bill, and virtually all of these senators spoke against it.[88] In many ways, because of the strong suburban opposition in the Senate, the rural senators had carried the day. The Senate bill was then sent back to the House, where it passed on a final vote 83 to 39, losing another seven votes amid growing controversy.[89]

The cities of Burnsville, Bloomington, and Shakopee brought suit against the bill almost immediately. One of the most vociferous opponents, Dakota County Commission Leo Murphy, declared that the fiscal disparities law was a threat to the free enterprise system. He said the thrust of the legislation is to "take from those who have and give to those who have not in a manner suggested by Karl Marx."[90] The bill was declared unconstitutional by the trial court, but that decision was overturned and the law upheld by the Minnesota Supreme Court in *Burnsville* v. *Onischuk*. The U.S. Supreme Court refused to hear the appeal. In February 1975, almost five years after the law was passed, the fiscal disparities law finally went into effect. In 1981, the southern suburbs again challenged the constitutionality of the law in *McCutcheon* v. *Minnesota*, where the law was upheld by the Minnesota Tax Court. This would be the last legal challenge, but there never has been any acquiescence from the southern suburbs with high property wealth. Representatives and state senators from the southern and western suburbs have tried to repeal the statute in virtually every session for the past twenty-five years.

The Metropolitan Fair Tax Base Act

In early 1995, with the full support of the North Metro Mayors Association, I introduced the Metropolitan Fair Tax Base Act, which created a

Map 3-8. Children Receiving Free and Reduced-Cost Lunches in Twin Cities Metro Elementary Schools,[a] 1993

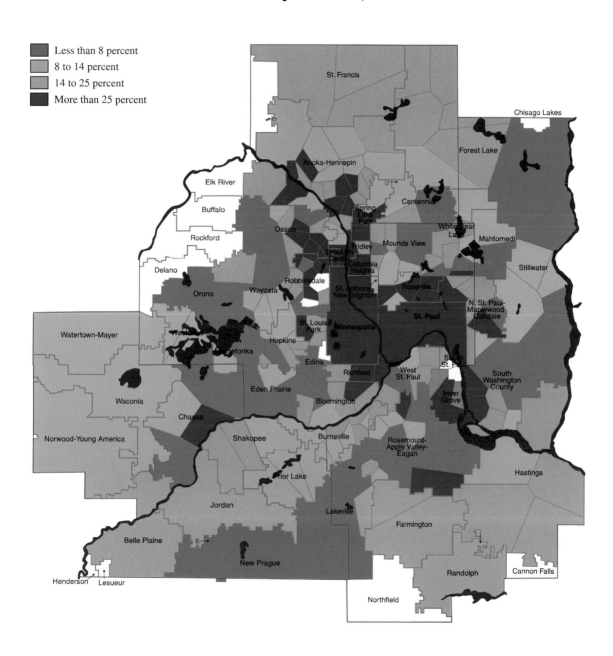

Less than 8 percent
8 to 14 percent
14 to 25 percent
More than 25 percent

St. Francis

Chisago Lakes

Forest Lake

Elk River

Anoka-Hennepin

Centennial

Buffalo

Spring Lake Park

White Bear Lake

Mahtomedi

Rockford

Osseo

Fridley

Mounds View

Brooklyn Center

Columbia Heights

Stillwater

Delano

Robbinsdale

St. Anthony New Brighton

Roseville

N. St. Paul-Maplewood-Oakdale

Orono

Wayzata

Watertown-Mayer

St. Louis Park

Minneapolis

St. Paul

Westonka

Minnetonka

Hopkins

South St. Paul

Edina

West St. Paul

South Washington County

Waconia

Eden Prairie

Richfield

Inver Grove

Chaska

Bloomington

Norwood-Young America

Shakopee

Burnsville

Rosemount-Apple Valley-Eagan

Hastings

Prior Lake

Jordan

Lakeville

Farmington

Belle Plaine

New Prague

Randolph

Cannon Falls

Henderson   Lesueur

Northfield

Source: Minnesota Department of Children, Families and Learning.

a. Each polygon represents one elementary school.

Cartography by Meridian Mapping, Minneapolis

Map 3-9. Minority Enrollment in Twin Cities Metro Area Elementary Schools,[a] 1993

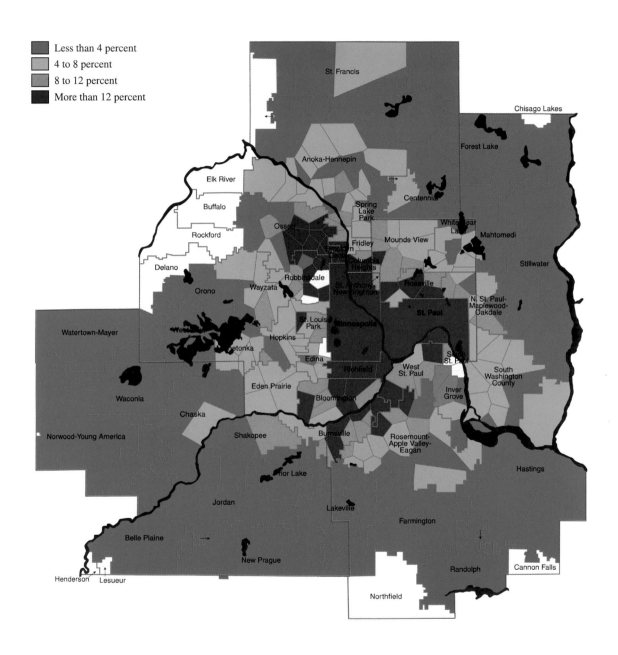

Less than 4 percent
4 to 8 percent
8 to 12 percent
More than 12 percent

Source: Minnesota Department of Children, Families and Learning.

a. Each polygon represents one elementary school.

Cartography by Meridian Mapping, Minneapolis

Map 3-10. Migration of White Preschool Children in Twin Cities Metro Area, 1990

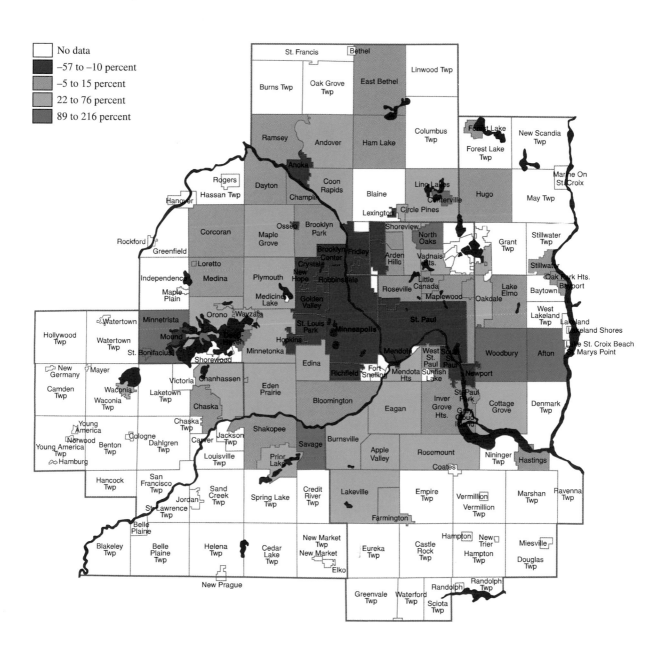

No data
−57 to −10 percent
−5 to 15 percent
22 to 76 percent
89 to 216 percent

Source: Bureau of the Census.

Cartography by Meridian Mapping, Minneapolis

Map 3-11. Twin Cities Metro Public School Closings and Openings, by School District[a]

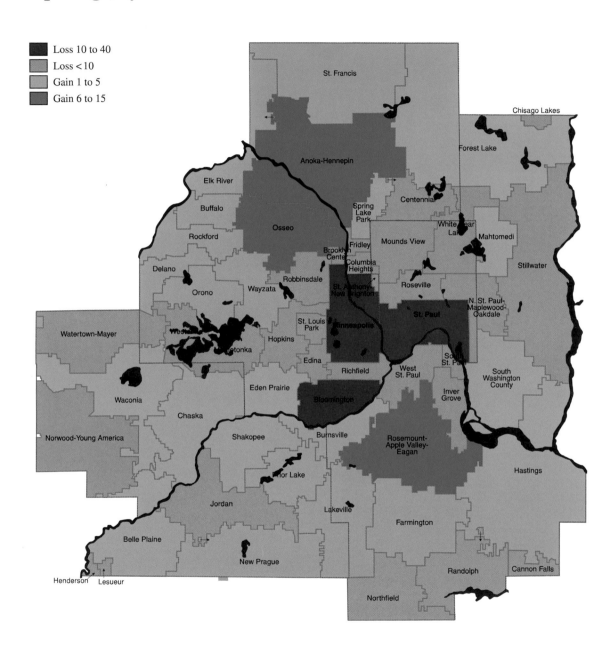

Loss 10 to 40
Loss <10
Gain 1 to 5
Gain 6 to 15

St. Francis

Chisago Lakes

Anoka-Hennepin

Forest Lake

Elk River

Centennial

Buffalo

Spring Lake Park

White Bear Lake

Rockford

Osseo

Fridley

Mounds View

Mahtomedi

Brooklyn Center

Delano

Robbinsdale

Columbia Heights

Stillwater

Orono

Wayzata

St. Anthony-New Brighton

Roseville

N. St. Paul-Maplewood-Oakdale

Watertown-Mayer

West

St. Louis Park

Minneapolis

St. Paul

Hopkins

Minnetonka

South St. Paul

Edina

West St. Paul

South Washington County

Richfield

Waconia

Eden Prairie

Inver Grove

Chaska

Bloomington

Norwood-Young America

Shakopee

Burnsville

Rosemount-Apple Valley-Eagan

Hastings

Prior Lake

Jordan

Lakeville

Farmington

Belle Plaine

New Prague

Randolph

Cannon Falls

Henderson   Lesueur

Northfield

Source: Minnesota Department of Children, Families and Learning.

a. Comparison based on sites in 1969 and 1990.

Cartography by Meridian Mapping, Minneapolis

Map 4-1. Change in Property Value, Twin Cities Region,[a] 1980–90

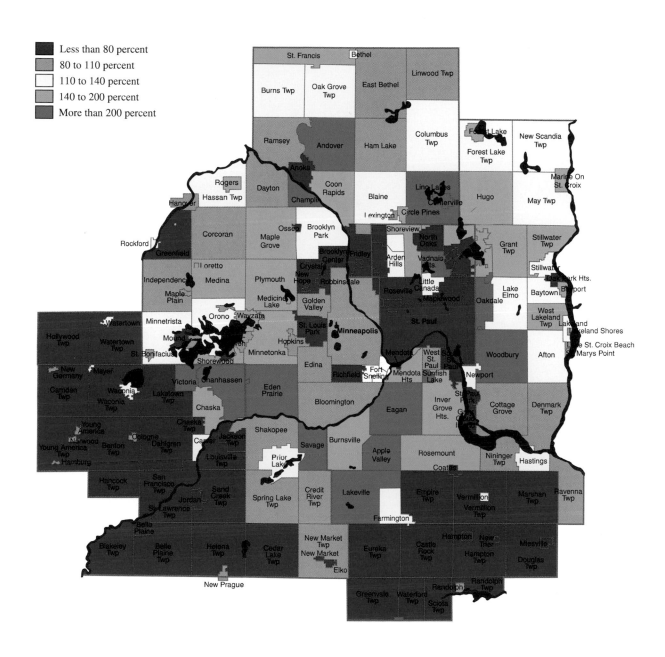

Legend:
- Less than 80 percent
- 80 to 110 percent
- 110 to 140 percent
- 140 to 200 percent
- More than 200 percent

Source: Minnesota House of Representatives, House Research Office.

a. Property value is the sum of land value and building value.

Cartography by Meridian Mapping, Minneapolis

Map 4-2. Effective Net Tax Capacity per Household, Post–Fiscal Disparities, Twin Cities Region, 1980–90

Legend:
- < $1,700
- $1,700 to $2,000
- $2,000 to $3,000
- $3,000 +

Source: Minnesota House of Representatives, House Research Office.

Cartography by Meridian Mapping, Minneapolis

Map 5-1. New Jobs in the Twin Cities, 1980–90

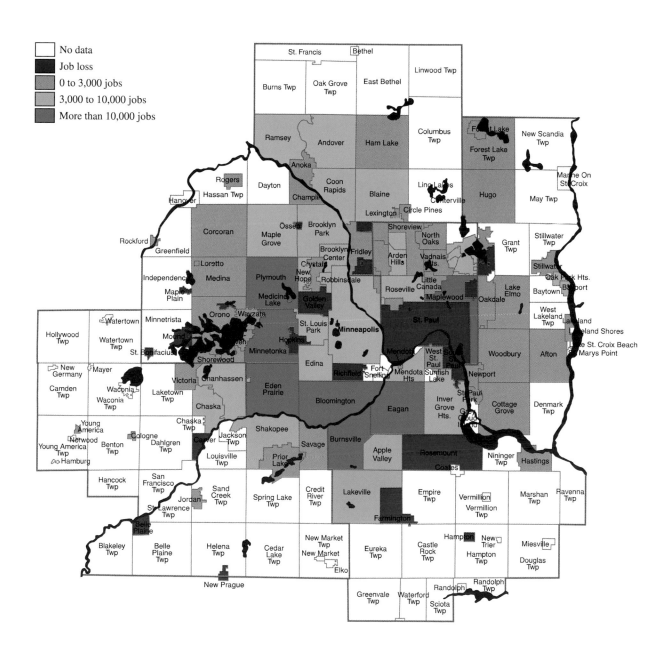

No data
Job loss
0 to 3,000 jobs
3,000 to 10,000 jobs
More than 10,000 jobs

Source: Metropolitan Council, Department of Jobs and Training, Minneapolis.

Cartography by Meridian Mapping, Minneapolis

Map 5-2. Major Highway Improvement Projects in the Twin Cities,[a] 1980–95

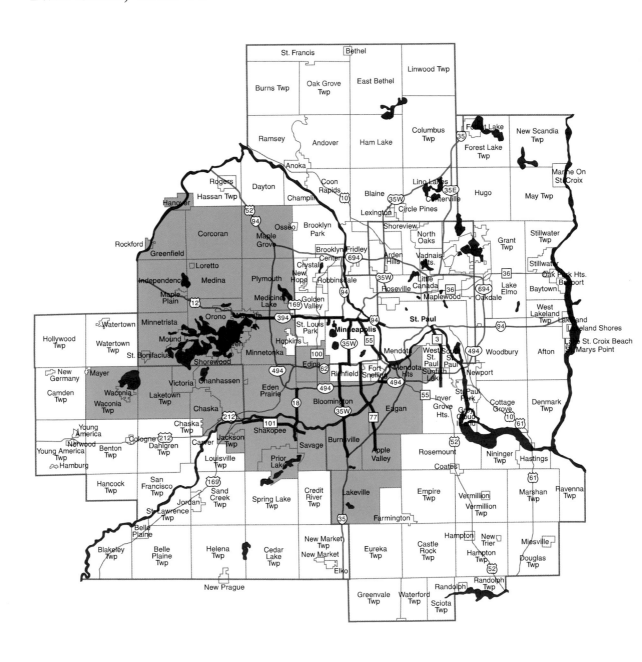

Source: Minnesota Department of Transportation.

a. Southern and western developing region is shaded.

Cartography by Meridian Mapping, Minneapolis

Map 5-3. Sewer Subsidy per Twin Cities Household

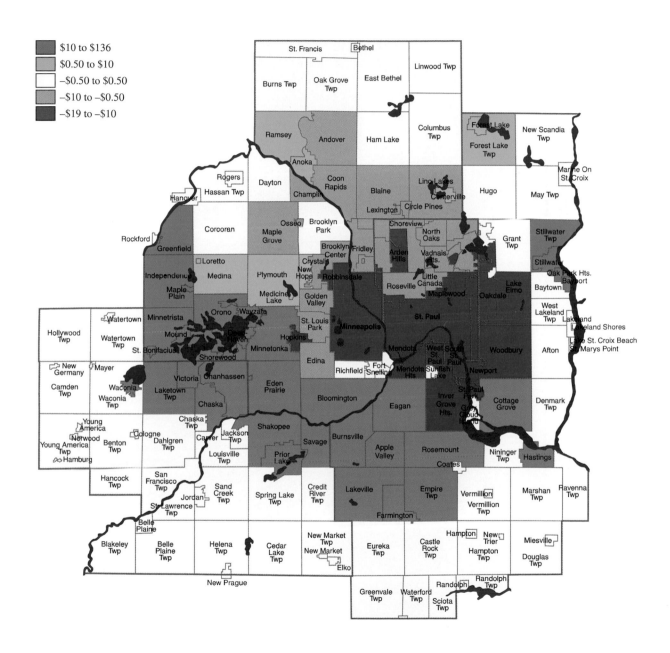

Legend:
- $10 to $136
- $0.50 to $10
- −$0.50 to $0.50
- −$10 to −$0.50
- −$19 to −$10

Sources: Principal investigation by Thomas Luce Jr., Barbara Lukermann, and Herbert Mohring,
"Regional Sewer System Rate Structure Study" (Minneapolis: Hubert H. Humphrey Institute of
Public Affairs, University of Minnesota, December 7, 1992); Metropolitan Waste Control Commission.

Cartography by Meridian Mapping, Minneapolis

Map 8-1. Portland, Oregon, Municipalities Divided into Regions

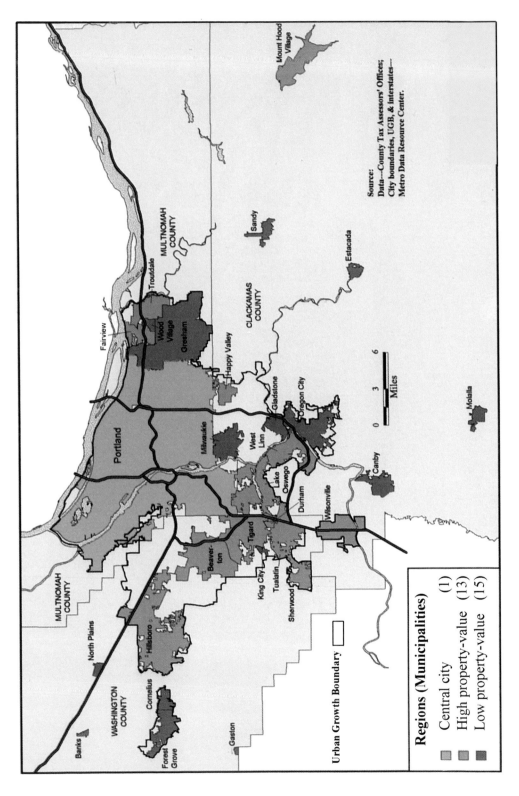

Regions (Municipalities)

Central city	(1)
High property-value	(13)
Low property-value	(15)

Urban Growth Boundary

Source:
Data—County Tax Assessors' Offices;
City boundaries, UGB, & interstates—
Metro Data Resource Center.

Source: Data—County Tax Assessors' Offices; City boundaries, UGB, and interstates—Metro Data Resource Center. Map created by Metropolitan Area Program, Minneapolis.

Map 8-2. Chicago Municipalities Divided into Regions

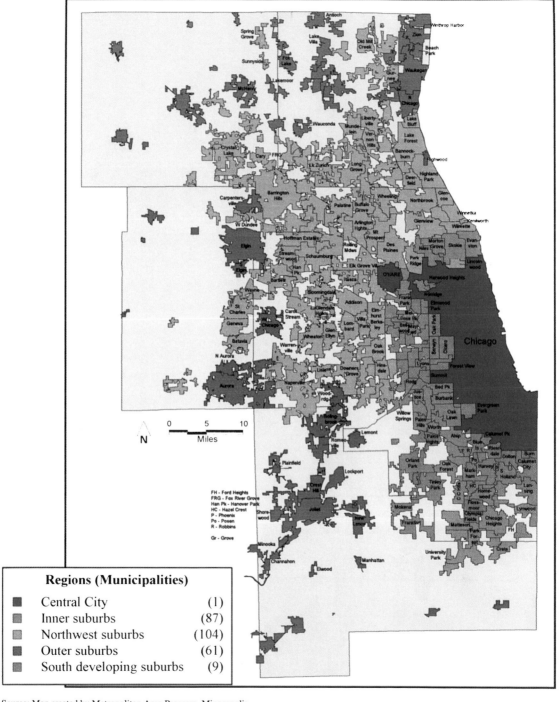

0   5   10
N   Miles

FH - Ford Heights
FRG - Fox River Grove
Han Pk - Hanover Park
HC - Hazel Crest
P - Phoenix
Po - Posen
R - Robbins

Gr - Grove

Regions (Municipalities)	
Central City	(1)
Inner suburbs	(87)
Northwest suburbs	(104)
Outer suburbs	(61)
South developing suburbs	(9)

Source: Map created by Metropolitan Area Program, Minneapolis.

Map 8-3. Philadelphia Municipalities Divided into Regions

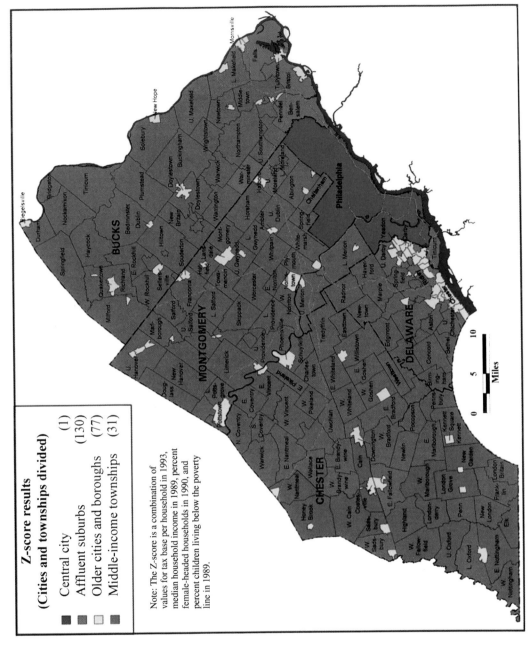

Z-score results
(Cities and townships divided)

■	Central city	(1)
■	Affluent suburbs	(130)
□	Older cities and boroughs	(77)
■	Middle-income townships	(31)

Note: The Z-score is a combination of values for tax base per household in 1993, median household income in 1989, percent female-headed households in 1990, and percent children living below the poverty line in 1989.

Source: Map created by Metropolitan Area Program, Minneapolis.

single unified regional tax base and redistributed almost $1 billion metrowide.[91] Instead of using the present fiscal disparities formula, the Fair Tax Base Act used "power equalization," a system pioneered by the Minnesota school aid formula. Power equalization allowed each municipality to levy off an equalized metropolitan tax base at a rate set locally. This system created more equity and also preserved the notion of local accountability in the setting of tax rates, which had become important in Minnesota statewide property tax debates. Through the Fair Tax Base Act, 30 percent of the region contributed tax base to the other 70 percent. Moreover, half of the new base added to a receiving city had to be used as a property tax cut. The North Metro Mayors Association held another summit in which they declared their support for this initiative.[92]

The subject of metropolitanism jumped to local television for the first sustained coverage—with a negative spin. The first story, on WCCO-TV, began: "Some call it socialism. . . ." A reporter walked up and down the streets of Edina, one of the region's most affluent cities, asking homeowners to comment on the possibility of a large local property tax increase that would benefit poor residents of Minneapolis. The responses were vitriolic, and the image communicated to the broad public was that the suburbs were in danger. KSTP-TV ran an almost identical story. The power of television was brought home by an onslaught of angry phone calls and a cooler attitude from many previously supportive members. It took several weeks of concerted effort to persuade WCCO to air a more balanced story.

Regional reform forces, politicians, churches, and virtually all of the member groups of the Alliance for Metropolitan Stability tried to persuade Representative Charlie Weaver Jr., son of the original author of the fiscal disparities law, to sponsor or at least support the Fair Tax Base Act. Weaver not only had been one of the legislature's staunchest defenders of the fiscal disparities law but also represented one of the region's most property-poor legislative districts. The Anoka-Hennepin school district, which he represents, was one of the region's lowest-spending districts and had one of the highest suburban drop-out rates. The city of Anoka, in the center of his district, also had deep social problems and few fiscal resources. If Weaver supported the bill, we believed that most of the eleven other Republicans in recipient districts would follow his lead, making the bill difficult to veto.

Weaver's comments in the press indicated his initial interest, which quickly cooled and became opposition. Following Weaver's lead, other Republican members who had shown interest in supporting the bill kept quiet. In the end, there were simply more Republican caucus members whose districts were contributors. Because some of the most prominent caucus members were also some of the largest contributors, the internal dynamics of the Republican legislative caucus rapidly squelched overt support for the bill.

In response to the negative television coverage and the rejection by Republicans in the legislature, the bill was scaled back, first to sharing the value of homes above $150,000 (as in 1994), then to sharing the value above $200,000, and finally to sharing only the *growth* in value above $200,000.[93] This lessened the richness of the pool but created even more recipients (83 percent of the metro population) and fewer contributors (17 percent). These continual concessions and compromises allowed moderate-recipient members in both parties to support the bill. It did not by any means reduce the hostility of the bill's main opponents from the wealthy western suburbs. Like the housing bill, the tax base–sharing bill was hard going. Take-no-prisoners–type hearings were fought in the subcommittee on property taxes and then in the full tax committee.[94] There was no Republican support for the bill until it reached the House floor.

Supporters of a variety of important public policy goals, including creating greater equity, resolving the growing mismatch between needs and resources, and eliminating fiscal zoning, supported the bill. But the political debate was far more centered on which communities would receive tax cuts and tax increases, whether the bill was "communistic" or a "gentle enhancement of a good Republican idea," and on a battle over studies concerning regional infrastructure and affordable housing.

It was undisputed that 83 percent of the region would get a tax cut under the bill. At the same time, because the bill dealt only with the *growth* of tax base above $200,000 in value, it did not take any current tax base away from any community and could not be portrayed as a mandatory tax increase. Therefore, some argued that the Fair Tax Base Act did not raise taxes in these communities but rather cut into a combination of future tax cuts, benefit improvements, or both. Put another way, the Fair Tax Base Act stemmed the increasing polarization of the region's tax base.

As with the original fiscal disparities bill in the early 1970s, daily charges in the media that the tax base–sharing bill was communistic or Marxist began to define the public debate. The original author of fiscal disparities was actually a Republican from the northern suburb of Anoka. Noting that the bill added $44 million to an existing program of $350 million of sharing, we maintained the tax base–sharing bill was simply "a gentle enhancement of a good Republican idea." We also concentrated on the message that the bill represented a property tax cut and better services to 83 percent of the region's residents.

The notion that tax base sharing was an outright theft from the southern suburbs also recurred frequently. It was countered by pointing to the large share of highway and sewer infrastructure provided from regional sources that went to Metropolitan Legislative Commission (MLC) suburbs, mostly developing ones to the south and west. "Was that spending a theft from the rest of the region?" we asked. The MLC and the Met Council produced a series of studies that showed that sewer and road expenditures were evenly divided throughout the region; debunked the Luce, Lukermann, and Mohring study of sewer rates that was completed pursuant to the 1991 legislation (which I have discussed); and declared that the region had no barriers to affordable housing. Each point was so thoroughly countered by experts that most opponents of tax base sharing abandoned such arguments.

Much of the committee debate was spent on a line of argument put forth by Representative H. Todd Van Dellen of Plymouth. A House research study done for him showed that the northern suburbs were spending slightly less of their income (around 2.5 percent versus 3 percent) on property taxes.[95] He argued that there should be no tax base sharing until northern-tier communities spent the same amount of their income on taxes.

This argument was a non sequitur, for the central issue was not who paid what percentage of income but rather what deleterious effect unequal tax bases would have on equity, regional polarization, and sprawl. Moreover, on its own terms it was incorrect. The League of Minnesota Cities showed quite clearly that Van Dellen's figures failed to take into account several important factors that would have biased his results.[96] Van Dellen also did not mention that MLC cities had an income 30 percent above average. Finally, notwithstanding all this, Minnesota's multitiered property tax system, in which homes valued above $72,000 are taxed at a higher rate than others, would bias the system to create higher tax rates in communities dominated by high-valued homes.

Instead of assisting his cause, Van Dellen's line of attack highlighted the multilayered inequities facing the northern suburbs. In addition to a small tax base that raised small resources, they had low household incomes. Their hard-pressed residents could not pay the higher-than-average taxes needed to provide average services. In the worst of both worlds, cities that were members of the North Metro Mayors Association often found themselves with the worst-funded municipal and school services in the region.

On the other side of the divide, MLC cities, with large tax bases and large household incomes, were (ironically) big tax-and-spenders. Instead of spending money on police and rebuilding aging infrastructure, as older cities did, they could lavish tax money on schools and parks, on larger-than-average government bureaucracies, and on above-average employee salaries and benefits. As a group, the MLC suburbs spent 50 percent more on government bureaucracy and 30 percent more on parks and also paid higher wages than the North Metro Mayors Association suburbs.[97] Their school district spending was also the highest in the suburbs. In response to Van Dellen's attack, the northern suburbs declared that if the MLC cities wanted lower taxes, they should cut their extravagant local services.

As the bill reached the full house, debate waxed long and angry in a replay of the original. The southern and western suburban members sounded exactly like their counterparts of a quarter of a century earlier, repeating the exact same phrases: "Robin Hood," "socialism," "communism," "theft." Unfortunately, the newspapers concentrated mainly on the personal attacks rather than on evaluating the bill's substance.[98] After extended debate, the full House backed the tax base–sharing bill by a 71 to 63 vote. Four Democrats, all representing high–tax base areas, voted against the bill. In an important step forward, three suburban Republicans from low–tax base areas voted in favor. An additional eight Republicans from the low–tax base suburbs, either bowing to internal party pressure or ideologically opposed to tax base sharing, opposed the bill. Some representatives from blue-collar, growing districts believed, against the evidence, that through hard work (and exclusive zoning) they could grow their way out of their fiscal troubles. Their vote against a tax cut and better services will likely become an election issue used against them in the next campaign.

In the Senate, the tax base–sharing bill sailed through the tax committee, only to fail unexpectedly on an initial floor vote. The Senate author, Steve Novak, had been so confident with his nearly two-thirds Democratic majority that he did not canvas the rural Democrats carefully enough. Entering the breach, the real estate lobby persuaded them to oppose the bill. After the bill's initial Senate failure, some persuasion by Democratic leadership and further lobbying by Senator Novak helped the bill pass on a second vote, 36 to 30. The bill was promptly vetoed.

In 1995, as controversy heated up over the bill, local professional regionalists harkened back to the seemingly Olympian consensus of 1971. In point of fact, the bill passed by a larger margin in 1995 in the Senate than it had in 1971. But for the conservative election of 1994, which did not affect the Senate, the bill would have also passed the House by a higher margin. Moreover, the acrimony of the debate was almost identical in both periods; by 1995 it may have even become more civil.

As the tax base–sharing bill neared the House floor for a vote, talk-radio hosts (in conjunction with the Republican caucus) launched a coordinated attack. The day before the floor vote, talk-radio host Jason Lewis, a former Republican candidate for Congress in Colorado, met with the Republican caucus and discussed a media strategy for dealing with the bill. On the floor of the House, Representative Mike Osskopp, a former talk radio host elected to the Minnesota legislature in 1994, repeatedly invoked Karl Marx when referring to the bill (or me). Jesse "the Body" Ventura, a former supporter who as mayor of Brooklyn Park had both endorsed tax base sharing and specifically supported parts of the MCSA, had retired from that post, moved to Maple Grove, and become a celebrated talk-radio host. He then switched sides and attacked our bill on his morning drive-time show: "Representative Myron 'the Communist' Orfield, his latest wealth-sharing strategy, I mean this guy really needs to go to China. I mean I think he'd be most happy there. . . . Oh Myron, Myron, Myron. You never realized the communists folded for a reason. You didn't figure it out, did you Myron?"[99]

Like the initial negative television coverage, the talk radio attacks weakened support for the bill in close districts. Moreover, because the attacks were so broad based and unfair, characterizing the controversy as one between the city and the monolithic suburbs, all of a sudden there was acrimony in beneficiary suburbs. Listeners mistakenly believed the bill amounted to a tax increase and poorer services, when the reality was just the opposite.

The Metropolitan Poverty Reduction Act

Southwest metro area Republicans again introduced their Metropolitan Poverty Reduction Act, with a few additional features. They used some of the resources in Governor Carlson's housing budget to create a regional fund for affordable housing. They also took the governor's proposal for local government aid budget reform (which tends to cut local government aid to much of rural Minnesota) and put the savings to further funding for a regional housing and revitalization pool. A bipartisan coalition of rural members roundly defeated this aspect of the proposal, and the bill wandered through several House committees, kept alive in the hope of reaching a compromise.

The Mondale-Long Metropolitan Livable Communities Act

During the 1995 legislative session, Senator Ted Mondale took the lead on affordable housing. Significant bills were also introduced by Representative Matt Entenza to codify the recently enacted regional blueprint housing language and by Representative Alice Hausman to make housing a regional system.[100] Despite strong opposition from the governor, these bills moved through the committees, keeping up pressure on fair housing issues.

Responding to the enormous pressure that had been building over the two vetoed housing bills, over the summer of 1994 newly appointed Met Council chair Curt Johnson and Ted Mondale, senator from Saint Louis Park, had begun negotiations on a bill ultimately called the Metropolitan Livable Communities Act (MLCA). Mondale and Johnson rapidly reached a compromise similar to the Metropolitan Reinvestment Act of 1994, which Mondale and I had cosponsored. As this compromise crystallized, however, both Mondale and Johnson began to criticize my past approach, saying that I had demonized the wealthy suburbs.[101] This approach gained support in the southwestern suburbs, which had been strenuous adversaries in the debate. The metropolitan newspapers, weary of the divisive battle over fair housing and sensing the possibility of some sort of bipartisan agreement, rapidly endorsed the Mondale-Johnson process.[102]

The initial Mondale bill gave the Met Council the power to negotiate goals with all regional communities, in line with the purposes of the Regional Blueprint. Closely resembling the Reinvestment Act in 1994, the most significant part of the bill had a gentle tax base–sharing formula that required all metropolitan communities to contribute a portion of their high-value home tax base to a regional housing pool. However, instead of specifying values above $150,000, it required each community to contribute to the pool all value on housing that was more than twice the average value of a home in that community.[103] A little more circuitous, this formula generally had a similar redistributive effect with a smaller housing pool. In the first year, it created $2.4 million in shared base, which grew a little each year. Like the Reinvestment Act, it allowed communities the choice of contributing their tax base to the shared pool or keeping it locally to provide affordable housing in compliance with Met Council–specified goals. Any city that had met its housing goal could use the money locally to upgrade housing stock.

Two other funds were created by the MLCA. The first abolished the Metropolitan Mosquito Control District, created in the 1950s to deal with a fierce local enemy, and gave its levy authority (about $12 million) to fund an environmental cleanup program. This amount was later halved to fund a program with such broad enabling language that it was difficult to pinpoint where the cleanup would be. The final fund scoured money from a variety of dormant metropolitan funds and unused tax levy authorities to create a $5 million account for a housing demonstration project. Ostensibly, it was to fund attractive, model, low-income projects to provide design mechanisms that might make them more acceptable to affluent, growing suburbs. As with the environmental cleanup fund, this fund was so broadly defined that it could be used for virtually any market-rate or expensive apartment complex on a transit corridor.

The Mondale-Johnson compromise was just the beginning, as the House Republican leaders still found it too strong and demanded further concessions to avoid another veto. In response, Senator Mondale added two provisions from the Republican bill that eliminated state taxes on building materials for affordable housing and created an urban homestead revitalization program. When this was insufficient, he began making serious concessions.

First, the provisions on high-valued home tax base sharing were made voluntary, essentially eliminating the most meaningful part of the bill. Mondale and others argued that incentives remained to contribute to the pool: exclusion of nonparticipants from use of the MLCA funds for environmental cleanup or housing; payment of past obligations for participation at a later date; and inclusion of a community's nonparticipation as a factor in Met Council allocations of regional infrastructure and regional funds. Only the last of these seemed important, and then only in the hands of a newly strong and assertive Met Council.

In another significant concession, the bill added a provision that forgave part of a loan to the wealthy southwestern city of Bloomington, Minnesota. In 1985 and 1986, the State of Minnesota had paid the principal value on the freeway improvements around the now famous Mall of America (the nation's largest) for an effective loan of $55 million. This shopping center added $700 million of assessed value to Bloomington's tax base, an amount equal to almost half of Saint Paul's commercial-industrial tax base. To secure the governor's approval, MLCA eased the terms of the Bloomington loan, saving that city about $7 million—more than twice the amount in the regional housing fund.

The third major concession gave power over the housing pool—to the extent that anyone voluntarily decided to contribute to it—to the metropolitan counties instead of the Met Council. This created a problem. Two counties that should be providing more affordable housing, Hennepin and Carver, had a conservative balance of power and would not and could not act. On the other hand, Ramsey and Anoka, which already had too much affordable housing, probably should not add any but could not act extraterritorially. Only Dakota County would be able to make effective use of the fund, if there was ever any money in it.

Little remained of the MLCA that hobbled to the floor of the legislature. The bill was still controversial only to its conservative Republican opponents. In essence, there was a provision left that gave the Met Council the statutory authority to negotiate goals and the ability to withhold regional services to cities that did not voluntarily participate in the regional housing fund (a power the council had asserted by regulation in the 1970s). A small amount of money would likely go to clean up industrial sites in the older part of the region and possibly toward a low-income housing demonstration project. In the end, the victory was more symbolic than substantive (much like the 1957 Civil Rights Act, the weak precursor of the 1964 act). The MLCA broke the deadlock, and the basic approach of the 1993 housing bill was accepted. Like the 1957 Civil Rights Act, MLCA was a platform on which a stronger and more enforceable act could be built. It also put the southwestern suburbs on notice: if things do not happen under the voluntary system, fair-housing forces will be back.

Maple Grove and the Implementation of the Livable Communities Act

In 1995, after the passage of the Livable Communities Act, the Met Council was scheduled to act on a request from the city of Maple Grove for a 1,000-acre MUSA expansion and a $43 million sewer interceptor ($71 million with carrying costs).[104] Maple Grove requested this infrastructure without making any changes in its restrictive, low-density housing market. In the end, the Met Council's negotiated agreement actually allowed Maple Grove to become more rather than less restrictive than ever before. This action undermined many of the high hopes and expectations built around the regional blueprint housing language and the Metropolitan Livable Communities Act.

A letter from the Met Council to Maple Grove, dated September 23, 1988, stated:

> [Maple Grove's] intent for the future is to build primarily high-cost housing. In its comments on [Maple Grove's comprehensive] plan, the Council expressed concern that the city not emphasize higher-priced single family housing at the expense of more affordable housing. Maple Grove has among the highest apartment rents in the metropolitan area, and among the highest minimum required apartment unit sizes. It is appropriate to reiterate the Council's comments on the 1987 plan update:

Maple Grove is encouraged to periodically evaluate its policy of encouraging primarily large-lot, single-family housing to ensure that housing continues to be available and affordable for people of varying incomes.[105]

In 1986, Joanne Barron of the Met Council staff wrote, "Although one of the stated goals of [Maple Grove's comprehensive plan] is to provide housing for all income groups, nothing in the plan would seem to encourage construction of moderate-cost housing."[106] Between 1975 and 1992, Maple Grove received $1.456 million in Community Development Block Grant funds from the U.S. Department of Housing and Urban Development. It did not use any of these funds for affordable housing.

The agreement declares in its preamble that it is not binding on Maple Grove. Specifically, "Relative to the diversity, tenure, density, and cost of housing developed in Maple Grove, the City cannot guarantee that its efforts will result in the achievement of all of its target goals and expectations."

With regard to unit density, the agreement asks Maple Grove to construct apartment buildings at a density of eleven units per acre. For twenty years, the Met Council has recommended a density of twenty units per acre. More troubling is the density requirement as it relates to single-family housing. The agreement allows single-family home construction to proceed at densities of 2.5 units per acre, or 17,000-square-foot lots. Even with Maple Grove's huge street requirements (which also contradict Met Council guidelines), the lots would still be more than 15,000 square feet. The Met Council's guidelines require 7,500-square-foot lots. Maple Grove's effective minimum lot size is currently 11,000 square feet. This new "requirement" therefore actually allows Maple Grove to build at even lower densities.

In the agreement, the Met Council "asks" that Maple Grove build 25 percent of its units for rental. Historically, Met Council guidelines have required 40 percent. Here again, nothing in the agreement binds Maple Grove to build any rental housing. In the first subdivision under development in Maple Grove, out of more than 450 units planned, only 40 (less than 10 percent) are rental units. In addition, these rents are specified as under $950 a month—hardly "affordable." The Met Council points to forty units to be developed to rent to tenants who are at 50 percent of the median income. However, these units were required as part of a settlement to a race discrimination lawsuit brought by Podawiltz/Hoyt Development, and the city had no choice but to build them. In response, the

153

Met Council notes that eighty-eight units of senior housing are to be built in Maple Grove and six units of existing market-rate family housing are to be subsidized for rental at 60 percent of the median income—all in response to the agreement. This hardly seems like much progress for adding a $43 million sewer interceptor and 1,000 acres of high-end land to the urban service area. Moreover, there is nothing in the agreement to ensure that these projects will actually be built.

In terms of affordability, the proposed agreement asks Maple Grove to ensure that only 6.4 percent of new units are affordable by Legal Aid Society estimates at $765 a month. The Met Council figures say $638 a month. The median rent in Maple Grove is currently $637—almost $200 above the Twin Cities region's median of $447, and among the highest average rents in the region. Whichever figures are used, the tiny required percentage of "affordable" units are renting for more than Maple Grove's present expensive stock. Many of the new jobs in Maple Grove pay $15,000 a year or less. A substantial percentage of the new housing ought to be affordable for these workers.

The agreement also failed to address several of the most restrictive aspects of Maple Grove's housing practices. Although the Met Council's advisory zoning standards discourage the use of floor area requirements, Maple Grove's are among the highest in the metropolitan area for single-family and multifamily housing.

In its settlement, the *Hollman* v. *Cisneros* lawsuit had provided millions of dollars for subsidized housing in suburbs like Maple Grove. When the plaintiffs offered to give the Met Council these units to assist in the housing agreement, the Met Council refused to even broach the subject, arguing that it would be too controversial. This was extremely disheartening. If the region could not make progress on affordable housing in a community that wanted new sewers that it could not afford, with money to build the housing already in place, how would anyone ever make any headway on this issue?

Before this agreement became final in late 1995, the Alliance for Metro Stability brought together 250 people and dozens of interest groups to protest the Maple Grove agreement. In coordinated testimony, the region's land use and environmental groups, its community development and housing advocates, advocates for the communities of color and poor residents, and transit advocates raised serious and unanswered questions about the agreement. The meetings were powerful enough so that, for the first time, the appointed council members from the central city opposed the agreement. But they were not powerful enough to modify it substantially.

The 1996 Legislative Session

The 1996 session was a short one, dominated (unfortunately for the House Democrats) by ethics controversies involving rural members. During that time, the legislature passed a model ordinance for sustainable development.[107] It also repealed the 1987 statute creating uniform sewer costs, in which the core of the region subsidized the fringe in a move that would have allowed the Met Council to return to a mode of sewer pricing. The governor vetoed this bill.[108] The legislature narrowly passed a bill to encourage stronger regional planning and to study tax base sharing in the Saint Cloud metropolitan area, a fast-growing community of 100,000 just northwest of the Twin Cities. Although the bill (sponsored by a legislator representing Saint Cloud) had bipartisan local authorship, the governor vetoed it, too.[109] Finally, the Iron Range communities of northern Minnesota passed a regional tax base–sharing bill that Governor Carlson was forced to sign as a provision of the tax bill. In the end, though I was saddened that the governor had put an end to so many worthy initiatives, I was pleased to see that regional movement was gaining new supporters and advocates in both the Twin Cities metropolitan area and other growing regions of the state.

8

Can Regional Coalitions
Work Elsewhere?

In response to growing regional social and economic polarization, between 1993 and 1996, the Twin Cities jump-started a long-dormant regional debate. In three years, it reorganized its regional planning council, transforming it from a $40-million-a-year coordinating agency to a $600-million-a-year regional governance structure with coordinated control over transit and transportation, sewers, land use, airports, and housing policy. It enacted an important regional affordable-housing bill, strengthened the regional land use system, and the legislature passed (but the governor vetoed) a major addition to regional tax-base sharing. Energy for regional reform is growing.

In the process of reenergizing regionalism and ranging metropolitan issues on our negotiating table, we have discovered that our problems are not unique and that the suburban monolith, thought to prevent all progress on regional issues, is a myth. Every metropolitan region in the United States faces the same problems, and several of them have expressed interest in the analytical methods we have applied to our problems. We would share with them some those methods and some of the lessons learned in building our coalition for regional solutions.

Applicability to Other Regions

Portland, Oregon, Chicago, and Philadelphia, in three different regions of the country, have the same social and economic pattern of polarization as the Twin Cities, to greater or lesser degrees. For each city, the demographic basis for forming regional reform coalitions between cities and less affluent suburban jurisdictions are explored in this chapter, using the same methodology applied to the Twin Cities. These cities were not chosen scientifically, but rather because local groups, supported by philanthropy, wanted to duplicate the Twin Cities' coalition-building regional model.[1] In Portland, the first region to undertake the analysis, the political response is already manifest; in the other cities, the political story is still a work in progress.

Portland, Oregon

Portland, Oregon, has a larger percentage of white residents and is somewhat less governmentally fragmented than the Twin Cities (table 8-1 and map 8-1).[2] The Oregon side of the region has twenty-nine cities, forty-two school districts, and three major metro counties. Like the Twin Cities, it has a regional coordinating body. Portland's Metropolitan Council is elected, however, and has the nation's strongest land use planning statute as a tool for shaping development. Portland is developing with a denser land use pattern and a more inclusive housing market at the outer edge than any of the other regions studied. There is less fiscal disparity than in the other regions, perhaps because there is less political fragmentation and the state land use law forces a wide variety of housing types. More balanced development is occurring all around the city, and more redevelopment is taking place in the central city and older suburbs than in the other metropolitan regions studied. Perhaps this is because Portland's land use framework has a growth boundary that arguably constrains development and such rapid population growth that new housing and construction in the region's favored quarter cannot be built fast enough.

Although problems are less acute in Portland than in other cities, similar patterns of regional polarization are at work. For example, the very small population of poor African-American residents is extraordinarily segregated in Portland, as it is in Minneapolis. Portland's poorest city schools are more than 70 percent African-American, compared with a regional population that is 3 percent African-American. Portland's relatively small core of poverty, with the region's highest concentration of African-American residents, is growing larger.

Despite relatively balanced regional growth and urban redevelopment, the older, socially burdened part of the region still cannot compete equally with the region's favored quarter, and the income and family structure in Portland's working-class neighborhoods and its working and middle-class older suburbs are weakening disproportionately. Portland, like the Twin Cities, also has a favored quarter in its southwest sector that has fewer social needs, dominates regional job growth, and has a comparatively large and fast-growing fiscal capacity. If Portland, like Min-

Table 8-1. Selected Portland, Oregon, Regional Statistics

	Central city	Low–tax base suburbs	High–tax base suburbs
Population, 1990	437,319	157,258	207,073
Households, 1990	187,262	59,897	80,504
Percentage of region's population, 1990	37.2	13.4	17.6
Median household income, 1989 (thousands of dollars)	25.6	29.6	38.3
Percentage children under age 5 in poverty, 1990	21.0	15.0	8.6
Percentage female-headed households with children, 1990	24.1	17.7	15.4
Percentage change in white children up to age 5 in 1980 and to ages 10–14 in 1990	no data	24.3	42.1
Percentage change in jobs, 1980–90	no data		
Market value per household, 1993 (thousands of dollars)	115.8	109.6	171.0
Percentage change in market value per household, 1983–93	–2.1	–6.7	6.2

Source: Metropolitan Area Program, Minneapolis.

neapolis, becomes more racially diverse, and if the western suburbs continue to dominate the region's growth, similar polarization pressures may build.

Many of Portland's outer suburbs have comparatively high concentrations of poor and minority households, and its outer poor suburbs are less readily distinguishable from the inner suburbs. Portland was therefore divided into three study regions rather than five: the central city, the low–property value suburbs, and the high–property value suburbs. The central city, together with the low–property value suburbs, represents about 65 percent of the region's population. Like the Twin Cities, the low–property value suburbs are closer to the city of Portland on such social measures as median incomes, female-headed households, and poor preschool children than to the high–tax base, developing suburbs, mainly in Washington County. Moreover, as in Portland, poverty and family instability in the low–property value suburbs increased measurably.

Portland's average tax base per household ($115,832) was about 90 percent of the regional average ($128,547) in 1994. Assessed value was much lower in the low–property value suburbs ($109,569) and much higher in the southwest suburbs ($170,952)—132 percent of the regional average.

In growth of real tax base per household in 1983–93, the southwestern, high–property value developing suburbs, strong to begin with, composed the only subregion to gain in property value per household after inflation. Portland actually lost 2 percent of its assessed value per household. The low–property value suburbs lost a striking 6.7 percent. As in the Twin Cities, as the resources to support local services were eroding, social needs increased dramatically in the low–property value suburbs. Again, the powerful southwestern developing suburbs were the gainers, with an increase of 6.2 percent.

From 1990 to 1994, as regional growth accelerated, assessed value also grew, by 27.1 percent per capita. Growth in assessed value was fairly uniform throughout the subregions, with the high–property value suburbs slightly above average at 29.4, the low–property value suburbs gaining ground at 30.7 percent, and Portland trailing the field with a 24.1 percent increase. During this period, Gresham, a low–tax base inner suburb, had an increase of 35.3 percent per capita above the regional average, but this was not high enough to begin closing the astounding gap with the mighty tax bases of southwestern communities such as Tigard, Tualatin, and Wilsonville. An analysis of tax base sharing shows that between 60 percent and 80 percent of the region would gain resources by a property tax–sharing system.

Job growth in the Portland area has been healthy overall but far from uniform within the region for the past decade and a half. From 1980 to 1990, jobs per capita increased by 13 percent, from 56.4 jobs per 100 people to 64.0 jobs per 100 people.[3] Jobs in Portland's bustling central business district and much of the city and older suburbs expanded between 5 percent and 10 percent, while jobs in the southwestern Washington County growth corridor grew by 25 percent.

Because Portland's metro governmental presence has accustomed the citizenry to thinking regionally, area activists readily understood the Twin Cities' coalition-building strategy. The new maps and polarization analysis fit well into the already established land use framework. The computer model of Portland's tax base sharing revealed that between 60 and 80 percent of the region could be winners. Within a month after my first visit, the Coalition for a Livable Future, an entity much like the Alliance for Metropolitan Stability in the Twin Cities, was formed in 1994. It now has thirty-four member groups, including 1,000 Friends of Oregon, the state's premier land use group; the Portland Urban League; and a broad collection of churches, environmental, and community development organizations.[4] The coalition's goals include strengthening Oregon's land use law and moving toward regional equity in tax base sharing and fair housing. In addition to creating a broader based and more sinuous support for land use, the coalition has persuaded the Metro Council to amend its "Regional Urban Growth Goals and Objectives" to strengthen its commitment to transit and affordable housing in the developing suburbs. At the instigation of the coalition, the council's Metro Policy Advisory Committee on growth planning has also added a new section on maintaining social and economic health in the older parts of the Portland metropolitan area. In 1996 the coalition began a broad-based effort to have a tax base sharing proposal debated in the Metro Council and in the Oregon legislature.

In May 1996, the coalition organized a "Metro Future Sabbath," on the Twin Cities model, as the kickoff for a grassroots drive to organize the region's churches in favor of metro reform. The initial meeting attracted 120 participants. Presenters included Robert Liberty, the executive director of 1,000 Friends of Oregon; Portland city commissioner Charlie Hales (also chair of the Metro Policy Advisory Committee); Bishop Ken Steiner of the Archdiocese of Portland; Rabbi Joey Wolf of Havurah Shalom Temple; and the Rev. Cecil Prescod, a pastor of the United Church of Christ.

Chicago, Illinois

Chicago, with 7.5 million people, is the nation's third-largest metropolitan region, finely divided into 262 cities, 244 school districts, and six counties (table 8-2 and map 8-2).[5] Its patterns of development and decline are far more dramatic than those of Minneapolis.[6] Instead of having one or two rings of suburban decline like Minneapolis, Chicago has over seven rings of declining suburbs on its south side, five to the west, and a thin ring of social change to the north.

Poverty is far more concentrated in many parts of Chicago's southern and western inner suburbs than in Minneapolis, social challenges are greater, and tax base resources are more limited. A drive through the empty malls and abandoned buildings of suburban Harvey, Markham, and Ford Heights recalls some of the third world's less favored areas. Chicago's other pole is the northwest quadrant, which has 80 percent of the new jobs and the strongest office markets, but only 20 percent of the region's residents.

Over the past decade, Chicago grew 4 percent in population and 40 percent in land area. "Grand Canyon"–like disparities characterize its fiscal situation.[7] In its declining southside suburbs, school districts with some of the region's highest school taxes spend $4,000 per pupil, while its northern and western suburbs, with their rich tax base and with the lowest school taxes in the region, spend $9,000. Chicago's problems are

Table 8-2. Selected Chicago Regional Statistics

	Central city	Inner suburbs	Outer suburbs	South developing suburbs	Northwest suburbs
Population, 1990	2,783,726	1,364,193	720,799	107,336	1,632,536
Households, 1990	1,025,174	503,820	242,870	36,044	590,134
Percentage of region's population, 1990	38.3	18.8	9.9	1.7	23.5
Median household income, 1989 (thousands of dollars)	26.3	37.8	36.7	49.6	54.1
Percentage children under age 5 in poverty, 1990	35.0	10.1	11.9	1.7	2.7
Percentage female-headed households with children, 1990	35.6	17.8	16.2	6.7	8.4
Percentage change in white children up to age 5 in 1980 to ages 10–14 in 1990	−29.2	−16.8	−12.1	34.6	11.7
Percentage change in jobs, 1980–90	−5.8	2.2	16.5	95.2	58.1
Market value per household, 1993 (thousands of dollars)	83.9	103.6	102.9	162.0	201.7
Percentage change in market value per household, 1980–93	50.7	25.3	26.4	45.1	48.2

Source: Metropolitan Area Program, Minneapolis.

immense, but a legion of declining, disenfranchised suburbs invite coalition building.

As these patterns of urban decline have played out over generations of growth in the Chicago metropolitan area, four distinct types of suburban communities have emerged: the socioeconomically declining inner suburbs; the outer-region satellite cities and low–tax capacity, developing suburbs; the northwestern region, commercial, high–tax capacity, developing suburbs; and the southern region, high–tax capacity, developing suburbs.[8] The city, the inner, older suburbs, and the satellite suburbs are home to 72 percent of the region's population.

The concentration of Chicago's population living in extreme poverty census tracts scarcely increased from 1980 (23.8 percent) to 1990 (25.5 percent), but the physical area of the distressed part of the city expanded at the second-fastest rate in the nation. The number of tracts in Chicago's area of extreme poverty increased by 36 percent (forty-seven tracts) during the 1980s. The number of census tracts considered poverty tracts, with between 20 percent and 39.9 percent of the residents poor, increased by 10 percent (thirty-seven tracts) over the decade.[9] As the core grew, Chicago's center was rapidly depopulating. Droves of people moved out of the distressed areas, pushed by the concentration effects of poverty into the middle-class sections of the city, the inner-ring suburbs, and beyond.

The city of Chicago had 72.9 percent non-Asian minority students. The inner suburbs had 34.4 percent and the outer suburbs 16.1 percent. Ten suburban school districts had a higher concentration of non-Asian minority students than the city schools. Twenty-two districts had more than 50 percent non-Asian elementary minority students, thirty-eight had more than 25 percent, and sixty-six had more than 10 percent. These figures contrast sharply with concentrations of 5.2 percent in the northwest developing suburbs and 1.2 percent in the southern developing suburbs. In these areas, 80 school districts had less than 1 percent and 143 districts had less than 5 percent non-Asian minority students.

Net losses of white preschool children from 1980 to 1990 ran to 29.2 percent in Chicago and 16.8 percent in the inner-ring suburbs. Thirty of these suburbs, mainly in the southern and western inner ring, had more rapid white flight than the city of Chicago. The northwestern and south developing suburbs gained, respectively, 12 percent and 35 percent more white children than were born in their communities over the decade.

In 1991, Chicago's crime rate was 11,623 serious crimes per 100,000 residents.[10] Nine suburbs, predominantly in the southern and western inner ring, had higher crime rates than Chicago's, and forty suburbs had crime rates above the regional average. In the insulated housing markets to the north, crime was low. Almost everywhere crime was low to begin with saw it decline further during the 1980s.

Most new highway spending went to support the northwest development boom. This vast supply of developmental infrastructure in restrictively zoned communities created a land use pattern that was particularly low density, economically inefficient, and environmentally dangerous. Between 1970 and 1990, the population of the metro area grew by 4 percent, while the land area expanded 46 percent for housing and 74 percent for commercial uses.[11]

The average tax base per household in the Chicago region was $121,007.[12] Chicago was at $83,884, or about two-thirds of the regional average. The outer-ring and inner-ring suburbs had low tax bases that were similar—$103,000 and $104,000, respectively. In all, fifty-nine suburbs (mainly on the southern and western inner ring) had less tax base per household than Chicago's, and 68 percent of the metropolitan population lived in cities with below-average tax bases. The northwest suburbs towered above the rest of the region at $202,000, and the south developing suburbs were not far behind, with an average of $162,000. On the high end were forty-eight cities with more than twice the regional average tax base per household and twenty-three with more than three times the regional average. Some of the largest tax bases per household were in a sector west of Midway Airport and south of O'Hare, owing to heavy commercial development in proximity to the two airports.

In the growth of real tax base per household over the decade, the northwestern developing suburbs (strong to begin with) saw the largest gains. Downtown development and loss of households fed Chicago's 50.7 percent increase (from $55,561 to $83,884 per household). Tax base growth was most sluggish in the inner and outer rings, respectively, at 25.3 percent ($82,705 to $103,608) and 26.4 percent ($81,391 to $102,850). As social needs proliferated, tax base declined in twenty-six cities, almost entirely in the western and southern inner suburbs. Again, the gainers were the northwestern developing suburbs, with a 48.2 percent increase (from $136,117 to $201,677 per household) and the south developing suburbs, with a 45.1 percent increase (from $111,676 to $162,002).

Among the 244 school districts in the Chicago region, the tax base disparity is 28 to 1. The largest tax bases are in the northwest developing suburbs and the lowest are in the southern suburbs, particularly the southern inner ring. Within the region, the disparity in annual spending per pupil amounts to 3 to 1. As in Minneapolis and Portland, computer modeling of Chicago's tax base sharing revealed that between 60 percent and 85 percent of the region's population and legislative districts would win under tax base sharing.

The six-county Chicago metropolitan region experienced a 13.5 percent increase from 1980 to 1990 in the number of jobs. Chicago lost 5.8 percent of its jobs over the decade, dropping from 1.56 million jobs in 1980 to 1.47 million jobs in 1990. Employment in the inner-ring suburbs increased by a modest 2.2 percent (16,000 jobs), but the outer-ring suburbs did much better, adding 48,000 jobs, a 16.5 percent increase. The geographically small south developing suburbs, with one-tenth the population of the large inner-ring suburbs, gained an extraordinary 27,000 jobs. The true employment leader was the northwestern suburban region with a 58.1 percent increase—458,000 jobs. The northwestern suburbs, by themselves, gained 80 percent of Chicago's new jobs during the 1980s. This meant that by 1990 almost two jobs were available for every household in this subregion, compared with barely one job per household in the inner-ring suburbs.

Chicago, under the leadership of the MacArthur Foundation, is just beginning to get out the message about regional polarization. A recent ballot initiative to take school funding off local property taxes passed in Chicago, the inner western and southern suburbs, and the satellite cities, but failed to gather the necessary votes statewide. More recently, the distinguished Ikenberry Commission, headed by the former president of the University of Illinois, has come forward with a call for greater statewide school equity. The Republican governor of Illinois, Jim Edgar, has bravely supported the commission's recommendations, but thus far his own party (which controls the state legislature) has refused to take action. Pressure is building for equity in the property-poor areas of the region.

Philadelphia, Pennsylvania

Philadelphia, the fifth-largest U.S. metropolitan area, is politically more fragmented than either Chicago or Minneapolis (table 8-3 and map 8-3).[13] The central city has a sprawling area of extreme poverty, but socioeconomic and racial change seem confined to the city neighborhoods and a few older inner boroughs in southeastern Delaware County and north of the city. Its pattern of suburban decline is not concentric but elongated, in a succession of older river towns and boroughs along the Delaware River Valley. Social needs are growing in a constellation of older boroughs tucked between growing townships throughout the region. The favored quarter in the Philadelphia region is a suburban growth center surrounding the King of Prussia corridor. Like its counterparts in Minneapolis and Chicago, this area encompasses a geographically small part of the region but dominates its economic growth.

Much of the Philadelphia region's suburban decline is occurring across the Delaware River around Camden, New Jersey, an area outside the scope of this study as well as the jurisdiction of the Pennsylvania legislature. On the Pennsylvania side of the region, almost half of the metropolitan population lives in the city of Philadelphia—hence its legislative strength. In terms of a political strategy in the state legislature, Philadelphia is the most politically powerful central city I have studied. In the other urban regions, between 30 percent and 40 percent of the total area population lives in the city.

Philadelphia in 1980 contained twenty-nine extreme poverty tracts—those where 40 percent or more of resident families lived in poverty. By 1990, this number had increased to thirty-seven tracts. The total number of households living in poverty tracts (areas with between 20 percent and 40 percent of the citizens below the poverty line) increased by 16 percent, from 205,405 in 1980 to 238,123 in 1990. By 1990, 41 percent of Philadelphia's 367 census tracts were poverty tracts.

Three distinct types of suburban communities have emerged in the Philadelphia metropolitan area: older cities and boroughs, middle-income townships, and affluent suburbs.[14]

Table 8-3. Selected Philadelphia Regional Statistics

	Central city	Low–tax base boroughs and cities	Low–tax base townships	High–tax base cities
Population, 1990	1,585,577	449,441	442,143	1,251,748
Households, 1990	603,075	174,688	160,491	444,954
Percentage of region's population, 1990	42.5	12.1	11.9	33.6
Median household income, 1989 (thousands of dollars)	24.6	31.4	37.1	51.5
Percentage children under age 5 in poverty, 1990	31.9	12.7	8.3	2.2
Percentage change in children under age 5 in poverty, 1979–89	–1.4	–19.7	–19.5	–52.6
Percentage female-headed households with children, 1990	35.8	21.7	13.4	7.7
Percentage change in white children up to age 5 in 1980 and to age 10–14 in 1990	–19.1	–18.5	–10.4	31.3
Percentage change in jobs, 1980–90	0.1	–2.7	18.5	50.3
Market value per household, 1993 (thousands of dollars)	57.4	95.4	119.3	202.5
Percentage change in market value per household, 1980–93	38.3	27.4	44.8	49.6

Source: Metropolitan Area Program, Minneapolis.

In the Philadelphia region (that is, strictly its Pennsylvania side), the concentration of school children eligible for free or reduced cost lunch ranged from 78.7 percent in Philadelphia to zero in the Spring-Ford district. Fifteen school districts had more than 20 percent poor students, and thirty-one districts had more than 10 percent. The highest concentration of poor were in Chester-Upland (62.9 percent), Norristown (45.7 percent), and Pottstown (44.4 percent). Most of these districts were older suburban communities. Ten school districts had less than 5 percent poor children.

The city of Philadelphia had 69.9 percent non-Asian minority students. The Chester-Upland district at 86.2 percent was fifteen points higher than the city. Seven suburban districts had more than 25 percent non-Asian elementary minority students; twenty districts had more than 10 percent. The most sharply defined corridor of non-Asian minority students is along the Delaware River Valley, particularly in Delaware County's inner, older suburbs. There is also a significant presence of such students in outer districts such as Coatesville (29.9) and Owen J. Roberts (27.5). In the affluent suburbs, twenty-five districts had less than 5 percent non-Asian minority students, and two districts had less than 1 percent non-Asian minority elementary students.

Between 1980 and 1990, Philadelphia and the older cities and boroughs lost roughly 19 percent of their white preschool children, while the middle-income townships lost 10.4 percent. Thirty-six Pennsylvania suburbs, mainly older cities and boroughs, had more rapid white flight than the city of Philadelphia. The counterpart of the exodus was a gain of preschool-age white children in 119 communities. The affluent suburbs alone gained 31 percent.

In 1993, the Philadelphia crime rate was 6,106 serious crimes per 100,000 residents. Crime was more rampant in some inner-ring suburbs than in the central city—for example, in Chester (12,692) and in Pottstown borough (6,255). At the other extreme, cities in the affluent suburbs were relatively crime free—for example, East Coventry (534), Northampton (746), and Bedminster (791).

Philadelphia's new infrastructure investment went northwest to support the development explosion from King of Prussia to Exton, into restrictively zoned low-density communities. Between 1970 and 1990, the population of the metro area grew by 3.8 percent, while the percentage of land used for urban purposes expanded by 36 percent.[15]

The average tax base per household in the Philadelphia region was $115,947, about half the regional average in Philadelphia proper ($57,366). The tax base in the affluent suburbs ($202,489) was 175 percent of the regional average. The tax base in older boroughs and cities was $95,431, 80 percent of the regional average, while the middle-income townships ($119,263) were just above average. Altogether, 57.8 percent of the Philadelphia metropolitan area's population lives in municipalities with tax bases below the regional average.

Despite a two-to-one disparity in annual spending per student, Philadelphia is not among the lowest metropolitan regions in educational outlays. Overall, Philadelphia spent $6,376, the tenth lowest of sixty-five school districts. Avon Grove at $5,454 and Coatesville at $5,483 in older Chester County were among the region's lowest-spending districts. The highest spenders were in highly exclusive housing markets such as Tredyffrin Easttown ($11,867) and Radnor ($10,881). In the Philadelphia region, our computer runs showed that more than 60 percent of the region would win under a tax base–sharing scenario.

From 1980 to 1990, jobs increased by 15 percent in the metropolitan region overall, a 13.6 increase in the number of jobs per capita. Philadelphia gained 0.1 percent in total jobs but, because of population loss, 6.6 percent in jobs per capita. The older cities and boroughs lost about 2.7 percent of their jobs and also experienced a small loss in jobs per capita. The middle-income townships gained 26,707 jobs over the decade, up

18.5 percent in jobs per capita. But the real story occurred in the affluent suburbs, which gained 235,939 new jobs, 90 percent of all job growth in the region. These suburbs experienced a 50 percent gain in the number of jobs and a 32 percent gain in the number of jobs per capita.

By all early indications, the need for equity runs deep in the Philadelphia community, especially in the case of the schools. Local land use groups like the Pennsylvania Environmental Council are taking the lead in the regional effort. Places like inner southeastern Delaware County, with the most rapidly increasing social needs in the region and the smallest tax base, have nowhere to go for help. As in Chicago, the demographics in Philadelphia are ripe for change.

Some Lessons in Coalition Building

These three metropolitan regions are finding the analytical methods tested in the Twin Cities to be handy tools for studying the dynamics of regional polarization. As they begin to form coalitions to break this pattern, progress—slow but real—suggests some lessons.

Lesson 1: Understand the Region's Demographics and Make Maps

Look for the declining older, low–tax base developing, and favored-quarter suburbs. Understand the local fiscal equity question and the local barriers to affordable housing. Measure road spending and land use. Seek out other regions' studies; finance and conduct others. Bring in the best scholars at area universities. In short, develop the most accurate and comprehensive picture of the region possible.

Use color maps to show trends. They are inexpensive to create, easy to reproduce for meetings or presentations, and truly worth a thousand words. Politicians, newspaper reporters, citizens groups, and other potential allies will not necessarily read reports or speeches, but they *will* look at color maps, over and over again. These maps will persuade them.

Lesson 2: Reach Out and Organize the Issue on a Personal Level

Political reform is about ideas, but individuals who are organizing bring it about. Political persuasion is about *selling* an idea to another person or group that has power. When regional trends are satisfactorily described,

167

some individual or group of people has to reach out, person to person, to make contact with the individuals and groups affected by them. Do not announce problems and disparities until after meeting these people.

Invite broad input from these individuals. Then lay out broad themes and the areas where regional progress is necessary—namely, affordable housing, tax base sharing, and land use planning. Talk about the experience of other states. Engage all affected constituencies in the crafting of legislation. This gives them all ownership and allows for adjustment to the peculiarities of the local terrain they know best—economic, physical, cultural, and political.

Lesson 3: Build a Broad, Inclusive Coalition

The coalition should stress two themes: It is in the long-term interest of the entire region to solve the problems of polarization, and it is in the immediate short-term interest of the vast majority of the region. The first argument is important for the long haul; the second gets the ball rolling.

A regional agenda, at the beginning, finds few elected altruistic supporters. The early political support for regional reform in the Twin Cities came entirely from legislators who believed their districts would benefit immediately or soon from part or all of our policy package. The politics of self-interest were particularly apparent in the housing bill, where the decisive suburban political support was largely defensive in character. The supporters believed that as long as the affluent, developing part of the region did not accept its fair share of affordable housing, the burden would fall on the older parts of the Twin Cities region. The low–tax base suburbs supported tax base sharing, because it gave them lower taxes and better services. They supported land use planning, because they did not want the developing suburbs to draw development away from them.

Lesson 4: "It's the Older Suburbs, Stupid"

Regional reformers should tape this message to their mirrors: The inner and low–tax base suburbs are the pivot point in American politics and are the reformers' key political allies. They were instrumental in electing Presidents Nixon, Carter, Reagan, and Clinton and an endless procession of officials in state office. The support of these suburbs alters the political dynamics. When regionalism becomes a suburban issue, it becomes possible. As long as regionalism is portrayed as a conflict between city and suburbs, the debate is over before it starts.

In this light, do not accept early rejection by these working-class, inner, older suburbs. These communities have been polarized for over a generation. Residential turnover and the growing impoverishment of their communities, the downturn in the U.S. economy for low-skilled workers, and relentless class- and raced-based political appeals have made many residents callused. Underneath they will soon realize that they need regionalism to have healthy, stable communities. They will come around as they come to see that a better future is possible, their alternatives are limited, cooperation will produce measurable benefits, and they have long-term, trustworthy friends in those who promote regionalism.

Lesson 5: Reach into the Central Cities to Make Sure the Message Is Understood

Central cities have a volatile political landscape. Without person-to-person contact in the inner city, the message will be misunderstood. Regionalism, if misperceived, threatens the power base of officials elected by poor, segregated constituencies. In this light, as in the older suburbs, the patterns of regional polarization must be reemphasized and the hopelessness of the present course revealed. Metropolitan reforms must not be presented as alternatives to existing programs competing for resources and power. Instead, they need to be seen as complements that would gradually reduce overwhelming central-city problems to manageable size and provide resources for community redevelopment through metropolitan equity. Fair housing is not an attempt to force poor minority communities to disperse but to allow individuals to choose—whether to remain or seek out opportunity, wherever it may be.

Lesson 6: Seek Out the Region's Religious Community

Politicians and self-interest arguments can move the agenda forward in the city and older suburbs. But they will not build a base of understanding in the affluent areas, and their determined opposition will slow progress. Churches and other houses of worship and religious organizations can bring a powerful new dimension to the debate—the moral dimension. How moral is it, they will ask, to divide a region into two communities, one prospering and enjoying all the benefits of metropolitan citizenship while the other bears most of its burdens? How moral is it to strand the region's poor people on a melting ice floe of resources at the region's core, or to destroy forests and farmland while older cities decline? Churches will broaden the reach of a regional movement. They can provide a legitimacy for its message in distrustful blue-collar suburbs, and understanding and a sense of responsibility and fair play in more affluent ones. Without the churches, the Twin Cities housing bill would not have been signed.

Lesson 7: Seek Out the Philanthropic Community, Established Reform Groups, and Business Leaders

Every day philanthropic organizations face the consequences of regional polarization, and their mission statements are often in line with regional reform. They can be important sources of financing for research and non-profit activities in support of regional solutions. The League of Women Voters can be helpful, as can entities like the National Civic League and established reform groups. All of these groups can confer establishment respectability to the regional cause. Many of these groups, by themselves, have been working on regional reform for a generation. In this light, seek their counsel as well as their support. Business leaders, particularly in the central business district and the older suburbs, can also be helpful and influential.

Lesson 8: Draw in Distinct but Compatible Issues and Organizations

In addition to the churches, the communities of color have a deep stake in this agenda, as do land use groups and a broad variety of environmental organizations that can reach into affluent suburbia. Women's and senior citizens' organizations, for example, want a variety of housing types in all communities for single mothers and retired people who cannot remain in their homes. These groups also want better transit. Regionalism is a multifaceted gemstone. In the power of its comprehensive solutions, it can show a bright face to many different constituencies to build broad support.

Lesson 9: With the Coalition, Seek Out the Media

Using factual information, suburban officials, churches, philanthropists, reform groups, and business leaders, seek out editorial boards, which by necessity must have a broad, far-reaching vision for the region. Reporters who have covered the same political stories over and over will be interested in something new and potentially controversial. They will like the maps, and straightforward news releases without too much theoretical discussion will get the message across.

Lesson 10: Prepare for Controversy

Professional regionalists have, over the years, explained away Minnesota's and Oregon's success with reforms as being the result of people's having reached some happy Olympian consensus. This is not true. Each reform was a tough battle, and each group of leaders had to build coalitions to weather intense opposition and controversy. This is how any important reform in politics comes about—from labor reform, to civil rights, to the women's movement. Reform never happens effortlessly or overnight. It entails building coalitions, creating power, and engaging in strenuous political struggle.

Lesson 11: Move Simultaneously on Several Fronts and Accept Good Compromises

Get as many issues moving as can effectively be managed, but not so many that nothing happens. Keep opponents busy and on the defensive. When many bills were moving in the Minnesota legislature, rarely were we completely defeated in any session. The governor of Minnesota vetoed the housing bill in 1993 but signed a land use reform bill. He vetoed housing in 1994 but signed the Metro Reorganization Act. He vetoed tax base sharing in 1995 but signed the housing bill. Had these bills not all been moving at once, no bill would have been signed. A platform for progress can be built step by step, bill by bill, session by session.

Parting Thoughts

By the year 2000, three out of four Americans will live in metropolitan regions with the same patterns of extravagant metropolitan development and of social and economic polarization described here. We cannot afford to throw away people and cities, and we must not accept anyone's doing so.

The agenda sketched here to deal with growing regional instability and disparities will evolve in the negotiation, reformulation, and synthesis that make up the political process. The issues are difficult, controversial—and of mutual concern. This is the real importance of this discussion: the realization that our metropolitan areas are suffering from a set of problems too massive for an individual city to confront alone, the same problems that have caused the decline and death of some of our largest urban centers. Unless we concentrate our efforts on finding new solutions, we can expect no better outcome in the future. It is my hope that the Twin Cities region and other regions can work together—reason together—to solve our common problems.

Some states, including Minnesota and Oregon, have made progress on parts of a metropolitan agenda, but none has confronted these issues comprehensively enough or early enough to turn the tide. We can learn much from the efforts of other metropolitan areas and much from their failures. Our problems are already big and urgent; we gain nothing by waiting to act.

Appendix

The Evolution of the Metropolitan Council

The Metropolitan Council was created in 1967 as a policysetting or planning agency.[1] It is composed of sixteen members, each representing a district and a chair, all appointed by the governor of Minnesota. From the beginning, forces have debated whether the council should be appointed or elected.

Until 1994, the council supervised the agencies created in response to specific needs for regional coordination: the Metropolitan Transit Commission, the Regional Transit Board, and the Metropolitan Waste Control Commission. In terms of the Metropolitan Airports Commission, the council continues to have the authority to review and approve certain capitol improvements of "metro significance" over $5 million at Minneapolis-Saint Paul International Airport and over $2 million at other regional airports, and of course has ultimate authority over the siting of a new airport.[2] In 1994, the waste control commission and the transit commission and board were abolished and, for the first time, the council assumed direct operational control over these services. Until 1994, the council appointed the members (except the chairs) of these agencies and had review authority over their capital budgets and requests for federal funds.[3] With less power over the Metropolitan Airports Commission, the council could only suspend certain of its capital projects. A tortuous debate always challenged the council's authority over these agencies, specifically where the line is drawn between its planning and operational authority. Periodically, the Minnesota legislature enlarged the council's formal review authority over agency budgets. But the agencies (with staffs and annual budgets that dwarfed the council's) grew independent and developed their own constituencies in the legislature, and they became determined to pursue their own courses of action without coordinating with each other or the council.

The Metropolitan Council Act of 1967 directed the council to develop a comprehensive plan to guide the region's growth. The plan, the Metropolitan Development Guide, has evolved chapters in ten areas: health, aviation, housing, recreational open space, transportation, solid waste management, sewage disposal, surface water management, water use and availability, and law and justice. Each chapter is a comprehensive statement of the policies and objectives that should control the region's development in that area. Housing, transportation, and sewage are the most relevant to this inquiry. The most recent chapter, the Regional Blueprint, replaces the Metropolitan Development Investment Framework (MDIF) for rural services policies and policies for reviewing Metropolitan Urban Service Area (MUSA) expansion requests. It also attempts to revise the framework for the work of pulling together and revising the previous chapters.

Housing

For regional housing, the June 1985 Housing Chapter of the Metropolitan Development Guide identifies four goals:

—Affordable housing "in a choice of locations for people of all income levels";

—Planning development of housing for all stages of life and for people with special housing needs;

—Maintenance and improvement of existing housing and neighborhoods; and

—Promoting energy efficiency in all housing, new and old, and encouraging all levels of government to become involved in providing affordable housing and facilitating its development.[4]

The significance of the council's housing mission is enhanced by its empowerment to serve as a regional housing and redevelopment authority, to administer the federal Section 8 program, and to review federal housing grant applications.[5] Throughout the 1970s the council developed one of the most ambitious plans for suburban affordable housing in the country.

Pursuant to this authority, the council adopted Policy 13 (later Policy 39), which gave it substantial leverage over suburban communities seeking funding: "In reviewing applications for funds, the Met Council will recommend priority in funding based on the local government's current provision of housing opportunities for people with low and moderate incomes, and its plans and programs to provide such housing opportunities in the future." Explaining this policy, the council notes that it "applies to all local applications for state and federal funding." Policy 34 calls for the council to use its review powers to encourage communities to meet the needs of low-income residents areawide rather than strictly locally. Policy 38 requires the council to apply its review guidelines to the housing elements of the comprehensive plans and development proposals of local communities. These council policies resulted in a dramatic improvement in the distribution of housing opportunities throughout the Twin Cities metropolitan area. The suburban share of subsidized housing grew from 10 percent in 1971 to 41 percent in 1983.

In the early 1980s, the Met Council stopped enforcing this policy but has never rescinded it. It argued (with questionable logic) that it no longer had sufficient federal housing resources to continue. Although massive federal waste control resources also disappeared during this period, the council created a regional funding source for sewers. It did nothing about housing.

The Regional Blueprint states that local comprehensive plans amendments and MUSA extensions will be reviewed for housing strategies and actions that will show that a community is providing its share of the region's low- and moderate-income and life-cycle housing.

Transportation

The guide chapter on transportation involves plans from many agencies: the Minnesota Department of Transportation; the seven county highway departments; city streets and public works departments; planning bodies at every level of government; and a wide range of business firms, citizens groups, and individuals who have ideas on how to use private cars more efficiently. These varied interests were brought together in the Transportation Advisory Board, created by the council in 1974 to develop transportation programs for the region.

The guide's transportation chapter spells out the policies under which the council will exercise its power to approve highway projects in the metropolitan area proposed by state or local governments. This power allows the council to play a critical role in the overall regional strategy by deciding how land will be used, what will be located where, and what the character of the region's overall development will be.

Sewerage

Likewise, the sewerage chapter could play a vital role in comprehensive regional planning. The council was established in response to the regional sewage problem. Its first major undertaking was development of an inte-grated waste management system, encompassing all sewage interceptors and wastewater treatment operations in the seven-county metropolitan area. The council's interest in the function is twofold: to ensure high standards of water quality and to control the location of new develop-ment. Again, though the potential of this concept is significant, how it has been carried out has been singularly unimpressive.

Under the forerunner to the Metropolitan Waste Control Commis-sion, the Minneapolis-Saint Paul Sanitary Sewer District had what might be described as marginal cost pricing. The cost of sewers rose with the in-terceptor's distance from the central treatment plant. This pricing struc-ture appropriately distributed the cost of expansion. But in 1969 the suburbs, using an average cost–pricing analysis, decided they were being overcharged. The solution that was found then, which began the reversal of fiscal burdens of expansion back to the urban core, was to regionalize the cost of treatment structures. In addition, future users were charged for underreserved capacity, which was eventually converted to an availability charge for new development. According to Robert Einsweiler, the Met Council's first executive director and current director of research for the Lincoln Land Institute, that "took the pressure off individual communities to be prudent."[6] In 1987, the Minnesota legislature totally regionalized the cost of all capital and operating expenses, making it virtually costless for individual communities to add sewer capacity.

The sewer policy is replete with conflicting, meaningless statements. In practice, policy has been dominated by the Waste Control Commission (now merged into the Met Council), an aggressive agency bent on maxi-mizing regional capacity. Through exceptions to the MUSA line, the vast excess regional sewerage capacity grew and grew. The profile presented by the council in sewerage and highway skirmishes is one of a low-density development promoter rather than a responsible manager of regional growth.

Metropolitan Development Investment Framework and the Regional Blueprint

The Regional Blueprint, which replaces the Metropolitan Development Investment Framework (MDIF), attempts to give coherence to council plans in other chapters of the development guide. It does this by estab-lishing an overall policy for supporting development with major regional facilities like sewers and highways and by setting the general direction of the Twin Cities metropolitan area's future development patterns.[7]

The blueprint contains procedures for guiding decisions about regional investment and development proposals submitted to the council for review, for preparing reports on the region's fiscal health and the degree to which council decisions reflects its policies, for helping to ensure that regional commissions carry out council policies, and for resolving issues resulting from changes in a community's expectation about its growth.

Land Use

The council's powers under the Metropolitan Development Guide were augmented by the Metropolitan Land Planning Act of 1976.[8] The act required all metropolitan cities to submit "comprehensive plans" to the Met Council. The plans had to be consistent with the growth projections and infrastructure planning of the council in its Metropolitan Development Guide. There are four metropolitan "systems," or policy areas, over which the council has strong regional authority by statute: transportation, airports, wastewater treatment, and open space. Under the Land Planning Act, a local government unit's comprehensive plan must contain a local land use plan, a transportation plan, and a community facilities plan.[9]

The Land Planning Act allows the council to require a local community to "modify a comprehensive plan or any part thereof which may have a *substantial impact* on or contain a *substantial departure* from metropolitan systems plans [emphasis added]."[10] These terms are broad and open ended, but the Met Council has narrowly construed its authority. Under a system of self-imposed restraint, the council will require a plan amendment only when the local comprehensive plan imposes a burden on a metropolitan system that "threatens its capacity"—a fairly cataclysmic event.[11] Consequently, the council has rarely used its authority to shape regional planning, and the Twin Cities region has continued to develop in an exceedingly low-density, restrictive, fragmented way.

The Metropolitan Agricultural Preserves Act of 1980 gave specific legislative approval for the council's concept of a metropolitan urban service area.[12] The law provides a tax advantage for farmland designated for agricultural purposes and gives the council the authority to approve such designation as part of the regional land planning system.

The Metropolitan Significance Act of 1976 charged the council with preparing criteria and procedures for identifying and reviewing matters having a major impact on the Twin Cities metropolitan area.[13] Under this act, the council may suspend matters considered to have metropolitan significance, for up to one year. It may block housing projects, shopping centers, and other major developments that, in its judgment, do not conform with regional plans.[14]

An impressive range of formal powers lies with the Met Council through the Metropolitan Development Guide and the Regional Blueprint, the Land Planning Act, the review of agency budgets, and the approval of certain federal funds for local units of government. How it has exercised these powers in the past dozen years has been unimpressive.

Track Record: Failure and Potential

Despite the regional authority embodied in the council and the existence of a superstructure for tackling the problems of the city and older suburbs, few problems have been solved. Instead, the Met Council has become part of the problem of regional economic polarization, helping exclusive, economically powerful communities to grow at the expense of the region. The council has neither promoted economic stability and equity nor provided consistent leadership to deal with regional conflict.

The Regional Blueprint and its predecessor, the Metropolitan Development Investment Framework, and many council planning documents acknowledge the interrelations between rapid peripheral growth and core stability, but this symbiosis has never been a significant part of the council's agenda. Since its founding, the council's central ethos has been planning efficient and cost-effective suburban growth—"good sprawl," former council staffer Ann Hurlburt called it. Until recently, this ethos has been reflected in the structural relationship between the council and regional agencies. The operating agencies—waste control, transit, and airports—were independent and self-financed. The council, an increasingly ineffectual planning agency, had little real control over the agencies' actions.

Finally, in 1991, the Minnesota legislature ordered the Met Council to study the health of the fully developed area. The results, summarized in a report entitled "Trouble in the Core," dismayed the council, which had never dealt effectively with regional conflict.[15]

An agenda for governmental action comes from many sources: government, business, advocacy, and good-government groups. In the early years, the best members and governors on regional issues were Republicans, and council members were strong. Instead of ducking confrontations, the council fought tremendous battles on suburban airports, sewers, suburban affordable housing, parks, and landfills.

Beginning in the early 1980s with Democratic governor Rudy Perpich, council appointees lacked a background in and an understanding of metropolitan affairs. Thereafter, the council's performance and ability to stand up for its authority began to decline rapidly. By the 1980s, when regional systems were in place to ensure efficient growth, the strong regionalists who had worked to establish these policies had retired. The new generation of Met Council members did not fully appreciate the significance of their predecessors' accomplishments and lacked a vision of how to carry a regional agenda forward. By the late 1980s, many council members actually opposed various basic regional principles. Without a commitment to regionalism and a vision of its future, the Met Council could not deal with the natural and healthy conflicts that arise from the original metropolitan enactments in the Twin Cities.

Concurrently, the leadership and ability of the Citizens League became less strong and resolute on regional issues. The league became a conservative reactive force, rather than a reform entity unafraid of the local controversy involved in regional legislation. During the 1980s, as the league became much more interested in many other issues such as school choice and scaling back state local government aid, the opponents of regional reform deeply damaged and almost destroyed the Met Council and the framework of regional legislative acts that had been put in place in the 1960s and 1970s.

Many of the metropolitan acts gave the council and its planners the ability to veto unwise or inefficient local growth decisions. Without a commitment or an agenda, carrying out these policies became difficult. Increasingly, developers who wanted profits and cities that wanted tax base lobbied and fought the council. Until the Land Stewardship Project (a nonprofit land use group) began to oppose development decisions in Washington County in the late 1980s and early 1990s, there had been no countervailing force. The central cities and older suburbs have been strikingly absent from these debates, despite their manifold interests. In time, council members and planners—consistently beaten by cities, real estate developers, and their lobbyists—either quit, were fired, or simply stopped saying "No." As the council receded from public attention, the regulated community captured the council, and council staff began to look for ways to help develop affluent communities.

As the Met Council has floundered, it has been sidestepped with increasing frequency on important regional decisions: siting of a regional racetrack (Canterbury Downs), a local World Trade Center, a regional zoo, and (most spectacularly) the Mall of America, a massive shopping complex that required equally massive new highway construction. The counties wrested control from the council over the issues of solid waste management and light-rail transit. Finally, the Minnesota legislature, responding to claims of unfair treatment by cities, gave local zoning decisions precedence over the council's metropolitan review powers conferred in the Land Planning Act. Similarly, arguing that the Metropolitan Transit Commission was not responding to suburban transit needs, the southwestern and east developing suburbs received permission to keep their local property tax contribution to the regional transit system and operate their own independent ones. By the early 1990s this step would throw regional transit into a fiscal crisis.

Each of these powers belonged by law to the Met Council, and many believe that a regional perspective would have resulted in better decisions. However, in each case the political powers of the state, the counties, or the cities overwhelmed the council's political power.[16] During all this time the Metropolitan Council presented virtually no affirmative legislative agenda.

In the mid-1990s, the advent of a newly reinvigorated regional agenda and a legislative power base in the central cities and inner and low–tax base suburbs helped to revitalize the Met Council. It was forced to consider issues such as housing, land use, and transportation in the context of what is happening at the region's core. Its progress, though unspectacular, has been a major improvement. After more than a decade of dormancy, the council helped spearhead the Livable Communities Act, improved language in the Regional Blueprint on affordable housing, put forth legislation to repeal the uniform sewer pricing policy, and is beginning to tentatively discuss denser land use patterns. An elected council would provide the needed impetus and regional leadership to bring about real progress on these and other issues.

Notes

Chapter One

1. See John D. Kasarda, "Inner-City Concentrated Poverty and Neighborhood Distress: 1970–1990," *Housing Policy Debate,* vol. 4, no. 3 (1993), p. 255. See also Paul A. Jargowsky and Mary Jo Bane, "Ghetto Poverty in the United States, 1970–1980," in Christopher Jencks and Paul E. Peterson, eds., *The Urban Underclass* (Brookings, 1991), p. 240.

2. A ghetto is a neighborhood with more than 40 percent of the residents living below the federal poverty line. A transitional or mixed neighborhood has between 20 and 40 percent of the residents in poverty. Kasarda, "Inner-City Concentrated Poverty."

3. Kasarda, "Inner-City Concentrated Poverty"; Paul Jargowsky, "Ghetto Poverty among Blacks in the 1980s," *Journal of Policy Analysis and Management,* vol. 13, no. 2 (1994), p. 288; Jargowsky and Bane, "Ghetto Poverty."

4. Douglas S. Massey and Nancy A. Denton, *American Apartheid: Segregation and the Making of the Underclass* (Harvard University Press, 1993).

5. After Milwaukee, Wisconsin; Detroit, Michigan; and Buffalo, New York. Jargowsky, "Ghetto Poverty among Blacks," p. 306.

6. U.S. Department of Commerce, Bureau of the Census, Data User Services Division, *1990 Census of Population and Housing,* Summary Tape File 3A (1992).

7. Jonathan Crane, "Effects of Neighborhoods on Dropping Out of School and Teenage Childbearing," in Jencks and Peterson, *The Urban Underclass,* pp. 299–320; Susan E. Mayer, "How Much Does a High School's Racial and Socioeconomic Mix Affect Graduation and Teenage Fertility Rates," in Jencks and Peterson, *The Urban Underclass,* pp. 321–41; Massey and Denton, *American Apartheid,* pp. 169–70; Dennis P. Hogan and Evelyn M. Kitagawa, "The Impact of Social Status, Family Structure, and Neighborhood on the Fertility of Black Adolescents," *American Journal of Sociology,* vol. 90, no. 4 (1985), pp. 825–55; Frank F. Furstenberg Jr. and others, "Race Differences in the Timing of Adolescent Intercourse," *American Sociological Review,* vol. 52 (August 1987), pp. 511–18; Elijah Anderson, "Neighborhood Effects on Teenage Pregnancy," in Jencks and Peterson, *The Urban Underclass,* pp. 375–98; Sara McLanahan and Irwin Garfinkel, "Single Mothers, the Underclass, and Social

Policy," *Annals of the American Academy of Political and Social Science,* vol. 501 (January 1989), pp. 92–104.

8. Massey and Denton, *American Apartheid.* See also James E. Rosenbaum and Susan J. Popkin, "Employment and Earnings of Low-Income Blacks Who Move to Middle-Class Suburbs," in Jencks and Peterson, *The Urban Underclass,* pp. 342–56; James E. Rosenbaum and others, "Social Integration of Low-Income Black Adults in Middle-Class White Suburbs," *Social Problems,* vol. 38, no. 4 (1991), pp. 448–61; James E. Rosenbaum, Marilynn J. Kulieke, and Leonard S. Rubinowitz, "White Suburban Schools' Responses to Low-Income Black Children: Sources of Successes and Problems," *Urban Review,* vol. 20, no. 1 (1988), pp. 28–41; James E. Rosenbaum and Susan Popkin, "Black Pioneers: Do Their Moves to the Suburbs Increase Economic Opportunity for Mothers and Children?", *Housing Policy Debate*, vol. 2, no. 4 (1991), pp. 1179–1213; James E. Rosenbaum and Julie Kaufman, "Educational and Occupational Achievements of Low Income Black Youth in White Suburbs," paper presented at the 1991 annual meeting of the American Sociological Association, Cincinnati, October 18. See also Schools section below.

9. Minnesota Department of Children, Families and Learning, unpublished data.

10. Minneapolis Police Department, unpublished data; U.S. Department of Commerce, *1990 Census of the United States.*

11. Dirk Johnson, "A Nice City's Nasty Distinction: Minneapolis Murder Rate Soars," *New York Times*, July 30, 1996, p. 1.

12. John D. Kasarda, "Urban Industrial Transition and the Underclass," *Annals of the American Academy of Political and Social Science,* vol. 501 (1989), pp. 26–47.

13. Minneapolis City Assessor and Minnesota Department of Revenue, unpublished data.

14. Minnesota Department of Jobs and Training, Research and Statistics Office, *Twin Cities Area Average Covered Employment, First Quarter 1992* (Minneapolis, June 25, 1993).

15. Minnesota Department of Children, Families and Learning, unpublished data.

16. Minnesota Department of Jobs and Training, Research and Statistics Office, *Twin Cities Area Average Covered Employment, First Quarter 1992* (Minneapolis, June 25, 1993).

17. Barbara L. Lukermann and Michael P. Kane, "Land Use Practices: Exclusionary Zoning, De Facto or De Jure: An Examination of the Practices of Ten Suburban Communities in the Twin Cities Metropolitan Area," Center for Urban and Regional Affairs, University of Minnesota, Minneapolis, April 1994; and supporting memordum from Robert Marthaler to Tim Thompson, "A Memo Concerning Lakeville's Zoning Ordinance and City Actions Incongruent with the Comprehensive Plan and Other Practices and Policies Effecting the Provision of Low to Moderate Income Housing," June 1, 1993.

18. U.S. Department of Commerce, *1990 Census of the United States.*

19. U.S. Department of Commerce, *1990 Census*; Dane Smith, "Legislature to Get Proposals to Mend Disparities," *Minneapolis Star Tribune*, December 11, 1992, p. 26A. See also J. Hanks and T. Lomax, *Roadway Congestion in Major Urban Ar-*

eas, 1982–1988 (College Station, Tex.: Texas Transportation Institute, Texas A&M University, 1990); cited in Minnesota Department of Trade and Economic Development, Business Development and Analysis Division, *Compare Minnesota: An Economic and Statistical Fact Book, 1992/1993* (Saint Paul, Minn.: 1992).

20. Personal communication from Al Schenkelberg, director, Highway Programming Section, Minnesota Department of Transportation, November 21, 1992. Ken Pekarek, Land Management Information Center, Minnesota Planning, assigned project code numbers from the Mn/DOT budgets provided by Mr. Schenkelberg to travel behavior inventory regions developed by the Metropolitan Council. This division of expenditures allowed regional spending values to be determined.

21. James N. Denn, "Mn/DOT Announces Reconstruction Plans for I-35W and I-494," press release from Minnesota Department of Transportation, January 12, 1993.

22. Metropolitan Council, "Preliminary GIS Land Use Report," Saint Paul, Minn., October 25, 1993.

23. Ibid.

24. Metropolitan Waste Control Commission, *Annual Reports* (Saint Paul, Minn.: 1971–94).

25. Thomas F. Luce, Jr., Barbara Lukermann, and Herbert Mohring, "Regional Sewer System Rate Structure Study," Hubert H. Humphrey Institute of Public Affairs, University of Minnesota, Minneapolis, December 7, 1992.

26. Minnesota Department of Revenue, unpublished data.

27. Minnesota Department of Children, Families and Learning, unpublished data.

28. Bureau of the Census, *1987 Census of Agriculture*, vol. 1, pt. 23 (Department of Commerce, 1989).

29. Minnesota Pollution Control Agency, Division of Water Quality, *Protecting Water Quality in Urban Areas* (St. Paul, Minn., 1989); Ann McCammon, "The Impact of Urban Sprawl on Water Quality in the Twin Cities Area," term paper, University of Minnesota Law School, Minneapolis, May 8, 1992.

30. Children's Defense Fund—Minnesota, "Children's Defense Fund—Minnesota Legislative Scorecard for 1991," Corrected Edition, St. Paul, Minn., August 1991.

31. Neal R. Peirce, *Citistates: How Urban America Can Prosper in a Competitive World* (Washington: Seven Locks Press, 1993).

32. David Rusk, *Cities without Suburbs* (Washington: Woodrow Wilson Center Press, 1993).

33. Anthony Downs, *New Visions for Metropolitan America* (Brookings and Lincoln Institute of Land Policy, 1994).

34. Peter Calthorpe, *The Next American Metropolis: Ecology, Community, and the American Dream* (New York: Princeton Architectural Press, 1993).

35. Office of the President, "Leadership and Coordination of Fair Housing in Federal Programs: Affirmatively Furthering Fair Housing, Executive Order 12892 of January 17, 1994," *Weekly Compilation of Presidential Documents*, January 24, 1994, pp. 110–14.

36. E. J. Dionne Jr., *Why Americans Hate Politics* (Simon & Schuster, 1991); Stanley B. Greenberg, *Middle-Class Dreams: The Politics and Power of the New*

American Majority (Times Books, 1995); Kevin Phillips, *The Politics of Rich and Poor. Wealth and the American Electorate in the Reagan Aftermath* (Random House, 1990); Kevin Phillips, *Arrogant Capital: Washington, Wall Street, and the Frustration of American Politics* (Boston: Little, Brown, 1994); Kevin Phillips, *Boiling Point: Republicans, Democrats, and the Decline of Middle-Class Prosperity* (Random House, 1993); Kevin Phillips, *The Emerging Republican Majority* (New Rochelle, N.Y.: Arlington House, 1969); Haynes Johnson, *Divided We Fall: Gambling with History in the Nineties* (W. W. Norton, 1994); William Greider, *Who Will Tell the People? The Betrayal of American Democracy* (Simon & Schuster, 1992); Thomas Byrne Edsall with Mary D. Edsall, *Chain Reaction: The Impact of Race, Rights and Taxes on American Politics* (W. W. Norton, 1991).

37. The Met Council was created in 1967 with jurisdiction in the seven regional counties of Hennepin, Ramsey, Anoka, Scott, Carver, Dakota, and Washington. Its members are appointed by the governor and (until 1994) had loose supervisory authority over separate regional transit, waste control, and airport agencies.

Chapter Two

1. Metropolitan Council, *Trouble at the Core: The Twin Cities under Stress,* Pub. No. 310-92-116 (Saint Paul, Minn., November 18, 1992).

2. John D. Kasarda, "Inner-City Concentrated Poverty and Neighborhood Distress: 1970–1990," *Housing Policy Debate,* vol. 4, no. 3 (1993), p. 255; Paul A. Jargowsky and Mary Jo Bane, "Ghetto Poverty in the United States, 1970–1980," in Christopher Jencks and Paul Peterson, eds., *The Urban Underclass* (Brookings, 1991), p. 240.

3. John S. Adams, "Housing Submarkets in an American Metropolis," in John Fraser Hart, ed., *Our Changing Cities* (Johns Hopkins University Press, 1991), pp. 108–26; Homer Hoyt, *The Structure and Growth of Residential Neighborhoods in American Cities* (Government Printing Office, 1939), reprinted in 1966 by the author with analysis of the 1960 census tract data; Ronald Abler and John S. Adams, *A Comparative Atlas of America's Great Cities: Twenty Metropolitan Regions* (University of Minnesota Press and Association of American Geographers, 1976); John S. Adams, *Housing America in the 1980s* (New York: Russell Sage Foundation, 1987).

4. In the Twin Cities metro area, the population increased 15.5 percent overall between 1980 and 1990. Bureau of the Census, *United States Population—Metropolitan Statistical Areas* (Department of Commerce, 1994).

5. Ibid.

6. Kasarda calls these extreme-poverty tracts; Jargowsky and Bane call them ghetto neighborhoods.

7. Kasarda, "Concentrated Poverty."

8. Ibid., pp. 290–93.

9. Ibid.

10. Bureau of the Census, Data User Services Division, *1990 Census of Population and Housing*, Summary Tape File 3A (Department of Commerce, 1992).

11. See Philip Meininger, "The Minneapolis Inner City: A Metropolitan Step-child, " draft (Minneapolis, Minn.: Minneapolis City Planning Department, 1993), p. 57. See also Erol R. Ricketts and Isabel V. Sawhill, "Defining and Measuring the Under-class," *Journal of Policy Analysis and Management*, vol. 7, no. 2 (1988), pp. 316–25.

12. See Jargowsky and Bane, "Ghetto Poverty"; Paul Jargowsky, "Ghetto Poverty Among Blacks in the 1980s," *Journal of Policy Analysis and Management,* vol. 13, no. 2 (1994), pp. 288–311; Douglas S. Massey and Nancy A. Denton, *American Apartheid: Segregation and the Making of the Underclass* (Harvard University Press, 1993).

13. Jargowsky, "Ghetto Poverty Among Blacks," p. 306.

14. About 20 percent lived in the southern and western developing suburbs, 15 percent in the inner suburbs, and less than 5 percent in the mid- and east developing suburbs. The highest concentrations of African-American suburban middle-class households were in two sectors: one to the south and one to the north. The southern sector includes Bloomington (249 African-American households), Eagan (243), and Burnsville (158). The northern sector includes Brooklyn Park (246) and Golden Valley (134). These suburbs are virtually all white. Both of these colonies of African-American middle-class residents follow the Adams sectoral housing model (see discussion of model above).

15. William Julius Wilson, *The Truly Disadvantaged: The Inner City, the Under-class, and Public Policy* (University of Chicago Press, 1987); Massey and Denton, *American Apartheid*; Christopher Jencks and Paul E. Peterson, eds., *The Urban Un-derclass* (Brookings, 1991); Nicholas Lemann, *The Promised Land: The Great Black Migration and How It Changed America* (Knopf, 1991); Nicholas Lemann, "The Ori-gins of the Underclass," *Atlantic Monthly,* vol. 257 (1986), pp. 31–55; Hope Melton, "Ghettos of the Nineties: The Consequences of Concentrated Poverty" (Saint Paul, Minn.: Department of Planning and Economic Development, November 10, 1993).

16. See generally George C. Galster, "A Cumulative Causation Model of the Un-derclass: Implications for Urban Economic Development Policy," in George C. Gal-ster and Edward W. Hill, eds., *The Metropolis in Black and White: Place, Power and Polarization* (New Brunswick, N.J.: Center for Urban Policy Research, 1992), pp. 180–215.

17. Wilson, *The Truly Disadvantaged,* p. 56.

18. Jonathan Crane, "Effects of Neighborhoods on Dropping Out of School and Teenage Childbearing," in Jencks and Peterson, *The Urban Underclass,* pp. 299–320; Susan E. Mayer, "How Much Does a High School's Racial and Socioeconomic Mix Affect Graduation and Teenage Fertility Rates?" in Jencks and Peterson, *The Urban Underclass,* pp. 321–41; Massey and Denton, *American Apartheid,* pp. 169–70; Den-nis P. Hogan and Evelyn M. Kitagawa, "The Impact of Social Status, Family Struc-ture, and Neighborhood on the Fertility of Black Adolescents," *American Journal of Sociology,*vol. 90, no. 4 (January 1985), pp. 825–55; Frank F. Furstenberg and others, "Race Differences in the Timing of Adolescent Intercourse," *American Sociological Review,* vol. 52 (August 1987), pp. 511–18; Elijah Anderson, "Neighborhood Effects on Teenage Pregnancy," in Jencks and Peterson, *The Urban Underclass,* pp. 375–98; Sara McLanahan and Irwin Garfinkel, "Single Mothers, the Underclass, and Social

Policy," *Annals of the American Academy of Political and Social Science,* vol. 501 (January 1989), pp. 92–104.

19. Crane, "Effects of Neighborhoods," pp. 299–320; Mayer, "Graduation and Teenage Fertility Rates," pp. 321–41; Massey and Denton, *American Apartheid,* pp. 169–70.

20. Massey and Denton, *American Apartheid,* pp. 180–82.

21. Joleen Kirschenman and Kathryn M. Neckerman, "'We'd Love to Hire Them, But . . . ': The Meaning of Race for Employers," in Jencks and Peterson, *The Urban Underclass,* pp. 203–32; Roger Shuy, "Teacher Training and Urban Language Problems," in Paul Stoller, ed., *Black American English: Its Background and Its Usage in the Schools and in Literature* (Dell, 1975), pp. 168–85.

22. John Baugh, *Black Street Speech: Its History, Structure, and Survival* (University of Texas Press, 1983), pp. 11–22; William Labov, *Language in the Inner City: Studies in the Black English Vernacular* (University of Pennsylvania Press, 1972); William Labov, "The Logic of Nonstandard English," in Stoller, *Black American English*; William Labov and Wendell Harris, "Defacto Segregation of Black and White Vernaculars," in David Sankoff, ed., *Diversity and Diachrony*, Current Issues in Linguistic Theory Series, vol. 53 (Philadelphia: Benjamins, 1986), pp. 1–24; William Labov, ed., *Locating Language in Time and Space* (Academic Press, 1980).

23. Kenneth B. Clark, *Dark Ghetto: Dilemmas of Social Power* (Harper & Row, 1965); Wilson, *The Truly Disadvantaged*; Massey and Denton, *American Apartheid,* pp. 148–58, 167; Elijah Anderson, *A Place on the Corner* (University of Chicago Press, 1978); Elliot Liebow, *Talley's Corner: A Study of Negro Streetcorner Men* (Boston: Little, Brown, 1967); Lee Rainwater, *Behind Ghetto Walls: Black Families in a Federal Slum* (Chicago: Aldine, 1970); Carol Stack, *All Our Kin: Strategies for Survival in a Black Community* (Harper & Row, 1974); Terry M. Williams and William Kornblum, *Growing Up Poor* (Lexington, Mass.: Lexington Books, 1985); Anderson, "Neighborhood Effects on Teenage Pregnancy"; Lemann, "The Origins of the Underclass"; Elijah Anderson, "The Code of the Streets," *Atlantic Monthly,* May 1994, pp. 80–94.

24. Elijah Anderson, "Sex Codes and Family Life among Poor Inner-City Youths," *Annals of the American Academy of Political and Social Science,* vol. 501 (January 1989), pp. 59–78; Anderson, "Neighborhood Effects on Teenage Pregnancy," pp. 382–98.

25. Anderson, "Sex Code"; Anderson, "The Code of the Streets."

26. Anderson, "The Code of the Streets"; Wesley G. Skogan, *Disorder and Decline: Crime and the Spiral of Decay in American Neighborhoods* (University of California Press, 1992), pp. 21–50; Ralon B. Taylor, Stephen D. Gottfredson, and Sidney Brower, "Attachment to Place: Discriminant Validity, and Impacts of Disorder and Diversity," *American Journal of Community Psychology,* vol. 13, no. 5 (1985), pp. 525–42; Massey and Denton, *American Apartheid,* pp. 137–39. See also Crime section below.

27. Massey and Denton, *American Apartheid,* p. 166.

28. John U. Ogbu, *Minority Education and Caste: The American System in Cross-Cultural Perspective* (Academic Press, 1978); John U. Ogbu, "Minority Status and Schooling in Plural Societies," *Comparative Education Review,* vol. 27, no. 2

(1983), pp. 168–90; Signithia Fordham and John U. Ogbu, "Black Students' School Success: Coping with the 'Burden of Acting White,'" *Urban Review,* vol. 18, no. 3 (1986), pp. 176–206; Signithia Fordham, "Racelessness as a Factor in Black Students' School Success: Pragmatic Strategy or Pyrrhic Victory?" *Harvard Educational Review*, vol. 58, no. 1 (1988), pp. 54–84.

29. This section is adapted from a draft article: Myron Orfield and Steven Cannon, "The Effect of Concentrated Poverty on Crime: A Case Study of Minneapolis, Minnesota," 1995.

30. The Federal Bureau of Investigation classifies criminal homicide, forcible rape, robbery, aggravated assault, burglary, larceny, motor vehicle theft, and arson as Part I or serious crimes. Violent crime, a subset of serious crime, includes criminal homicide, forcible rape, robbery, and aggravated assault. In order to compare the level of crime across jurisdictions, crime rates are used. The crime rate is the number of crimes committed per hypothetical 100,000 residents. For example, in Minneapolis's Whittier neighborhood, 2,082 serious and 282 violent crimes were committed in 1983. Because Whittier had 13,051 people, it had a serious crime rate of 16,075 and a violent crime rate of 2,161 in that year. Unless otherwise specified, the crime rate for a given community is based on the community average for the years 1989, 1990, and 1991. Similarly, unless otherwise noted, changes in crime rate reflect the change between the community average crime rate in 1980, 1981, and 1982 and its average crime rate in 1989, 1990, and 1991.

31. Based on 1987–89 statistics, Minneapolis neighborhoods can be divided into five categories for the purposes of violent crime (see table 2-1).

32. The exception is Hilltop, a tiny municipality that encompasses a trailer park and a liquor store, with a crime rate of 10,141 per 100,000 residents.

33. For this section, local news broadcasts were analyzed from a random sample of 1,800 10 p.m. transcripts acquired from a local independent contractor working for a transcribing service. Each broadcast transcript includes the start and end time for every story, along with a descriptive paragraph specifying content. The sample stories were coded by the Minnesota Center for Survey Research into one of eighteen major categories (sports, crime, weather, and so on; see appendix). The center then computed the mean number of seconds spent per broadcast on each category (figure 2-1 and maps 2-6 to 2-8). This coding project was funded by the Center for Race and Poverty at the University of Minnesota.

34. Michael Freeman, "Networks Double Crime Coverage in '93, Despite Flat Violence Levels of US Society," *Mediaweek,* March 14, 1994, p. 4; Mark Brunswick, "Crime Stories: You Get a Lot of Them When You Pick Up the Paper or Turn on the TV News. But What You Are Watching and Reading Is Only a Sliver of What Is Going On out There," *Minneapolis Star Tribune*, January 7, 1994, p. 22A; Brian Lambert, "Where Is Responsibility in TV Crime Coverage?" *Saint Paul Pioneer Press*, February 6, 1994, p. 1E; Steve Perry, "The Way WCCO and KARE 11 Cover Crime News Is, Well, Criminal," *City Pages (of the Twin Cities),* February 2, 1994, p. 12.

35. Minnesota Sentencing Guidelines Commission, "Sentencing Practices: Highlights and Statistical Tables" (Minneapolis, February 1995).

36. Stations sell an average of almost one-third of the allotted news time to advertisers. The highest-rated station charges roughly $8,000 per minute during the 10 p.m. broadcast. It collects about $20 million of advertising revenue each year from its weekday 10 o'clock broadcast alone. The local station with the highest ratings for the two weekday evening news programs (6 p.m. and 10 p.m.) annually earns $10 million more on advertising than the runner-up.

Stations spend another quarter of the local news broadcast on elaborate coverage of weather and sports. Of the remaining fifteen minutes, stations devote about four minutes to crime, sex, and disaster stories. These stories are promoted aggressively by sensational teaser advertisements that are often far more lurid than the actual stories. Another five minutes constitute what, in the age of Rupert Murdoch, has become known as "infotainment"—a combination of stories on subjects like celebrities, park openings, and small adorable animals. For example, one station spent several days covering a small white dog lost in a cemetery, while another reviewed Hillary Clinton's most recent hairstyles. More than half of the final six minutes is devoted to general consumer awareness and health issues—things such as the safety of medical procedures or other products. *Strikingly, networks devote fewer than three minutes to national, state, and local politics and community issues.* Frequently, the small amount of time that is spent here is devoted to ethical scandals, with almost no discussion of underling policy issues. In the end, crime and infotainment together take up almost twice the time devoted to national, state, local, and community news combined. See Myron Orfield, "The News, Please: TV Plays Up Crime, Pays Little Head to Policy Issues," *Minneapolis Star Tribune*, June 16, 1996, p. A23.

37. Phil Rosenthal, "TV Violence Study Is a Bruising Indictment," *Star Tribune*, February 10, 1996, p. E3. The National Television Violence Study, released February 7, 1996, indicated that 57 percent of all television shows on broadcast and cable television contained violence. See also Michael Freeman, "Networks Doubled Crime Coverage in '93, Despite Flat Violence Levels in U.S. Society," *Mediaweek*, March 14, 1994, p. 4; Marriane W. Zawitz and others, "Highlights from 20 Years of Surveying Crime Victims: The National Crime Victimization Survey, 1973–92," report prepared for the Bureau of Justice (Washington: U.S. Department of Justice, Office of Justice Programs, Bureau of Justice Statistics, 1993), p. 7.

38. Paul Klite, Robert A. Bardwell, Jason Setzman, "A Day in the Life of Local TV News in America," *Rocky Mountain Media Watch,* Content Analysis No. 5, January 11, 1995, pp. 1–3.

39. Ibid., p. 10; Timothy J. Hudson, "Consonance in Depiction of Violent Material in Television News," *Journal of Broadcasting and Electronic Media*, vol. 36, no. 4 (Fall 1992), pp. 411–25. Hudson's research led him to agree with one colleague, who had previously noted, "There does seem to be a general notion [among news managers] as to what makes a suitable news package" (p. 21).

40. Ibid.

41. Minnesota Planning, "Troubling Perceptions: 1993 Minnesota Crime Survey" (Minneapolis, January 1994), pp. 5–6; James H. Watt, Mary Mazza, and Leslie

Snyder, "Agenda-Setting Effects of Television News Coverage and the Effects Decay Curve," *Communication Research,* vol. 20, no. 3 (June 1993), p. 411.

42. Throughout the 1980s, criminal sentences remained roughly constant until 1989, when a dramatic increase in criminal sentencing for violent offenders occurred. Sentence lengths increased by 70 percent for assault in the first degree, 60 percent for aggravated robbery, and 100 percent for criminal sexual conduct in the third degree involving force. Overall, the average pronounced sentence in 1989 of 37.7 months increased by almost one-third to 48.6 months in 1992. Minnesota Sentencing Guidelines Commission, "Minnesota Sentencing Guidelines and Commentary" (Minneapolis, August 1, 1993).

Although crime rates have fluctuated and generally declined, arrest rates have increased dramatically. Thus the number of offenders sentenced for felony convictions increased by 60 percent from 1986 to 1993, from just over 6,000 to 9,600. Similarly, throughout the 1980s and early 1990s, 20 percent of convicted felons have been sentenced to prison. The growth in the volume of cases has caused the number of offenders sent to prison to increase from 825 in 1981 to 2,064 in 1993. Minnesota Sentencing Guidelines Commission, "Sentencing Practices: Highlights and Statistical Tables" (Minneapolis, February 1995), pp. 4, 6, 18–21.

The resulting pressure of increased sentencing and arrest rates has caused the state prison population to more than double from 2,244 in 1985 to 4,591 in 1995 and a projected 6,671 in 2005. In 1995, the legislature approved a bonding appropriation of more than $80 million for new state prisons and again substantially increased criminal penalties. Minnesota Planning Commission, "Paying the Price: The Rising Cost of Prison" (March 1996), p. 7.

43. *Hills* v. *Gautreaux*, 425 U.S. 284 (1976).

44. Susan J. Popkin, James E. Rosenbaum, and Patricia M. Meaden, "Labor Market Experiences of Low-Income Black Women in Middle-Class Suburbs: Evidence from a Survey of Gautreaux Program Participants," *Journal of Policy Analysis and Management*, vol. 12, no. 3 (1993), pp. 556–73.

45. James E. Rosenbaum and Susan J. Popkin, "Employment and Earnings of Low-Income Blacks Who Move to Middle-Class Suburbs," in Jencks and Peterson, *The Urban Underclass*; James E. Rosenbaum and others, "Social Integration of Low-Income Black Adults in Middle-Class White Suburbs," *Social Problems,* vol. 38, no. 4 (1991), pp. 448–61; James E. Rosenbaum, Marilyn J. Kulieke, and Leonard S. Rubinowitz, "White Suburban Schools' Responses to Low-Income Black Children: Sources of Successes and Problems," *Urban Review,* vol. 20, no. 1 (1988), pp. 28–41; James E. Rosenbaum and Susan Popkin, "Black Pioneers: Do Their Moves to the Suburbs Increase Economic Opportunity for Mothers and Children?" *Housing Policy Debate,* vol. 2, no. 4 (1991), pp. 1179–1213; James E. Rosenbaum and Julie Kaufman, "Educational and Occupational Achievements of Low Income Black Youth in White Suburbs," paper presented at the annual meeting of the American Sociological Association, Cincinnati, October 18, 1991. See also Schools section below.

46. Rosenbaum and Popkin, "Employment and Earnings," p. 355.

47. Ibid., p. 352.

48. Ibid.

49. Rosenbaum and Kaufman, "Educational and Occupational Achievements," pp. 4–8.

50. Ibid., p. 8.

51. Ibid.

52. Rosenbaum and others, "Social Integration," pp. 454–55.

53. Ibid., pp. 455–57.

54. Gary Orfield, "Ghettoization and Its Alternatives," in Paul E. Peterson, ed., *The New Urban Reality* (Brookings, 1985), p. 163.

55. Pierre de Vise, "Social Change," in Dick Simpson, ed., *Chicago's Future* (Champaign, Ill.: Stripes Publishing Company, 1976), pp. 113–22.

56. Loic J. D. Wacquant and William Julius Wilson, "Poverty, Joblessness, and the Social Transformation of the Inner City," in Phoebe H. Cottingham and David T. Ellwood, eds., *Welfare Policy for the 1990s* (Harvard University Press, 1989), p. 92.

57. Ibid.

58. John D. Kasarda, "Urban Change and Minority Opportunities," in Peterson, *The New Urban Reality,* pp. 33–67; John D. Kasarda, "Urban Industrial Transition and the Underclass," *Annals of the American Academy of Political and Social Science,* vol. 501 (January 1989), pp. 26–47.

59. Nicholas Lemann, "The Myth of Community Development," *New York Times Magazine*, January 2, 1994, p. 27; Lemann, *The Promised Land,* pp. 109–222; David Rusk, *Cities without Suburbs* (Washington: Woodrow Wilson Center Press, 1993), pp. 44–47.

60. David Rusk, research supported by the Twentieth Century Fund.

61. See generally Roy E. Green, ed., *Enterprise Zones: New Directions in Economic Development* (Newbury Park, Calif.: Sage Publications, 1991); Thomas G. Donlan, "Danger Zones: The Required Ingredient in an Enterprise Zone Is Enterprise," *Barron's,* June 22, 1992, p. 10; Glenda Glover and J. Paul Brownridge, "Enterprise Zones as an Instrument of Urban Policy: A Review of the Zones in South Central Los Angeles," *Government Finance Review,* vol. 3 (June 1993), pp. 15–17; Neal R. Peirce, "Enterprise Zones—No Great Shakes," *National Journal*, vol. 29 (July 17, 1993), p. 1828; Elizabeth Larson, "Network News: Enterprise Zones Ignore the Importance of Social Networks," *Reason*, vol. 25 (April 1994), p. 17; Richard Pomp and others, "Can Tax Policy Be Used to Stimulate Economic Development?" *American University Law Review,* vol. 29, no. 207 (1979–80), pp. 207–33; Paul Kantor and H. V. Savitch, "Can Politicians Bargain with Business? A Theoretical and Comparative Perspective on Urban Development," *Urban Affairs Quarterly,* vol. 29, no. 2 (1993), pp. 230–55; Elizabeth M. Gunn, "The Growth of Enterprise Zones: A Policy Transformation," *Policy Studies Journal,* vol. 21, no. 3 (1993), pp. 432–49; Otto J. Hetzel, "Some Historical Lessons for Implementing the Clinton Administration's Empowerment Zones and Enterprise Communities Program: Experiences from the Model Cities Program," *Urban Lawyer,* vol. 26, no. 1 (1994), pp. 63–81; Jeffrey L. Katz, "Enterprise Zones Struggle to Make Their Mark," *Congressional Quarterly*

Weekly Report, July 17, 1993, pp. 1880–83; Timothy J. Bartik, *Who Benefits from State and Local Economic Development Policies* (Kalamazoo, Mich.: W. E. Upjohn Institute for Employment Research, 1991), pp. 17–62; Laura McClure, "Enterprise Zones Have Negligible History of Success," *National Catholic Reporter*, November 13, 1992, p. 9; Glenda Glover, "Enterprise Zones: Incentives are Not Attracting Minority Firms," *Review of Black Political Economy*, vol. 22 (Summer 1993), pp. 73–99.

62. Anthony Downs, in his book *New Visions for Metropolitan America* (Brookings and Lincoln Institute of Land Policy, 1994), repeatedly outlines the necessity of sweeping metropolitan reform and then dismisses the possibility of political success because of the monolithic opposition of the suburbs.

63. All statistics in the following section are U.S. Census data unless otherwise noted.

64. Minnesota Department of Revenue, unpublished data. The net tax capacity of a property is a statutorily determined percentage of the property's market value. The percentage relates to how the property is used (for example, residential homestead versus agricultural). A taxing jurisdiction's tax rate is determined by dividing its total levy by the sum of the net tax capacities of all property within the jurisdiction. The property tax for any property is derived by multiplying the property's net tax capacity by the tax rate of each taxing jurisdiction in which the property is located.

65. Minnesota Department of Revenue, unpublished data.

66. Minnesota Department of Public Safety, Office of Information Systems Management, *Minnesota Crime Information—1980, 1990* (Minneapolis, 1981, 1991).

67. As this dynamic has run its course in larger metropolitan areas, the consequences can be extreme. For example, the property wealth of East St. Louis, Missouri, can only cover the expenses of its school system for one month a year—the rest is provided by emergency state aid. East St. Louis can no longer afford public garbage collection, and this function is performed by a group of volunteer nuns for a city of more than 40,000 people. David Rusk, lecture presented at Landmark Center, Saint Paul, Minn., September 17, 1993.

68. See Housing section below.

69. Stanley B. Greenberg, *Middle Class Dreams: The Politics and Power of the New American Majority* (Times Books, 1995).

70. Although the term "midregion" is primarily geographic, it also applies to the household income level of these suburbs.

71. Minnesota Department of Revenue, unpublished data; see also Fiscal Disparities section below. Of the twenty-one largest metropolitan areas in 1994, the Twin Cities' median sale price for a single-family home was the ninth lowest at $101,500. The prices ranged from Tampa–St. Petersburg with a median single-family home price of $76,200 to Los Angeles–Long Beach with a median price of $197,900. Bureau of the Census, *Statistical Abstract of the United States: 1995* (Department of Commerce, 1995), p. 731.

72. Ibid.

73. Minnesota Department of Children, Families and Learning, unpublished data; see also Schools section below.

74. Minnesota Department of Public Safety, Office of Information Systems Management, *Minnesota Crime Information—1980, 1990* (Minneapolis, 1981, 1991).

75. Ibid.

76. See Urban Stability Memo, memo by author, September 14, 1991; namely, Afton, Arden Hills, Bloomington, Corcoran, Deephaven, Eden Prairie, Edina, Lake Elmo, Lakeville, Medina, Mendota Heights, Mound, Plymouth, Savage, Shakopee, Spring Park, Vadnais Heights, Waconia, Wayzata, Woodbury, and Woodland.

77. Robert Charles Lessor & Co. (Santa Fe, N. Mex.), one of America's leading real estate consulting firms, calls metropolitan subareas like the southern and western developing suburbs "favored sectors." When advising major clients to locate facilities, they systematically search for subregions with the greatest presence of executive housing, high-end local retail malls, recent highway improvements, employment growth, low commercial real estate vacancy rates, and high share of regional economic growth. They judge these areas the most viable for a wide variety of business endeavors. See Christopher Leinberger, Managing Partner, Robert Charles Lessor & Co., memorandum to author, Re: Robert Charles Lessor & Co. Metropolitan Overview Analysis (MOA) methodology, August 16, 1994.

78. Robert Reich, "Revolt of the Anxious Class," speech to the Democratic Leadership Council, Washington, November 22, 1994.

79. Striking was the transition that occurred in the seat of Phil Carruthers, the Democratic Majority Leader of the House. Carruthers was elected from working-class Brooklyn Center, a perennial democratic and labor stronghold. As Brooklyn Center underwent a jarring social transition in the late 1980s and early 1990s, Carruthers's margin declined from 67 percent in 1988 to 52 percent in 1992. In neighboring Columbia Heights, another democratic, pro-labor, working-class suburb in severe transition, Wayne Simoneau's margin declined from 77 percent in 1974 to 55 percent in 1992. Democrats lost this seat in a 1995 special election.

80. Timothy Egan, "The Serene Fortress: A Special Report. Many Seek Security in Private Communities," *New York Times*, September 3, 1995, p. 1A.

Chapter Three

1. Jomills H. Braddock II and James M. McPartland, "The Social and Academic Consequences of School Desegregation," *Equity & Choice* (February 1988), p. 5; Gary Orfield and Carole Ashkinaze, *The Closing Door: Conservative Policy and Black Opportunity* (University of Chicago Press, 1991), p. 131; James E. Rosenbaum, Marilyn Kulieke, and Leonard S. Rubinowitz, "Low-Income Black Children in White Suburban Schools: A Study of School and Student Responses," *Journal of Negro Education,* vol. 56, no. 1 (1987), pp. 35–43.

2. Braddock and McPartland, "Social and Academic Consequences of School Desegregation;" Orfield and Ashkinaze, *The Closing Door*; Rosenbaum, Kulieke, and Rubinowitz, "Low-Income Black Children in White Suburban Schools."

3. Susan E. Mayer, "How Much Does a High School's Racial and Socioeconomic Mix Affect Graduation and Teenage Fertility Rates?" in Christopher Jencks and Paul E. Peterson, eds., *The Urban Underclass* (Brookings, 1991), pp. 321–41; Jonathan Kozol, *Savage Inequalities: Children in America's Schools* (Crown, 1991); Robert L. Crain and Rita E. Mahard, "School Racial Composition and Black College Attendance and Achievement Test Performance," *Sociology of Education*, vol. 51, no. 2 (1978), pp. 81–101; Peter Scheirer, "Poverty, Not Bureaucracy: Poverty, Segregation, and Inequality in Metropolitan Chicago Schools" (University of Chicago, Metropolitan Opportunity Project, 1989).

4. Braddock and McPartland, "Social and Academic Consequences of School Desegregation."

5. H. G. Bissinger, "We're All Racist Now," *New York Times Magazine*, May 29, 1994, pp. 26–55.

6. Unless otherwise indicated, spending data are derived from the 1992–93 fiscal year and race and socioeconomic data from the 1994–95 fiscal year.

7. Laws of Minnesota 1971, extra session, chapter 31, articles 15, 16, and 20.

8. Unless otherwise specified, spending figures are for the 1993–94 fiscal year.

9. A large-scale metropolitan equity lawsuit brought by districts with lower property wealth recently failed. See *Skeen* v. *Minnesota Department of Education*, 505 N.W.2d 299 (Minn. 1993).

10. *Booker* v. *Special School District No. 1,* 351 F. Supp. 711 (D. Minn. 1972); Minn. R. 3535. See discussion below.

11. Affordable housing is discussed in chapter 6.

12. See *Booker* v. *Special School District No. 1*, 351 F. Supp. 799 (D. Minn. 1972).

13. The federal court dissolved its supervision of the Minneapolis desegregation plan in reliance on the Commissioner's commitment to maintain desegregation. See affidavit of John J. Feda, Commissioner of the Minnesota Department of Children, Families and Learning (April 29, 1983), in the court file of *Booker* v. *Special School District No. 1*, No. 4-71 Civ. 382 (D. Minn. June 8, 1983). See also Minnesota Rule 3535.

14. Free lunch and minority data are from the Minnesota Department of Children, Families and Learning, unpublished data.

15. Gary Orfield and Franklin Monfort, *Status of School Desegregation: The Next Generation* (Alexandria, Va.: National School Boards Association, Council of Urban Boards of Education, 1992), p. 39.

16. Public entities sometimes distort or render meaningless important statistics to avoid reporting potentially unpopular facts. Drop-out rates are not an accurate reflection of the percentage of students who do not graduate from high school; no one says that they are. Drop-out rates are simply the product of a formula that is the sum of all the students who do not *withdraw* from school for a list of specified reasons. For example, if over the summer a student decides not to return to school in the fall, he is classified as a withdrawal, not a dropout. As the number of withdrawal categories

mounts, the figures released as dropouts become altogether meaningless. In such a way, school officials who do not want to reveal unpopular information prevent the public from having any idea of how well its schools are functioning.

The best way to determine the real drop-out rate is to follow a group of students all the way through high school—a linear analysis. This is expensive and time consuming. A second method, used by the U.S. Department of Education, counts the number of children entering a given ninth-grade class in a school district and subtracts the number that graduate four years later. To the extent transfers in or out are limited, this figure is accurate. It loses validity as the number of transfers in or out increases disproportionately. For discussion purposes in this section, completion rates will be measured by this method and the figure reported will reflect the average completion rate between 1984 and 1991.

17. On the census tract level, the best way to track white, school-related flight is to calculate the net loss of preschool white children between census periods. Because of the high correlation between being white and middle class, it is also a reasonably good surrogate for middle-class family flight. In 1980 in Minneapolis, there were 17,021 white preschool children up to 4 years old. Ten years later, only 10,041 white children remained in the 10- to 14-year-old age group.

18. Minneapolis City Planning Department, *Minneapolis Home Ownership 1986* (Minneapolis, 1986), pp. 11–12.

19. Bill McMahon, Minneapolis City Planning Department, unpublished data from *Minneapolis Homeowners 1993* survey.

20. The 1993 survey, which had become more precise, indicated that 32 percent of the movers with preschool children planned to move within the metropolitan area, while the remaining 13 percent would move outside the Twin Cities. Minneapolis City Planning Department, *Minneapolis Homeowners 1993*, p. 23.

21. Orfield and Ashkinaze, *The Closing Door,* p. 141.

22. Ibid.

23. Ibid., p. 124.

24. Scott Seiler, untitled term paper, Hamline Law School, Saint Paul, Minn., January 5, 1992. See also Sue Urahn, legislative analyst, Minnesota House of Representatives House Research, memorandum to author, re: Testing and Dropouts in the Minneapolis Public Schools, January 29, 1992, which notes that the California Achievement testing norms require reporting special education students as a part of the testing pool and that Minneapolis did not report such students scores as a part of the testing pool. However, Larry Sawyer, an active parent in the late 1980s, completed a study using data from the Minneapolis Public Schools Complete Profiles of Performance dating back to the 1970s, which convincingly shows test scores dropping.

25. Scheirer, "Poverty, Not Bureaucracy;" Orfield and Ashkinaze, *The Closing Door,* pp. 138–40.

26. *Minneapolis Branch of the National Association for the Advancement of Colored People* v. *State of Minnesota,* District Court, Fourth Judicial District, Docket Number MC 95-014800. The case was closely modeled in a lawsuit in Connecticut;

see *Sheff v. O'Neil*, 238 Conn. 1, 678 A.2d 1267 (1996), in which the plaintiffs prevailed under a similar theory before the Connecticut Supreme Court.

27. Gary Orfield and Franklin Monfort, *Racial Change & Desegregation in Large School Districts: Trends Though the 1986–87 School Year* (Alexandria, Va.: National School Boards Association, Council of Urban Boards of Education, 1988), p. 9; Ibid., "School Desegregation," p. 39.

28. See discussion of sectoral housing markets in chapter 2.

29. Kevin Diaz, "Weapons Law Awaits Students: They'll Face Felony If They Are Armed," *Minneapolis Star Tribune*, August 27, 1993, p. 1B.

30. The districts with low poverty rates to the south and west and east (including Rosemount, Randolf, Waconia, and Stillwater) had less than 7 percent noncompletion. On the other hand, blue-collar districts such as Shakopee (19 percent), Prior Lake (13 percent), Saint Francis (25 percent), Forest Lake (14 percent), Inver Grove Heights (18 percent), and Anoka (15 percent) had alarmingly high drop-out rates.

31. Metropolitan Council, *Supplement to the Inventory of Twin Cities Metropolitan Area Public School Facilities* (Minneapolis, 1993), p. 12; Minnesota Department of Children, Families and Learning, *School District Profiles*, 1992; Department of Children Families and Learning, *February 1996 Enrollment Projections*, 1996.

32. Ibid.

33. Ibid., p. 12.

Chapter Four

1. Kathy Novak and Steve Hinze of the Minnesota House Research Department determined how much affordable housing was available in each city and suburb of the Twin Cities metropolitan area at the different levels of income. Their analysis was based on data from the 1990 U.S. Census for rental units and 1992 Minnesota Department of Revenue files on assessor's market value for owner-occupied units. It was assumed for this analysis that owner-occupied homes were 100 percent mortgaged. Also, a market-rate mortgage interest rate and the specific property tax rate for each individual city were applied.

2. This relatively simple picture is obscured by at least two factors. First, some parts of the region have a greater than average amount of affordable housing and some much less. Second, a considerable number of people live in housing that is either more or less expensive than they can afford.

3. The central cities have 164 percent of their fair share of households at 50 percent of the median (35 percent) and 144 percent of fair share at 80 percent (56 percent). The central cities have three times their fair share of units affordable at 50 percent (67 percent) and 80 percent (91 percent) of the metropolitan median income.

4. The inner suburbs have 94 percent of their fair share of households at 50 percent of the median income (20 percent) and 101 percent at 80 percent (39 percent). They have more than twice the corresponding number of units affordable at these levels.

5. Waconia (144 percent fair share [FS]), Spring Park (141 percent FS), Wayzata (117 percent FS), Shakopee (100 percent FS) and Chaska (97 percent FS); Woodland (14 percent FS), Minnetonka Beach (17 percent FS), Mendota Heights (18 percent FS), Maple Grove (20 percent FS), and Deephaven (24 percent FS).

6. All three developing groups appear to have approximately half their fair share of households below 50 percent of the median (11.05 percent to 12.23 percent) and two-thirds of their fair share of households below 80 percent of the median (24.10 percent to 25.93 percent). These subregions have much more than their fair share of units affordable at 50 percent and 80 percent of metropolitan median income, with the mid-developing suburbs having somewhat more affordable housing in these groups that the other developing suburbs.

7. Minnesota Planning, Metropolitan Council, and the Minnesota Housing and Finance Agency, "Making the Connection: Linking Housing, Jobs, and Transportation," Minneapolis, December 1993.

8. *Hollman* v. *Cisneros,* No. 4-92-712 (D. Minn.). See also Barbara L. Lukermann and Michael P. Kane, "Land Use Practices: Exclusionary Zoning, De Facto or De Jure: An Examination of the Practices of Ten Suburban Communities in the Twin Cities Metropolitan Area" (Center for Urban and Regional Affairs, University of Minnesota, April 1994).

9. Minnesota Planning, "Making the Connection," pp. 26, 28.

10. Lukermann and Kane, "Land Use Practices," p. 18.

11. Minnesota Planning, "Making the Connection," pp. 28, 25.

12. Minnesota Planning, "Making the Connection," p. 25. See also American Farmland Trust, "Density-Related Public Costs," Washington, 1986, which found that property taxes on a 2.5-acre developed lot are 40 percent higher than on a developed lot of one-third of an acre.

13. Minnesota Planning, "Making the Connection," p. 27.

14. Lukermann and Kane, "Land Use Practices," pp. 19.

15. Minnesota Planning, "Making the Connection," p. 28.

16. Ibid.

17. Lukermann and Kane, "Land Use Practices," p. 18.

18. Minnesota Planning, "Making the Connection," pp. 28–29.

19. Lukermann and Kane, "Land Use Practices," pp. 17–19.

20. Minnesota Planning, "Making the Connection," p. 31.

21. Lukermann and Kane, "Land Use Practices," p. 17.

22. Minnesota Planning, "Making the Connection," pp. 39–40; Lukermann and Kane, "Land Use Practices," p. 20.

23. Lukermann and Kane, "Land Use Practices," pp. 25–29.

24. Minnesota Planning, "Making the Connection," p. 31.

25. Lukermann and Kane, "Land Use Practices," p. 6.

26. Minnesota Planning, "Making the Connection," p. 23.

27. Lukermann and Kane, "Land Use Practices," p. 20.

28. Minnesota Planning, "Making the Connection," pp. 31–34.

29. Ibid., p. 34.

30. Ibid.

31. Duane Windsor, *Fiscal Zoning in Suburban Communities* (Lexington, Mass.: Lexington Books, 1979); Barbara Sherman Rolleston, "Determinants of Restrictive Suburban Zoning: An Empirical Analysis," *Journal of Urban Economics*, vol. 21, no. 1 (1987), pp. 1–21; Michael J. Wasylenko, "Evidence of Fiscal Differentials and Intrametropolitan Firm Relocation," *Land Economics,* vol. 56, no. 3 (1980), pp. 339–49; Robert Cervero, "Jobs-Housing Balancing and Regional Mobility," *American Planning Association Journal,* vol. 55 (Spring 1989), pp. 136–50.

Chapter Five

1. John F. Kain, "Housing Segregation, Negro Unemployment, and Metropolitan Decentralization," *Quarterly Journal of Economics,* vol. 82 (May 1968), pp. 175–97.

2. John D. Kasarda, "Urban Industrial Transition and the Underclass," *Annals of the American Academy of Political and Social Sciences*, vol. 501 (January 1989), pp. 26–47.

3. Ibid.

4. For further discussion of the pros and cons of the spatial mismatch hypothesis, see Joseph D. Mooney, "Housing Segregation, Negro Employment and Metropolitan Decentralization: An Alternative Perspective," *Quarterly Journal of Economics,* vol. 83 (May 1969), pp. 299–311. See Hutchinson (1974); Farley (1987); Inlanfedt and Sjoquist (1990–92); Offner and Saks (1971); Friedlander (1972); Harrison (1974); Leonard (1986); all in Kathy Novak, "Jobs and Housing: Policy Options for Metropolitan Development," Minnesota House of Representatives, Research Department, Minneapolis, February 1994; David Elwood, "The Spatial Mismatch Hypothesis: Are the Teenage Jobs Missing in the Ghetto?", in Richard B. Freeman and Harry J. Holzer, eds., *The Black Youth Employment Crisis* (University of Chicago Press, 1986), pp. 147–85; Citizens League, "Why We Should Build More Inclusive Communities: The Case for a Regional Housing Policy in the Twin Cities Metropolitan Region—Final Report of the Committee on Housing Policy and Metropolitan Development" (Minneapolis, May 1994), pp. 22–25; Minneapolis City Planning, "Changes in the Minneapolis Labor Force and the Growing Living Wage Employment Gap" (Minneapolis, October 1993).

5. Osseo (–53 percent), Hopkins (–35 percent), Richfield (–22 percent), South Saint Paul (–18 percent), Saint Anthony (–17 percent), Columbia Heights (–15 percent), Golden Valley (–16 percent), Moundsview (–11 percent), and North Saint Paul (–10 percent).

6. Mike Kaszuba, "Demand Draws City Workers to Suburbs," *Minneapolis Star Tribune*, April 18, 1994, p. 1B.

7. Minneapolis City Assessor's Office, unpublished data.

8. Ibid.

9. Douglas Porter, "Regional Governance of Metropolitan Form: The Missing Link in Relating Land Use and Transportation," in *Transportation, Urban Form and the Environment: Proceedings of a Conference, Beckman Center, Irvine, California,*

December 9 12, 1990 (Washington: Transportation Research Board, National Research Council, 1991); Eric Sheppard, "Modeling and Predicting Aggregate Flows," in Susan Hanson, ed., *The Geography of Urban Transportation* (New York: Guilford, 1986), pp. 91, 95; Alan Pisarski, *Commuting in America, A National Report on Commuting Patterns and Trends* (Westport, Conn.: Eno Foundation for Transportation, Inc., 1987).

10. Herbert Mohring and David Anderson, "Congestion Pricing for the Twin Cities Metropolitan Area," report prepared for the Minnesota Legislature (Minneapolis, January 7, 1994).

11. Minn. Stat §§ 473.167, 473.171; see also "Study of Minnesota's Surface Transportation Needs, Report to the Governor and the Legislature, 20 Year Transportation Program," Transportation Study Board, Saint Paul, Minn., 15 January 1991, pp. 27–30.

12. Minnesota Department of Transportation Press Release, "Mn/DOT Announces Reconstruction Plans for I–35W and I–494," January 12, 1993.

13. Metropolitan Council Information Bulletin, "How Does the Twin Cities Compare? 1990 Census Rankings of the Twenty-Five Largest Metropolitan Areas," Publication No. 620-92-023 (Saint Paul, Minn., March 1992), p. 14.

The Metropolitan Council "Metropolitan Development Guide," p. 47, states: "A congestion-free highway system would produce negative impacts on transit usage which would make it increasingly difficult to serve transit dependent people. These negative impacts would especially affect central cities and first-ring suburbs." During the nation's most intense period of highway construction (1945–70), transit ridership dropped from 23.3 billion rides per year to 7.3 billion. The decline in transit ridership continues.

14. J. Hanks and T. Lomax, *Roadway Congestion in Major Urban Areas, 1982– 1988* (Lubbock, Tex.: Texas A&M University, Texas Transportation Institute, 1990), cited in Minnesota Department of Trade and Economic Development, Business Development and Analysis Division*, Compare Minnesota: An Economic and Statistical Fact Book, 1992/1993* (Minneapolis, 1992).

15. Robert Cervero, "Jobs-Housing Balancing and Regional Mobility," *American Planning Association Journal,* vol. 55 (Spring 1989), p. 136; Robert Cervero, "Jobs-Housing Balance as Public Policy," *Urban Land* (October 1991), p. 10. John Williams, a researcher for the Minnesota House of Representatives, has duplicated Cervero's research in the Twin Cities metropolitan area and had similar results.

16. U.S. Department of Commerce, Bureau of the Census, Data User Services Division, *1990 Census of Population and Housing,* Summary Tape File 3A (1992).

17. See Norman Draper, "For Many, Drive Time Seems Eternal: Northern Suburbs Have it the Worst, Census Shows," *Minneapolis Star Tribune*, July 18, 1992, p. 1B (based on analysis of the 1990 Census).

18. Mohring and Anderson, "Congestion Pricing."

19. Public Law 102–240 (H.R. 2950); Minnesota Constitution Article 14, Section 10.

20. Yale Rabin, "Highways as a Barrier to Equal Access," *Annals of the American Academy of Political Science,* vol. 451 (1974), pp. 22–35. See generally Metropolitan

Council, "Trouble at the Core: The Twin Cities Under Stress," Publication No. 310-92-116 (Saint Paul, Minn., November 18, 1992).

21. Metropolitan Council Wastewater Services, *1995–1999 Capital Improvement Program and 1995 Capital Budget* (Minneapolis, adopted December 15, 1994), p. 10.

22. Metropolitan Council Environmental Services, *Capital Improvment Program* (Minneapolis, adopted December 21, 1995), p. 4-3.

23. Ibid. at appendix A, pp. 1–5.

24. Thomas F. Luce, Jr., Barbara Lukermann, and Herbert Mohring, "Regional Sewer System Rate Structure Study" (Minneapolis: Hubert H. Humphrey Institute of Public Affairs, University of Minnesota, December 7, 1992). Significant additional costs were incurred because in the southern and western region, many of the treatment plants were built on the Minnesota River. Minnesota is heavily polluted by non–point source farm runoff and hence the sewer plants must treat waste water to a much higher standard on that river than on the Mississippi.

25. Luce and others, "Regional Sewer System," pp. 67–68.

26. Metropolitan Council Information Bulletin, "How Does the Twin Cities Compare?," p. 14.

27. Bureau of the Census, Data User Services Division, *1987 Census of Agriculture* (Department of Commerce, 1988).

28. Metropolitan Council, unpublished data, 1993.

29. The State Planning study found that 85 percent of the developing suburbs had lot sizes that exceeded the 7,500 square feet recommended by the Met Council; Lukermann and Kane found that all of the high-growth suburbs exceeded the recommended density.

Chapter Six

1. David Rusk, lecture at Landmark Center, Saint Paul, Minn., September 17, 1993.

2. Paul E. Peterson, ed., *The New Urban Reality* (Brookings, 1985).

3. David Rusk, lecture at Landmark Center, Saint Paul, Minn., September 17, 1993.

4. Douglas S. Massey and Nancy A. Denton, *American Apartheid: Segregation and the Making of the Underclass* (Harvard University Press, 1993).

5. In the 1992 presidential election, metropolitan area House districts with more than 30 percent of the people in poverty had a 50.6 percent voter turn-out, while districts with less than 5 percent had an 84.6 percent turnout. The Urban Coalition [of Minneapolis and Saint Paul], "Poverty and Voter Turnout in the 1992 Election" (Minneapolis, June 1994).

6. Also called at the time "gilding the ghetto" by John H. Kain and Joseph J. Persky and "ghetto enrichment" by Anthony Downs. See John H. Kain and Joseph J. Persky, "Alternatives to the Gilded Ghetto," *Public Interest* (Winter 1969), pp. 74–

8/; Anthony Downs, "Alternative Futures for the American Ghetto," *Daedelus* (Fall 1968), pp. 1331–78.

7. Nicholas Lemann, *The Promised Land: The Great Black Migration and How it Changed America* (Knopf, 1991).

8. David Rusk, research supported by the Twentieth Century Fund, New York.

9. See Twin Cities RISE!, "Closing the Work Skills Gap: Implications for Development of a Skills-Based Jobs Preparation Program for Twin Cities Adults" (Minneapolis, March 1994).

10. Charles Murray, *Losing Ground: American Social Policy, 1950–1980* (Basic Books, 1984); Lawrence M. Mead, *Beyond Entitlement: The Social Obligations of Citizenship* (Free Press, 1986).

11. Nicholas Lemann, "The Myth of Community Development," *New York Times Magazine*, January 9, 1994, pp. 27–35; Lemann, *The Promised Land.*

12. Murray, *Losing Ground.*

13. George C. Galster and Edward W. Hill, eds., *The Metropolis in Black and White: Place, Power and Polarization* (New Brunswick, N.J.: Center for Urban Policy Research, 1992).

14. Anthony Downs, *New Visions for Metropolitan America* (Brookings and Lincoln Institute of Land Policy, 1994), pp. 109–10.

15. Advisory Commission on Regulatory Barriers to Affordable Housing, "'Not in My Back Yard': Removing Barriers to Affordable Housing" (Department of Housing and Urban Development, 1991). Richard Nixon's HUD secretary, George Romney, was very supportive of moving affordable housing to the suburbs as a way to help stabilize central-city neighborhoods.

16. Massey and Denton, *American Apartheid,* p. 214.

17. Examples include Mayor Freeman Bosley Jr. of Saint Louis, Mo., who in the face of dramatically improved graduation rates for city students atter.ding suburban Saint Louis schools, called repeatedly for an end to school busing. The NAACP strongly opposed Bosley's efforts. See Jo Mannies, "Mayor Wants to End School Busing: City Neighborhoods Suffering, He Says," *Saint Louis Post Dispatch*, September 27, 1993, p. A1.

18. The Voting Rights Act of 1973 urges the drawing of legislative and congressional districts so as to maximize minority voting power to elect minority public officials. It does this by creating as many 65 percent–minority districts as possible. The level is set at 65 percent because of low turnout among minority voters. See *Thornberg* v. *Gingles,* 478 U.S. 30 (1986). Anything higher than this percentage is packing; anything below is diluting the strength of minority voting blocks.

19. David Rusk, *Cities Without Suburbs* (Washington: Woodrow Wilson Center Press, 1993).

20. Massey and Denton, *American Apartheid,* p. 89. The problems arise from the fact that most whites do not want to live in neighborhoods that are more than 10 percent African-American. Ibid., pp. 91–93.

21. Minneapolis City Planning Department, "Minneapolis Homeowners 1993" (Minneapolis, 1993).

22. Mark Alfers, Dakota County Housing and Redevelopment Authority, letter to author, May 17, 1994.

23. Minneapolis Public Housing Authority, letter to author, August 1994.

24. However, it must be remembered that about two-thirds of the poor people in this metropolitan area are white and would not be affected by racial prejudice.

25. Douglas Massey, lecture at Landmark Center, Saint Paul, January 20, 1994.

26. James E. Rosenbaum and others, "Social Integration of Low-Income Black Adults in Middle-Class White Suburbs," *Social Problems,* vol. 38, no. 4 (1991), pp. 448–61.

27. Barbara L. Lukermann and Michael P. Kane, "Land Use Practices: Exclusionary Zoning, De Facto or De Jure: An Examination of the Practices of Ten Suburban Communities in the Twin Cities Metropolitan Area" (Minneapolis: University of Minnesota, Center for Urban and Regional Affairs, April 1994), pp. 53–57; and supporting memordum from Robert Marthaler to Tim Thompson, "A Memo Concerning Lakeville's Zoning Ordinance and City Actions Incongruent with the Comprehensive Plan and Other Practices and Policies Effecting the Provision of Low to Moderate Income Housing," June 1, 1993.

28. For a particularly powerful account and study of this phenomenon, see Thomas Bier, "Public Policy Against Itself: Investments that Help Bring Cleveland (and Eventually Suburbs) Down," in A. Schorr, ed., *Cleveland Development: A Dissenting View* (Cleveland: David Press, 1991), pp. 43–52.

29. Mike Kaszuba, "In Northern Metro, You Can't Always Get What You Want," *Minneapolis Star Tribune*, August 3, 1994, p. 1A; Steve Brandt, "Encroaching Poverty Drains Suburban Businesses," *Minneapolis Star Tribune*, August 1, 1994, p. 1A; Jennifer Waters, "Simon vs. Rouse in Regional Mall Squall," *City Business (of Minneapolis/Saint Paul)* (July 1995), pp. 21–27.

30. American Farmland Trust, "Density-Related Public Costs" (Washington, 1986).

31. Dana Schroeder, "Fiscal Disparities Pool Increases after 3-Year Decline," *Minnesota Journal*, February 20, 1996, p. 5.

32. See generally, William R. Morrish and Catherine R. Brown, *Planning to Stay* (Minneapolis: Milkweed Editions, 1994); William R. Morrish and Catherine R. Brown, *Tracing the Community: Connections of Phalen Creek and Trout Brook* (Minneapolis: Design Center for the American Urban Landscape, 1992); William R. Morrish and Catherine R. Brown*, Reinvisioning Public Housing Within the Neighborhood: A Design Study Process* (Minneapolis: Design Center for the American Urban Landscape, 1993).

33. Personal communication with John Borchert, Minneapolis, May 1992.

34. See discussion of Atlanta below.

35. Carnegie Foundation for the Advancement of Teaching, *School Choice: A Special Report* (Princeton, N.J., 1992).

36. Gary Orfield and Franklin Monfort, "Status of School Desegregation: The Next Generation" (Alexandria, Va.: National School Boards Association, Council of Urban Boards of Education, 1992), vol. 39, p. 23; Christina Meldrum and Susan

Eaton, *Resegregation in Norfolk, Virginia: Does Restoring Neighborhood Schools Work?*, report prepared for the Harvard Project on School Desegregation (Cambridge, Mass., May 1994).

37. Atlanta represents a particularly sad example of those who believed that segregation and neighborhood schools were a panacea for arresting school decline. In the "Atlanta Compromise," the outer suburbs and white business community helped blacks gain political control over the central city school system in exchange for Atlanta's abandoning its effort to achieve metropolitan desegregation. The state pumped huge new resources into Atlanta, and the school system implemented all the state-of-the-art reforms. Its results were a disaster for the Atlanta schools. Not only did whites flee, but so did middle-class African-Americans and the graduation rates and test scores declined dramatically.

Strikingly, of the cities where white enrollment has been the most stable over the last two decades, three of the top six have operated metropolitanwide desegregation programs since the early 1970s. In addition, two of them are rapidly growing counties in prosperous metropolitan areas. The third is Washington, D.C., the nation's most heavily African-American school district. More than half of the twenty districts with the smallest white losses implemented mandatory city-suburban busing twenty years ago. The data show that mandatory metropolitan-scale busing does not convert school districts to virtually all minority status. On the contrary, metropolitan busing has been occurring for a generation in many of the systems with the most stable share of white enrollment.

38. Systems with neighborhood schools were not the only cities to experience white flight. Cities with mandatory intra-city busing (that is, not involving the suburbs) also lost white students: Boston (49 percent), Denver (31 percent), and Minneapolis (34 percent). These types of systems encourage flight by allowing close-by suburbs to avoid any responsibility for desegregation. Cities with voluntary magnet plans also experienced significant loss of white students.

39. Jomills H. Braddock II and James M. McPartland, "Social and Academic Consequences of School Desegregation," *Equity & Choice*, vol. 4 (February 1988), pp. 5–10, 63–73; see also "Selected Excerpts" from "Desegregation Policy Analysis: A Report Prepared by the Minnesota Department of Education and Submitted to the State Board of Education" (Minneapolis, January 19, 1988), p. 7.

40. Personal communication with Carol Johnson, assistant superintendent, Minneapolis Public Schools, summer 1991.

41. Downs, *New Visions,* pp. 180–81.

42. 1000 Friends of Oregon and the Home Builders Association of Metropolitan Portland, "Managing Growth to Promote Affordable Housing: Revisiting Oregon's Goal 10," executive summary (Portland, Ore., September 1991), p. 3.

43. Ibid.

44. 1000 Friends and Home Builders, "Managing Growth"; Liberty, "Oregon's Comprehensive Growth Management," p. 10379.

45. 1000 Friends and Home Builders, "Managing Growth."

46. Ibid.

47. Gordon S. Wood, *The Creation of the American Republic, 1776–1787* (W. W. Norton, 1972).

48. Rusk, *Cities Without Suburbs,* p. 34.

49. Ibid., p. 82.

50. See Liberty, "Oregon's Comprehensive Growth Management."

51. *Village of Burnsville* v. *Onischuk,* 301 Minnesota 137, 222 N.W.2d 523 (1974), appeal dismissed 95 S.Ct. 1109, 420 U.S. 916, 43 L.Ed.2d 388.

Chapter Seven

1. See Metropolitan Council, *Trouble at the Core; The Twin Cities Under Stress,* Publication No. 310-92-116 (Saint Paul, November 18, 1992); Metropolitan Council, *Keeping the Twin Cities Vital: Regional Strategies for Change in the Fully Developed Area,* Publication No. 78-94-022 (Saint Paul, 15 February 1994).

2. *Metropolitan Infrastructure Stability Act of 1992,* 77th Session, H.F. 1778.

3. Deborah A. Dyson, Minnesota State House Research, memorandum to author, "History of Sewer Cost Allocation Change," January 28, 1992.

4. See Thomas F. Luce, Barbara Lukermann, and Herbert Mohring, "Regional Sewer System Rate Study" (Minneapolis: Hubert H. Humphrey Institute of Public Affairs, December 7, 1992); Herbert Mohring and David Anderson, "Congestion Pricing for the Twin Cities Metropolitan Area," Report to the Minnesota Legislature, January 7, 1994.

5. The process of creating these maps and their impact is described in some detail in Laura Lang, "Representative Uses Maps to Make a Point," *Government Technology,* vol. 6 (September 1993), pp. 12–13.

6. The process of coalition building is described in Neal R. Peirce, "Mapping Out a Citistate's Future", *National Journal,* vol. 25 (October 23, 1993), p. 2551; Neal Peirce, "Twin Cities, A Regional Leader Again?", *Nation's Cities Weekly,* vol. 17 (August 29, 1994), p. 2; Paul Glastris, "A New City-Suburbs Hookup," *U.S. News & World Report,* July 18, 1994, p. 28; Dane Smith, "Legislature to Get Proposals to Mend Disparities," *Minneapolis Star Tribune,* December 11, 1992, p. 26A; Peter Leyden, "Twin Cities' Woes No Longer Stop at the Gates to Suburbia," *Minneapolis Star Tribune,* December 11, 1992, p. 1A; Steve Berg, "Must Suburbs Be Abolished to Save Cities?", *Minneapolis Star Tribune,* July 11, 1993, p. 1A; Lynda McDonnell, "Switch Sought in Regional Growth," *Saint Paul Pioneer Press,* February 7, 1993, p. 1B; Linda Fullerton, "Urban Visionary or Suburban Villain," *Saint Paul Pioneer Press,* April 17, 1994, p. 1B; John Kostouros, "Urban Flight, Suburban Blight," *Minnesota's Journal of Law & Politics,* vol. 7 (March 1993), p. 24; Norman Draper, "Attack on the Suburbs: In Outer Ring, A Scramble to Offset Aura of Horn of Plenty," *Minneapolis Star Tribune,* March 19, 1993, p. 1A.

7. *Hollman* v. *Cisneros,* No. 4-92-712 (D. Minn.).

8. Ibid., Amended Answer of Defendants Cora McCorvey and Minneapolis Public Housing Authority and Cross-Claims Against Federal Defendants and Metro Defendants, April 8, 1994.

9. Metropolitan Area League of Women Voters, "Metropolitan School Desegregation and Integration Study" (Minneapolis, 1990).

10. Citizens League, "Why We Should Build More Inclusive Communities: The Case for a Regional Housing Policy in the Twin Cities Metropolitan Region—Final Report of the Committee on Housing Policy and Metropolitan Development" (Minneapolis, May 1994).

11. Smith, "Legislature to Get Proposals"; Dane Smith, "Bill Seeks to Balance Metro Growth with Opportunities," *Minneapolis Star Tribune,* February 19, 1993, p. 3B; Lynda McDonnell, "Plans to Strengthen the Urban Core Unveiled," *Saint Paul Pioneer Press,* February 19, 1993, p. 1C; Editorial, "Metro Imbalance is a Problem for All," *Minneapolis Star Tribune,* March 26, 1993, p. 20A.

12. *Comprehensive Choice Housing Act of 1993,* 77th Session, H.F. 671.

13. The road penalties were in a separate transportation bill, 77th Session, H.F. 623.

14. The six Republicans in communities that would benefit from the MCSA were Charlie Weaver (Anoka), Jim Rhodes (Saint Louis Park), Theresa Lynch (Andover), Brad Stannius (White Bear Lake), Doug Swenson (Forest Lake), Dennis Ozment (Rosemount), and Connie Morrison (Burnsville). In addition, Tim Pawlenty (Eagan) represented communities that had made great progress on low-income housing. Further, Peggy Leppik (Golden Valley) represented a community that, though quite affluent, bordered the rapidly expanding poor neighborhoods of north Minneapolis and was beginning to show increases in poverty in its schools.

15. Editorial, "The Met Council Takes a Housing Dive," *Minneapolis Star Tribune*, March 27, 1993, p. 14A; Polly Bowles, testimony before the Jobs, Energy, and Community Development Committee, Minnesota Senate, March 3, 1993.

16. Mike Kaszuba, "Met Council Chair's Affordable Housing Agenda Faces First Test," *Minneapolis Star Tribune*, August 28, 1995, p. 1B.

17. Bill Salisbury, "Lawmakers Remain True to the Game," *Minneapolis Star Tribune*, May 16, 1994, p. 1B.

18. Although Johnson early on in 1993 began to refer to quotas in the housing bill, the first press account of this does not occur until 1995. See Mike Kaszuba, "Met Council Chair's Affordable Housing Agenda Faces First Test," *Minneapolis Star Tribune*, August 28, 1995, p. 1B.

19. Letter from Governor Arne Carlson to author, April 23, 1993; Dane Smith, "Carlson Opposes Plan to Cut Suburb-City Gap," *Minneapolis Star Tribune,* April 22, 1993, p. 1B.

20. Letter to Governor Arne Carlson from author, April 24, 1993.

21. Author's letter to the governor, April 24, 1993. By way of analogy, I noted that efforts to advance state compliance with federal policy objectives by means of withholding categorical aids are at least as old as the New Deal. The policy goals of Title IX (sex-based discrimination in education) and most federal civil rights statutes were enforced in this manner. Further, the Metropolitan Council's own dormant hous-

ing policy was enforced by similar means, through the A-95 review process, throughout the 1970s. During this period, substantial federal rather than state grants were withheld by the council when communities created barriers to low- and moderate-income housing.

22. Carlson letter to author, April 23, 1993.

23. Adam Platt, "Suburban Gauntlet: A War of Waffly Words at the Capitol," *Twin Cities Reader*, May 12, 1993, p. 4.

24. Lynda McDonnell, "IRS Fail to Halt Low Cost Suburb Housing Move," *Saint Paul Pioneer Press,* April 22, 1993, p. 1B.

25. Letter from Governor Arne Carlson to author, May 18, 1993.

26. First, the governor asserted that no housing legislation was needed because the Metropolitan Council already had sufficient authority in this area. In response, the council did do much of what is directed in the housing bill in the 1970s under Metropolitan Council Policy 13/39 (see housing section in the appendix, page 174). However, for a variety of reasons, the council abandoned this responsibility. The intent of the housing bill was to move the council back into this process with explicit state support and in a more comprehensive and important way. Second, though it served no purpose to narrowly construe the council's authority, a clarification of legislative intent would strengthen the council's hand in providing affordable suburban housing.

Second, the governor objected to the requirement that the Metropolitan Council must set priorities for developing affordable housing in "inverse proportion" to a community's past efforts to provide such housing. He claimed this could result in the production of affordable housing in areas without jobs. In response, we stated that the inverse proportion rule (the "worst go first" rule) merely modified the act's more basic requirement to remove barriers and make affirmative efforts in communities that are rich in entry-level jobs.

The North Metro Mayors Association insisted on the inverse proportion rule. They feared the council would, following the path of least resistance, further concentrate low-income housing in the northern suburbs. The northern suburbs had no objection to providing their fair share of such housing, but wanted to assure that all communities would participate in this regional responsibility. Even so, I and other pro-housing forces had repeatedly told the governor's lobbyists that we would eliminate this provision if it meant that a housing bill would be signed.

Third, the governor objected that the housing bill was premature because the council was revising their housing guide. The council, made up of the governor's appointees who had endorsed the act, disagreed. Further, those who worked in the affordable housing field uniformly believed that this legislation would have greatly helped the council facilitate a more comprehensive choice of housing in affluent, restrictive communities.

27. Editorial, "Now's the Time for Metro Leadership," *Minneapolis Star Tribune*, December 12, 1992, p. 14A.

28. 77th Session, H.F. 641.

29. 78th Session, H.F. 1053.

30. Editorial, "A Chance for Fundamental Metropolitan Reform," *Minneapolis*

Star Tribune, February 17, 1993, p. 12A; Editorial, "Give Metro Reform a Second Chance," *Minneapolis Star Tribune*, April 26, 1993, p. 12A.

31. Editorial, "Keep Trying for an Elected Met Council," *Minneapolis Star Tribune*, April 13, 1993, p. 14A; Editorial, "Metro Reform: Let This Be Year for Election, Agency Merger," *Minneapolis Star Tribune,* February 17, 1994, p. 24A.

32. Metropolitan Council, *Regional Blueprint: Twin Cities Metropolitan Area*, Publication No. 78-94-057 (Saint Paul, September 22, 1994).

33. Laws of Minnesota 1976, ch. 127; Minn. Stat. §§ 473.851-473.872 (1994).

34. Minn. Stat. § 462.352, subd. 6, 7, and 8.

35. Minn. Stat. § 473.175, subd. 1. (emphasis provided).

36. See Brian Ohm, Assistant Counsel, memorandum to Metropolitan Council, Re: Authority of the Metropolitan Council Under the Metropolitan Land Planning Act (October 11, 1991), in which the assistant counsel to the Metropolitan Council (now a professor of land use at the University of Wisconsin Law School) urges a reluctant council to use its authority under the Land Planning Act.

37. Laws of Minnesota 1980, ch. 566; Minn. Stat. §§ 473H.01–473H.18 (1994).

38. Metropolitan Land Use Planning Act, 77th Session, H.F. 622/S.F. 449; Minn. Stat. §§ 473.145 et. seq.

39. The bill also amended the Uniform Conservation Easement Act to ensure that easements will be given consideration in the determination of assessments levied against the land.

40. Dennis Cassano, "Bill Would Ease the Squeeze on Metro Area's Rural Neighbors," *Minneapolis Star Tribune*, April 6, 1993, p. 1B.

41. 77th Session, H.F. 623/S.F. 474.

42. Metropolitan Public Works Training Act, 77th Session, H.F. 721; the same bill was introduced in 1994, 78th Session, H.F. 2152.

43. Dane Smith, "Bill Seeks to Balance Metro Growth with Opportunities," *Minneapolis Star Tribune,* February 19, 1993, p. 3B.

44. Mike Kaszuba, "Maple Grove Tables Low-Income Project After Angry Meeting," *Minneapolis Star Tribune*, November 18, 1993, p. 1B.

45. Mike Kaszuba, "Maple Grove Low-Income Housing OK'd," *Minneapolis Star Tribune,* December 21, 1993, p. 7B.

46. Kaszuba, "Maple Grove Tables Low-Income Project."

47. See generally, Ibid.; Editorial, "Maple Grove: A Night Ruled by Fear and Prejudice," *Minneapolis Star Tribune,* November 21, 1994, p. 34A; Mike Kaszuba, "Townhome Plan Puts Maple Grove on Defensive," *Minneapolis Star Tribune*, December 20, 1993, p. 1B; Mike Kaszuba, "Maple Grove Low-Income Housing Ok'd: But Strict Rules May Scuttle Storm-Tossed Development," *Minneapolis Star Tribune,* December 21, 1994, p. 1B; Mike Kaszuba, "Maple Grove Accused of Bias Against Housing Deal," *Minneapolis Star Tribune*, January 5, 1994, p. 1B; David Carr, "Suburban Outrage," *Twin Cities Reader*, November 24, 1993, p. 5; Britt Robson, "The Last Good Place to Live: Welcome to Maple Grove, Where They Defend the Middle-Class Dream By Any Means Necessary," *City Pages (Minneapolis),* March 2, 1994, p. 8; Bradley A. Hoyt, "Maple Grove Attempts to Foil Much Needed Housing Pro-

ject," *Minneapolis Star Tribune,* December 18, 1993, p. 17A; Editorial, "Maple Grove: Doing, and Undoing, the Right Thing," *Minneapolis Star Tribune,* December 23, 1993, p. 12A.

48. Mike Kaszuba, "Maple Grove Housing Project Approved," *Minneapolis Star Tribune,* March 12, 1994, p. 1B; Editorial, "Maple Grove: The Fair-Minded Reclaim Their City," *Minneapolis Star Tribune,* March 12, 1994, p. 16A.

49. Minnesota Planning, Metropolitan Council, and the Minnesota Housing and Finance Agency, "Making the Connection: Linking Housing, Jobs, and Transportation" (Minneapolis, December 1993). See also Steve Brandt, "Metro Suburbs Lag in Creating Affordable Housing, Study Says," *Minneapolis Star Tribune,* April 29, 1994, p. 5B.

50. Editorial, "Back to the Future: A Metro Plan Right Out of the '50s," *Minneapolis Star Tribune,* January 6, 1994, p. 18A.

51. Steven Dornfeld, "Governor, Panel May Not See Eye to Eye on How to Retool the Metropolitan Council," *Saint Paul Pioneer Press,* January 17, 1994, p. 10A.

52. See Mike Kaszuba and Steve Brandt, "Suburban Zoning Shuts Out the Poor," *Minneapolis Star Tribune,* February 28, 1994, p. 1A; Mike Kaszuba, "Suburbs Often Cite Columbia Heights Woes," *Minneapolis Star Tribune,* March 1, 1994, p. 1A; Steve Brandt, "Developer Fights to Build Townhouses in Mendota Heights," *Minneapolis Star Tribune,* March 2, 1994, p. 1B; Steve Brandt, "Burnsville Uses Team Approach to Make Room for 'Working Poor'," *Minneapolis Star Tribune,* March 3, 1994, p. 1A. See also 78th Session, H.F. 2758; Dane Smith, "Suburban IRs Unveil Poverty Reduction Bill: Plan Would Build Low-Income Housing in Wealthier Areas," *Minneapolis Star Tribune,* February 9, 1994, p. 1B; Bob Von Sternberg, "Met Council Offers Plan to Save the Cities," *Minneapolis Star Tribune,* February 10, 1994, p. 3B; Bill Salisbury, "Anti-Poverty Plan Allots Responsibility to Suburbs," *Saint Paul Pioneer Press,* January 27, 1994, p. 1A; Editorial, "Mixed Brew: A Compromise on Housing the Poor?", *Minneapolis Star Tribune,* February 18, 1994, p. 16A.

53. In the 1995 session of the legislature, in a major defeat for organized labor, the Chamber's workers' compensation reform was adopted. At this writing, this reform has not yet led to improved conditions in the older part of the region.

54. Comprehensive Choice Housing Act of 1994, 78th Session, H.F. 2171; Linda Fullerton, "Legislator's Bill Calls on Suburbs for Housing Aid," *Saint Paul Pioneer Press,* February 25, 1994, p. 1C; Mike Kaszuba, "Orfield Resumes Housing Effort," *Minneapolis Star Tribune,* February 25, 1994, p. 2B; Editorial, "He's Back: Orfield Stays Tough on Fair Housing," *Minneapolis Star Tribune,* 4 March 1994, p. 20A.

55. Editorial, "Zoning Barriers: Building Suburban Walls Against the Poor," *Minneapolis Star Tribune,* December 19, 1993, p. 30A; Editorial, "A Place to Live: Low-Income Housing Can Help Suburbs, Too," *Minneapolis Star Tribune,* December 27, 1993, p. 8A; Editorial, "Housing: Desegregate it, Like Schools, Metrowide," *Minneapolis Star Tribune,* February 5, 1994, p. 14A; Editorial, "Housing: Allow One-for-One Replacement Metrowide," *Minneapolis Star Tribune,* March 11, 1994, p. 16A; Editorial, "Compromise Needed in Housing Debate," *Saint Paul Pioneer Press,* March 20, 1994, p. 18A; Editorial, "Affordable Housing Bill: Carlson Must Do More

than Threaten a Veto," *Saint Paul Pioneer Press,* April 27, 1994, p. 8A; Editorial, "He's Back! Orfield Stays Tough on Fair Housing," *Minneapolis Star Tribune,* March 4, 1994, p. 20A; Editorial, "Mixed Brew: A Compromise on Housing the Poor?", *Minneapolis Star Tribune,* February 18, 1994, p. 16A; Editorial, "'Mean Ol' Myron': The Issue is Housing, Not Orfield," *Minneapolis Star Tribune,* April 21, 1994, p. 22A; Editorial, "Back to Work: Legislators Start Off With a Full Plate," *Minneapolis Star Tribune,* February 22, 1994, p. 12A; Editorial, "It is Definitely Time to Adjourn Session," *Saint Paul Pioneer Press,* May 17, 1993, p. 6A.

56. Editorial, "Met Council: A Housing Plan With Teeth—Maybe," *Minneapolis Star Tribune,* June 7, 1994, p. 10A.

57. Steve Brandt, "Low-Income Housing Compromise Deflated," *Minneapolis Star Tribune,* April 13, 1994, p. 4B; Steve Brandt, "Orfield Gives Ground in Effort to Disperse Affordable Housing," *Minneapolis Star Tribune,* April 20, 1994, p. 1B.

58. Steve Brandt and Mike Kaszuba, "Carlson-DFLer Discord Could Close Door on Housing Legislation," *Minneapolis Star Tribune,* March 27, 1994, p. 1B; Ronald Clark, "Combating Trouble at Urban Core," *Saint Paul Pioneer Press,* March 20, 1994, p. 18A; Editorial, "'Mean Ol' Myron': The Issue is Housing, Not Orfield," *Minneapolis Star Tribune,* April 21, 1994, p. 22A; Ronald Clark, "Legislative Bullies Attack the Messenger, Ignore the Message About Urban Ills," *Saint Paul Pioneer Press,* April 17, 1994, p. 16A; John Brandl, "Debate Orfield's Proposals, Not His Ability," *Minneapolis Star Tribune,* March 21, 1994, p. 11A; John Kostouros, "Brother Can You Spare a Dime?", *Minnesota's Journal of Law & Politics,* vol. 50 (July 1994), p. 33.

59. Dane Smith, "House Again OKs Orfield Housing Bill; Carlson Set to Veto," *Minneapolis Star Tribune,* April 23, 1994, p. 1B; "Carlson Vetoes Bill that Targeted Low Income Housing Dispersal," *Minneapolis Star Tribune,* May 10, 1994, p. 4B.

60. Letter from Governor Arne Carlson to author, May 9, 1994.

61. Myron Orfield, "Memorandum to Interested Parties Re: Governor's 1994 Housing Veto," May 10, 1994.

62. Editorial, "Orfield Extra: A Broader View of Housing the Poor," *Minneapolis Star Tribune,* May 31, 1994, p. 12A.

63. Editorial, "Met Council: A Housing Plan With Teeth—Maybe," *Minneapolis Star Tribune,* June 7, 1994, p. 10A.

64. Editorial, "Housing: Met Council Still Isn't Leading," *Minneapolis Star Tribune,* August 6, 1994, p 14A.

65. 78th Session, H.F. 2276.

66. Over the years, as the council has floundered without commitment or vision, it has been sidestepped with increasing frequency on important regional decisions. First, the state exempted the citing of a regional racetrack (Canterbury Downs), a local World Trade Center, and a regional zoo from the Met Council's authority. Similarly, a truly massive shopping complex, the famous Mall of America (which has had an enormous effect on the region's retail industry and required massive new supporting highway infrastructure) was removed entirely from Met Council significance review. Second, the counties wrested control from the council over solid waste

management and light-rail transit. Finally, the legislature, responding to claims of unfair treatment by cities, gave local zoning decisions precedence over metropolitan review powers contained in the Land Planning Act. Similarly, arguing that the MTC was not responding to suburban transit needs, the southwestern and east developing suburbs received permission to "opt out"—that is, to keep their local property tax contribution to the regional transit system, and operate independent transit systems.

67. House Rule 1.17 states: "Any Senate File received by the House, accompanied by a message announcing its passage by the Senate, shall be referred to the appropriate standing committee in accordance with [House] Rule 5.05." House Rule 5.05 states: "Except as provided in Rule 1.17 and Rule 5.06, each bill, advisory bill and resolution shall, after first reading, be referred by the Speaker to the appropriate standing committee or division thereof." Hence we argued that an appropriate committee was any committee that had jurisdiction over the bill.

68. During this time, representatives from the Saint Paul Ecumenical Alliance of Congregations (SPEAC) and other church groups began to publicly question Representative Osthoff about his opposition to metropolitan-based reforms. At his endorsing convention for renomination, angry neighborhood groups grilled him about his opposition to an elected council and prevented him from receiving a nomination by acclamation. This made him all the angrier.

69. The ferocity of the rural counties is difficult to understand. The rural cities supported an elected Met Council, following the lead of the metro cities. The metro counties opposed an elected council, and the rural counties may have been following their lead. The Association of Minnesota Counties also had an active presence lobbying against the bill—trying, many thought, to enhance their membership.

70. Dane Smith, "Bill to Make Met Council Elected is Narrowly Defeated in House," *Minneapolis Star Tribune*, April 29, 1994, p. 1B.

71. Dane Smith, "House Votes to Group Metropolitan Agencies," *Minneapolis Star Tribune,* May 3, 1994, p. 2B; Dane Smith, "Transit Service Turned Over to Met Council," *Minneapolis Star Tribune*, May 6, 1994, p. 1B; Gary Dawson, "3 Agencies Put Under Metro Council Control," *Saint Paul Pioneer Press*, May 6, 1994; Editorial, "Metro Reform: A Job Well Done Can Only Lead to More," *Minneapolis Star Tribune,* May 9, 1994, p. 10A.

72. *Metropolitan Reinvestment Act*, 78th Session, H.F. 2174. In the previous session, we had introduced a bill (77th Session, H.F. 677) to tighten up tax increment financing in wealthy suburbs and expanded language regarding urban enterprise zones.

73. For the flavor of the debate, see David M. Childs, Manager, City of Minnetonka, "Orfield Bill Would Shift Tax Rates Unfairly and Affect School Aid [counterpoint piece]," *Minneapolis Star Tribune,* March 14, 1994 p. 12A; Myron Orfield, "Defenders of the Status Quo Ignore a Growing Regional Crisis [response]," *Minneapolis Star Tribune,* March 19, 1994, p. 19A.

74. Comprehensive Land Use Planning Act of 1994, 78th Session, H.F. 2126.

75. Dennis Cassano, "Control Urban Sprawl? Wheels are Turning," *Minneapolis Star Tribune*, March 1, 1994, p. 1B; Editorial, "Sprawl Control: Oregon Law Might Work for Minnesota Too," *Minneapolis Star Tribune*, March 5, 1994, p. 14A; Dennis

Cassano, "Scott County's Move to Control Lot Size May Not Stop 2 Projects," *Minneapolis Star Tribune*, March 21, 1994, p. 1B.

76. In 1996, its members included Citizens for a Better Environment, the Community Stabilization Project, the Institute for Agriculture and Trade Policy, the Jewish Metropolitan Organizing Project, the League of Women Voters of Minnesota, the Metropolitan Interfaith Coalition on Affordable Housing, Minnesotans for an Energy Efficient Environment, the National Association for the Advancement of Colored People (Minneapolis Branch), the National Organization for Women, the Neighborhood Transportation Network, the Office for Social Justice (Archdiocese of Minneapolis and Saint Paul), the Saint Paul Ecumenical Alliance of Congregations, the South Minneapolis Livability Project, the Urban Coalition, and the Urban Ecology Coalition.

77. John R. Roach, "Moral Principles Should Help Guide Metro Area's Growth," *Minneapolis Star Tribune*, October 18, 1994, p. 15A.

78. Lynda McDonnell, "Religious Leaders Call for Support for Cities," *Saint Paul Pioneer Press,* January 13, 1996, p. 3F; Bob von Sternberg, "Congregations Unite to Fight Urban Woes," *Minneapolis Star Tribune*, January 11, 1996, p. 3B.

79. Dennis Cassano, "Council Maps Regional Plan For Metro Area: Goals Are to Create More Housing, Ease Poverty," *Minneapolis Star Tribune*, September 18, 1994, p. 1B.

80. Metropolitan Council, *Regional Blueprint: Twin Cities Metropolitan Area*, Publication no. 78-94-057 (Saint Paul, September 22, 1994), p. 51.

81. Alan Dale Albert, "Sharing Suburbia's Wealth: The Political Economy of Tax Base Sharing in the Twin Cities," bachelor's thesis, Harvard University, March 1979, p. 113.

82. Ibid., p. 152.

83. Peter Ackerberg, "Not Understood, Fiscal Disparity Proposal Delayed," *Minneapolis Star*, April 17, 1971, p. 14B.

84. Steven Dornfeld, "Dakota County Officials Protest Tax-Sharing Plan for Metro Area," *Minneapolis Tribune*, April 18, 1971, p. 10A.

85. Donnie Carr, "South Area Officials Attack Fiscal Disparity, Metro Taxing Authority," *Saint Paul Dispatch*, August 12, 1971, p. E5.

86. Ibid.

87. Betsy Becker, "Tax Share Bill Draws Dakota Fire," *Saint Paul Pioneer Press*, April 14, 1971, p. 26A.

88. "Tax-Base Pool Bill Advances: Plan Designed for Cities Area," *Minneapolis Star*, June 2, 1971, p. 1A.

89. In 1995, the House fiscal disparities bill would pass 71–63 and the Senate bill 36–30. By 1995, almost 40 percent of the suburban members supported the bill, a considerable increase from the 25 percent that did in 1970. Moreover, had the vote been taken before the new Gingrich Republicans had been seated, there is no doubt that more than half the suburbs would have supported it and it would have passed the House and Senate by a higher margin than it had twenty-five years before.

90. Jack Rhodes, "Dakota County Commissioners Seek Stay of Fiscal Disparities Law," *Saint Paul Dispatch,* September 25, 1974, p. 58.

91. Metropolitan Fair Tax Base Act, 79th Session, H.F. 431.

92. Mike Kaszuba, "Suburban Summit to Tackle Affordable Housing," *Minneapolis Star Tribune*, September 24, 1994, p. 1B ; Molly Guthrey, "Orfield Drums up Support for Equity Among Cities," *Saint Paul Pioneer Press,* October 6, 1994, p. 1B.

93. Tom Luce, "Regional Tax Base Sharing: The Twin Cities Experience," in Helen F. Ladd, ed., *Local Government Tax and Land Use Policy* (Brookings and Lincoln Institute of Land Policy, forthcoming). See also "Legislature Taps Shared Base, Considers Exapanding Pool," *Minnesota Journal*, vol. 13 (February 20, 1996), p. 6.

94. Mike Kaszuba, "Suburbs Clashing over Orfield Proposal: North Pitted Against South in Fight to Get Piece of Rich Tax Base,*" Minneapolis Star Tribune*, March 11, 1995, p. 1A.

95. H. Todd Van Dellen, memorandum to House Members, Re: H.F. 431, March 23, 1995.

96. Jim Asplund, Flaherty & Koebcle, letter to author, March 30, 1995.

97. Minnesota Office of the State Auditor, "Revenues, Expenditures, and Debt of Minnesota Cities Over 2500 in Population" (Minneapolis, December 31, 1993).

98. Gary Dawson, "Shared Tax Base For Metro Area Urged," *Saint Paul Pioneer Press*, January 26, 1995, p. 1C; Patricia Lopez Baden, "Orfield Calls for Metro-Area Tax Pool," *Minneapolis Star Tribune*, January 26, 1995, p. 1B; Doug Grow, "Listen to that Young Politician with the Venerable Ideas," *Minneapolis Star Tribune*, January 27, 1995, p. 3B; Editorial, "Metro Tax Base: A Need for Fairness All Around," *Minneapolis Star Tribune*, January 28, 1995, p. 14A; Editorial, "Tax Sharing: Making a Good Program Work Better," *Minneapolis Star Tribune*, February 21, 1995, p. 8A; Mike Kaszuba, "Suburbs Clashing"; Steve Brandt, "Groups Launch Campaign for Tax-Base Sharing," *Minneapolis Star Tribune*, March 27, 1995, p. 3B; Debra O'Connor, "Metro Property Tax Bill May Make Winners of Us All," *Saint Paul Pioneer Press*, March 19, 1995, p. 3B; Jim Ragesdale, "House Panel Approves Share-the-Wealth Plan," *Saint Paul Pioneer Press*, March 15, 1995, p. 2B; Jim Ragesdale, "Bill Shifting Tax Money to Cities OK'd," *Saint Paul Pioneer Press*, May 5, 1995, p. 1A; Dane Smith, "House Backs Tax-Sharing Proposal," *Minneapolis Star Tribune*, May 5, 1995, p. 1B; Jim Ragesdale, "Property Tax-Sharing Bill Fails," *Saint Paul Pioneer Press*, May 10, 1995, p. 1B; Patricia Lopez Baden, "Tax-Sharing Bill Fails in Close Senate Vote," *Minneapolis Star Tribune*, May 10, 1995, p. 1B; Patricia Lopez Baden, "In About-Face, Senate Backs Metro Tax-Sharing Bill," *Minneapolis Star Tribune*, May 11, 1995, p. 1A; Jim Ragesdale, "Senate Reconsiders Tax-Share Bill, Passing Measure on Second Vote," *Saint Paul Pioneer Press*, May 11, 1995, p. 1C; Jim Ragesdale, "Carlson Vetoes Bill Pooling Property Taxes in Metro Area," *Saint Paul Pioneer Press*, May 20, 1995, p. 1F.

99. City of Brooklyn Park Resolution #1994-115, #1991-53.

100. Respectively, 79th Session, H.F. 1114, and 79th Session, H.F. 1258.

101. Ted Mondale, "For Metro Solutions We Must Pull Together," *Minneapolis Star Tribune*, March 3, 1995, p. 15A; Citizens League Speech.

102. Editorial, "A Reasoned Approach to Address Problems," *Saint Paul Pioneer Press*, March 12, 1995, p. 22A; Editorial, "It's Time for Accord on Affordable Hous-

ing," *Saint Paul Pioneer Press*, March 22, 1995, p. 6A; Editorial, "A Major Moment—At Last, Accord on Affordable Housing," *Minneapolis Star Tribune*, May 20, 1995, p. 20A; Editorial, "Welcome Change," *Saint Paul Pioneer Press,* May 21, 1995, p. 20A.

103. 79th Session, H.F. 1156/S.F. 1019.

104. To put this in perspective, this single exception is half as large as the sum of exceptions to the Portland Oregon regional growth boundary over twenty years.

105. Copy of letter supplied by Joanne Barron, Met Council staff.

106. Cited in Tim Thompson, "Memo Concerning Maple Grove's Zoning Ordinance and Comprehensive Plan and Their Impact on the Development of Low- and Moderate-Income Housing," memo to David Kett (Minneapolis: Metropolitan Council, 1986), p. 23.

107. 79th Session, H.F. 1800/S.F. 1655.

108. 79th Session, H.F. 2556/S.F. 2194, vetoed March 28, 1996.

109. 79th Session, H.F. 2330/S.F. 2107, vetoed March 27, 1996.

Chapter Eight

1. This analysis is also being undertaken in Baltimore, Pittsburgh, Seattle, Cleveland, and San Francisco. It is being completed under the auspices of the National Growth Management Leadership Project and the newly formed American Land Institute and its Metropolitan Area Program.

2. The research was completed for the Coalition for a Livable Future with funds provided by the Northwest Area Foundation and the U.S. Department of Housing and Urban Development. This description and analysis applies only to the three Oregon counties: Washington, Clackamas, and Multnomah. One-fifth of the region's population (300,000 people) live in Clark County in the state of Washington.

3. The jobs data are collected by county subarea. County subareas are broad, contiguous geographical units that usually encompass more than one city, although the city of Portland itself contains four county subareas. There are 20 county subareas in the Portland metro area, 19 in Oregon, and one in Washington.

4. The members of the Coalition for a Livable Future include the American Institute of Architects (Portland Chapter), the Association of Oregon Rail and Transit Advocates, the Audubon Society of Portland, the Bicycle Transportation Alliance, the Columbia River Inter-Tribal Fish Commission, the Columbia River Region Inter-League Organization of the League of Women Voters, the Community Development Network, Ecumenical Ministries of Oregon, Environmental Commission of the Episcopal Diocese of Oregon, Fans of Fanno Creek, Hispanics in Unity for Oregon, Housing Partners, Inc., Jobs With Justice, Livable Oregon (formerly Oregon Downtown Development Association), Metro Community Development Corp., Multnomah County Community Action Commission, Network Behavioral Health Care, Inc., Northwest Housing Alternatives, 1000 Friends of Oregon, Oregon Housing Now Coalition, Portland Citizens for Oregon Schools, Portland Community Design, Portland Housing

Center, Portland Impact, REACH Community Development Corp., ROSE Community Development Corporation, Sensible Transportation Options for People, Sunnyside Methodist Church, Sustainable Oregon, Tualatin Riverkeepers, Urban League of Portland, the Wetlands Conservancy, Willamette Pedestrian Coalition, and XPAC (the Political Action Committee of the X Generation).

5. The Chicago research was supported by the John D. and Catherine T. Mac-Arthur Foundation, the Donnelley Foundation, the National Growth Management Leadership Project, and Strachan Donnelley. The region studied was the six-county Illinois region under the purview of the Northeast Illinois Planning Commission.

6. Minneapolis developed initially as a satellite to the thriving Chicago economy of the late nineteenth century. See generally William Cronon, *Nature's Metropolis: Chicago and the Great West* (W.W. Norton, 1991).

7. Neal Peirce, speech presented at the Metropolis Project Fall Seminar, Catigny, Illinois, October 27, 1995.

8. The Chicago-area municipalities were divided into regions based on their ratings in four areas: tax base per household, female-headed households as a percentage of total households with children, percentage of poor preschool children, and median household income. All four factors, weighted equally, were aggregated to arrive at a master score for the town. Above-average towns received a positive score and were generally assigned to two categories: "northern and western high–tax capacity, developing suburbs" and "southern developing suburbs"; below-average towns received a negative score and were in general further categorized as "inner and southern" or "outer, low–tax capacity, developing" suburbs. The city of Chicago, because of its size and the depth of its challenges, was put in its own category, "central city."

The socioeconomically declining inner and southern suburbs are experiencing detrimental socioeconomic changes moving sectorally out of the city. These communities share a combination of comparatively high and increasing childhood poverty and single parentage, low and declining median incomes, and comparatively small tax bases that are growing slowly, stagnant, or declining. In short, these communities are defined by a combination of increasing social needs and/or low local resources. A few communities in this category are currently stable and not experiencing dramatic change but are so geographically surrounded by others that are, that their long-term stability is threatened.

The outer-region, low–tax capacity, developing suburbs (the outer developing suburbs) tend to be extensions of middle- and working-class neighborhoods beyond the circumferential highways, communities of new immigrants from more rural settings to metropolitan Chicago, and older satellite cities (some now beginning to grow again) that have become firmly embedded in the region. These communities, often with a property tax base composed mainly of inexpensive single family homes and apartment buildings and/or a declining industrial base, do not have sufficient resources to adequately support basic public services. Though the older satellite cities (which do not think of themselves as suburbs at all) have high levels of social need, most of these communities have lower and more stable levels of poverty than the inner city. Further, because these communities are experiencing growth and are at the edge of the metropolitan area, they see their concerns as distinct from the fully developed communities experiencing direct city problems. These communities also have much deeper interests in the provision of new infrastructure and the continued pace of new outward development that the inner part of the region.

The northern and western high–tax capacity, developing suburbs (the northern and western developing suburbs, known as the favored quarter) are suburbs that are in many ways the polar opposite of the inner and southern suburbs. These communities share a combination of comparatively low, sometimes decreasing childhood poverty and single parentage, high and increasing median incomes, and comparatively large tax bases that are growing. In short, these communities are defined by a combination of small social needs and/or high local resources.

This group is a small growth area in the southern suburbs that is a pale reflection of the favored northern and western quarter, although substantially better off than the other groups of suburbs. They are distinguished from the northern and western developing suburbs in that they are physically separated from them and have competing views on infrastructure issues, such as the allocation of regional highway dollars and the location of regional airports.

9. John D. Kasarda, "Inner-City Concentrated Poverty and Neighborhood Distress: 1970–90," *Housing Policy Debate,* vol. 4, no. 3 (1994), pp. 253–302, especially pp. 286–94.

10. The part-one crime category includes murder, rape, robbery, aggravated assault, burglary, theft, motor vehicle theft, and arson (*Crime in Illinois 1993* [Springfield, Ill.: Illinois State Police, Division of Forensic Services and Identification, Bureau of Identification, 1993], p. 6.)

11. Bureau of the Census, Data User Services Division, *1987 Census of Agriculture* (Department of Commerce, 1988); John A. Buck, "Chicago: The Conurbation Conundrum," speech to the Young Executives Club of Chicago, October 15, 1992.

12. The "equalized assessed value" is a figure that is equal to one-third of property value. Illinois calculates this figure because properties are taxed on only one-third of their total value.

13. In Philadelphia, research is being undertaken for the Pennsylvania Environmental Council (PEC) with support from the William Penn Foundation, PEC, and the National Growth Management Leadership Project.

14. All statistics in this section are from the U.S. Census, unless otherwise noted. For the purposes of the following analysis, the Philadelphia region is the five-county Pennsylvania region under the jurisdiction of the Delaware Valley Regional Planning Council. The Philadelphia-area municipalities were divided into regions based on their ratings in four areas: tax base per household, female-headed households as a percentage of total households with children, percentage of poor preschool children, and median household income. All four factors, weighted equally, were aggregated to arrive at a master score for the town. Above-average towns received a positive score and were assigned to the category "affluent suburbs"; below-average towns received a negative score and were further categorized by their type—borough or township. The two resulting categories were labeled "Older cities and boroughs" and "middle-income

townships." The city of Philadelphia, because of its size and the depth of its challenges, was put in its own category, "central city."

15. Bureau of the Census, Data User Services Division, *1987 Census of Agriculture* (Department of Commerce, 1988).

Appendix

1. Laws of Minnesota 1967, ch. 896.

2. "Metropolitan Significance is Defined in Statute for Airports," see Minn. Stat. 473.621, subd. 6 and 7.

3. In terms of transit, the former Regional Transit Board members appointed the members of the Metropolitan Transit Commission.

4. The 1985 revision of the council's housing policy plan sets forth forty-four policies with detailed objectives and guidelines for municipalities, developers, financial institutions, citizens groups, and state and regional agencies. Its extensive detail reflects the council's responsibilities as the Metropolitan Housing and Redevelopment Authority, as the administering agency for federal Section 8 rent-assistance programs under the Housing and Community Development Act of 1974, and as the regional review agency for federal grant applications.

5. Minnesota Laws 1974, ch. 359, § 3 (originally codified at § 473.17).

6. Memo from Robert Einsweiler to Alice Ingerson, both at Lincoln Institute, "Re: Comments of Book Manuscript of Metropolitics," July 1995.

7. Specifically, the Metropolitan Development Investment Framework had established eight planning zones. Four are part of the metropolitan urban service area (MUSA). It is council policy to channel future growth within the "MUSA line" to bring about broad savings by increasing efficiency in using and enlarging existing facilities.

The eight planning zones are defined as the metropolitan centers or central business districts; the regional business concentrations; the fully developed area; the areas surrounding the metropolitan centers in the city and the first-ring suburbs that have been largely developed; the developing area within the metropolitan urban service area where the region's future growth is expected to be; the freestanding growth centers; and the smaller, spatially separated urban centers with a full range of services that can accommodate a wide variety of land uses. The last two planning zones are (and are intended to remain) outside the metropolitan urban service area: rural centers and commercial agricultural areas, and the general rural use area. Although these concepts are not used in such detail in the Regional Blueprint, it refers to the urban area, the rural area, and freestanding growth centers.

8. Laws of Minnesota 1976, ch. 127; Minn. Stat. §§ 473.851–473.871 (1994).

9. Minn. Stat. § 473.859.

10. Minn. Stat. § 473.175, subd. 1.

11. See Brian Ohm, Assistant Counsel, memorandum to Metropolitan Council, Re: Authority of the Metropolitan Council under the Metropolitan Land Planning Act

(October 11, 1991). Ohm, now a professor of land use at the University of Wisconsin Law School, urged a reluctant council to use its authority under the Land Planning Act.

12. Laws of Minnesota 1980, ch. 566; Minn. Stat. §§ 473H.01–473H.18 (1994).

13. Laws of Minnesota 1976, ch. 321; Minn. Stat. § 473.173 (1994).

14. The council also had significant power over solid waste and regional sporting issues. The Metropolitan Solid and Hazardous Waste Act of 1976 directed the council to prepare a long-range policy plan for collecting and processing solid and hazardous waste, assigned the implementation of the plan to county governments, and empowered the council to finance the counties' acquisition of landfills through the use of regional bonds. The Waste Management Act of 1980 rescinded the council's authority over hazardous waste, shifting responsibility for planning and approving hazardous waste facilities to a new Minnesota Waste Management Board. It also increased the council's responsibility and authority for sitting landfills. The 1985 solid waste amendments to the 1980 Waste Management Act mandated that waste disposal facilities in the metropolitan area discontinue receiving municipal solid waste after January 1, 1990. This provision represented a major initiative to drastically reduce the region's dependence on landfills for disposal of solid waste and to direct efforts toward recycling, reuse, and resource recovery. See generally Minn. Stat. §§ 473.801–849. This power was repealed in 1995 and was transferred to the state Office of Environmental Assessment.

The Metropolitan Sports Facilities Commission Act of 1977 gave the council general financial oversight over the commission's operation, including the authority to issue bonds for a domed stadium. The law detailed fourteen conditions that the council was to require of the commission. But the council was specifically denied authority to approve the stadium site, a matter of considerable controversy. Under the law, the council has continuing authority for approving the commission's operating budget. See generally Minn. Stat. §§ 473.551–599.

15. Metropolitan Council, "Trouble at the Core: The Twin Cities Under Stress," staff report (Minneapolis, November 18, 1992).

16. Citizens League, "Projects or Issues of Regional Significance Removed from Metropolitan Council Leadership," handout at hearings on the Metropolitan Reorganization Act of 1994.

Index